"When my friend Mark Thompson joined Schwab forty years ago during our IPO, we discovered a shared belief in the American dream—investing in the development of visionary leaders who build enduring companies, strong teams, and great service. *CEO Ready* reflects that spirit with clear, timely direction for those seeking greater responsibility."

—**CHARLES SCHWAB,** founder, Charles Schwab Corporation

"*CEO Ready* is an excellent resource for individuals aiming to make an impact within their organizations. Byron Loflin and Mark Thompson present an engaging narrative, complemented by real-world examples, to help readers develop key competencies necessary for effective leadership."

—**NELSON GRIGGS,** President, Nasdaq

"*CEO Ready* offers the grounded clarity that boards and executives need to prepare leaders for the top job. Mark Thompson and Byron Loflin provide an excellent approach to CEO readiness—a master class in thinking strategically about the role."

—**RAM CHARAN,** CEO and Board Adviser; bestselling author of thirty-six books

"*CEO Ready* shines a light on what it takes to lead with purpose—something I've seen firsthand in our CEO Jean Oelwang's bold leadership at Virgin Unite and in my friend Mark Thompson's enduring commitment to her journey. For two decades he's championed Jean and our team, and *CEO Ready* embodies the mindset that prepares leaders like her to make a lasting impact."

—**SIR RICHARD BRANSON,** founder, Virgin Group

"*CEO Ready* unites two powerful forces—Byron Loflin, architect of boardroom excellence, and Mark Thompson, confidant to world-class CEOs in make-or-break moments. Their hard-won wisdom delivers a rare, practical guide for aspiring and sitting CEOs—and for boards committed to choosing, developing, and supporting the right chief executive."

—**MARIE LALLEMAN,** Chair and Non-Executive Director at leading global tech firms

"Becoming a CEO is a leap that requires not just new skills, but the humility to grow in unexpected ways. *CEO Ready* helps you reflect on what it means to lead with both head and heart in what may be the most defining role of your career."

    —**HUBERT JOLY,** former CEO, Best Buy; Senior Lecturer, Harvard Business School; and bestselling author, *The Heart of Business*

"*CEO Ready* delivers actionable strategies that prepare leaders to step confidently into senior roles. This rare book draws on the impressive experience of Mark Thompson, the world's number one CEO coach, and board governance expert Byron Loflin—two of the most sought-after advisers to the world's most influential leaders."

    —**JIM YONG KIM, MD,** Vice Chair, Global Infrastructure Partners; former President, World Bank Group

"I wish I'd had this book when I became chief executive of *Inc.* and *Fast Company*! No one prepares you for the turf battles on your team, legacy inefficiencies, pressure from the board and investors, or your own blind spots. *CEO Ready* puts those challenges in perspective with practical wisdom drawn from decades of coaching the world's most renowned CEOs."

    —**ERIC SCHURENBERG,** Editor in Chief, Amplify Publishing Group; former CEO, *Inc.* and *Fast Company*

"*CEO Ready* is arguably the single best resource out there for helping insiders and outsiders grow into serious contenders for the biggest job of their lives. Every board believes it's at a crossroads—and selecting the right CEO is mission critical, which is my life's work. Mark Thompson, the world's top CEO coach, brings unmatched insight into preparing executives for that role."

    —**JAMES M. CITRIN,** Leader, CEO Practice and Coleader, Board Practice, Spencer Stuart

"Launching our moon shot for autonomous mobility challenged us to grow, align, and deliver on a transformative vision. Mark's warmth, care, and coaching supported us as true partners—helping turn that vision into reality. *CEO Ready* shares the steady-handed insight and experience that helped us navigate the scale and complexity of leadership."

—**AICHA EVANS**, CEO, and **JESSE LEVINSON**, CTO, Zoox/Amazon

"*CEO Ready* synthesizes Mark Thompson and Byron Loflin's lived wisdom—a compass for leading with trust. As AI systems grow more capable, we as leaders must grow more courageous through self-discovery, empathy, and service. Mark's coaching has been enriching and profound for me and my team."

—**SRIKANTH VELAMAKANNI,** cofounder and Group CEO, Fractal; Vice Chairman, NASSCOM

"Mark's coaching was transformative for me and for Pinterest's growth to over 570 million users. In *CEO Ready*, he and Byron Loflin bring the EQ and IQ insights necessary to push through ambiguity and prepare for complex management transitions."

—**EVAN SHARP**, cofounder, Pinterest; founding team, West Co.

"Leading a global brand with a 150-year legacy demands humility and fierce resolve from our team, and these are essential ingredients of our culture. We are mission driven and focused on helping people live gracious, healthy, and sustainable lives by living on the leading edge of design and technology. During this time of rapid transformation, my friend and adviser Mark Thompson has been an experienced sounding board and coach to me and our senior team—and *CEO Ready* reflects the insight he brings to his work."

—**DAVID KOHLER**, Chair and CEO, Kohler Co.

"Mark and Byron are sought-after advisers to the world's most influential leaders and trusted partners and friends. In *CEO Ready*, Mark and Byron help leaders rise to their highest potential—under pressure, in the spotlight, and when it counts most."

—**PAU GASOL**, NBA Hall of Fame and Olympic Gold Medalist

"*CEO Ready* provides a method to the madness of making the transition to chief executive. Mark Thompson's guidance lifted me during my toughest moments as a first-time CEO. He challenged and inspired me to grow—and helped me lead Team USA's historic performance at the Summer Olympics. I'm humbled and grateful to him for being there when I needed it most."

—**SARAH HIRSHLAND**, CEO, US Olympic & Paralympic Committee

"The key to good journalism is to see things steady and see them whole. In Mark Thompson's work, he shows that the same is true of great leadership. In *CEO Ready*, he and Byron Loflin offer a frank, deeply informed guide for rising leaders navigating the quiet politics and personal reckonings that come with preparing for the top job. This is a field manual for those who aspire not just to lead but to lead wisely—and to leave behind a legacy that becomes a model for others."

—**JOHN DICKERSON**, coanchor, CBS Evening News

"Stepping into the CEO role demands a new level of vision, discipline, and presence—even after decades in the industry. In *CEO Ready*, Mark Thompson and Byron Loflin sharpen your edge with rigor and relevance while supporting you with care, kindness, and authenticity. Ultimately, you will be transformed into a better version of yourself."

—**CARLOS ABRAMS-RIVERA**, CEO, Kraft Heinz Company

"Mark bolstered my confidence to grow into the CEO role and partner with our extraordinary founder, David Chang. *CEO Ready* echoes the methods with which he challenged and supported me and served as a sounding board as I grew a global culinary brand as a first-time CEO."

—**MARGUERITE MARISCAL**, CEO, Momofuku, and **DAVID CHANG**, founder, Momofuku; celebrity chef

"Mark Thompson has been a trusted coach and sounding board. Together we've strengthened our team and leadership impact in the fast-paced world of gaming. *CEO Ready* is a powerful guide for anyone serious about scaling themselves and their organizations."

—**PAUL CAIRNS**, Chief Business Officer, Electronic Arts

"Thinkers50 named Mark Thompson a Coaching Legend in 2023, and *CEO Ready* shows why. Mark and Byron reject off-the-shelf shortcuts in favor of the value of deep, data-driven insights. They bring real operating insight and disciplined analysis to CEO readiness. This book is essential for leaders serious about earning—and excelling in—the top job."

—**GEOFF SMART,** founder and Chairman, ghSMART

"What do CEOs need in today's dynamic tech environment, where workers feel more vulnerable than ever? A CEO must be the 'Chief Inspiration Leader,' galvanizing their employees' best energies and facing forward with positive power. Mark Thompson and Byron Loflin project the right balance. *CEO Ready* will change businesses for good."

—**LORD MICHAEL HASTINGS, CBE,** House of Lords, United Kingdom

"*CEO Ready* codifies the invaluable wisdom of these extraordinary counselors to develop and empower the highest-performing CEOs and their board partners to drive market-leading value for all stakeholders. Byron Loflin and Mark Thompson's combined insights uniquely transform executive leadership. The organizations I serve are proof of their magic!"

—**STEPHEN POWELL,** Director, OneSpaWorld; Managing Director, Mufson, Howe, Hunter & Co.

"*CEO Ready* distills decades of hard-earned leadership insight. Mark Thompson and Byron Loflin equip rising CEOs not only to survive the boardroom but to thrive within it. This book is both a guide and a gift to the next generation of high-impact leaders."

—**PAUL MENGERT,** CEO, Association Management Group (AMG); Community Associations Institute's Educator of the Year

"Mark has been a great partner in helping me and my team unlock deeper self-awareness and strategic influence, balancing high performance with trust and psychological safety. Becoming 'CEO ready' is a continuous journey for leaders striving to grow and lead more effectively."

—**JESPER NORDENGAARD,** CEO, Dechra Pharmaceuticals; former President, North America, Colgate-Palmolive

"In every CEO community session with Mark, I found a rare and trusted space to reflect—not just on strategy but on the human side of leadership. *CEO Ready* is a powerful companion for anyone preparing to lead at the highest level."

—**JAN CARLSON**, Chair, Ericsson; Board Director, Volvo; and former CEO, Veoneer/Qualcomm

"Mark Thompson, the world's number-one CEO coach, and Byron Loflin, the founder and head of Nasdaq's Center for Board Excellence, have created an indispensable readiness guide for aspiring chief executives. *CEO Ready* transforms ambition into boardroom credibility with unflinching honesty. It's required reading for anyone serious about earning—and excelling—as CEO."

—**SCOTT OSMAN** and **JACQUELYN LANE**, cofounders, 100 Coaches Agency

"During my first ninety days as president, Mark was invaluable: a trusted sounding board offering the seasoned objectivity that only comes from guiding dozens of C-suite transitions. His guidance helped me prepare for and navigate many nuances of the transition at the highest level. In *CEO Ready*, he and Byron Loflin encapsulate that wisdom into a clear, actionable framework for any executive stepping into a top role. This isn't just guidance—it's the strategic advantage every new leader needs."

—**STEPHEN LAZARUS**, President and CFO, OneSpaWorld

"When I was president of KIND, Mark Thompson consistently encouraged my growth with kindness and integrity. His coaching—and his global network—deeply enriched my journey. *CEO Ready* reflects that generosity, helping leaders prepare with clarity, connection, and character for what's next."

—**JUAN MARTÍN ALONSO**, CEO, Agrolimen; former President, Mars/KIND

"Thank you, Mark, for building a trusted CEO community, where leaders can speak candidly, prepare for their next career leap, and refocus their goals. *CEO Ready* reflects the spirit of our many leadership plan review sessions—practical, courageous, and human. It's an essential guide to impactful leadership."

—**DEANNA MULLIGAN,** CEO, Ceres Life Insurance Company; former Chair, President, and CEO, Guardian Life; and Board Member, Vanguard Group

"*CEO Ready* boils down the preparation every aspiring leader needs, with a clear outline about how values-based leadership begins long before you move into the corner office. A must-read for anyone striving to lead with purpose, self-awareness, and lasting impact."

—**HARRY M. J. KRAEMER JR.,** former Chairman and CEO, Baxter International; Clinical Professor of Leadership, Northwestern's Kellogg School of Management

"Over the past five years, I've had the privilege of taking part in Mark Thompson and Marshall Goldsmith's Leadership Plan Review sessions, spending dozens of weekend hours with fellow CEOs. It's a life-enriching community, where we brainstorm for the next quarter and the next chapter. Drawing from that shared experience, *CEO Ready*—coauthored with Nasdaq's Byron Loflin—is an essential strategic resource for leaders preparing to take on the biggest job of their lives."

—**MARGO GEORGIADIS,** cofounder and CEO, Montai Therapeutics; former President and CEO, Ancestry; former CEO, Mattel; and former President, Google North America

"Mark Thompson loves preparing CEOs for the biggest jobs of their lives—and you won't find a better advocate for you on that journey. *CEO Ready* is a bold, practical guide for leaders and boards who are serious about building capability at the top."

—**SANDY OGG,** founder, CEO.works; former Operating Partner, Blackstone

"There are few people you can truly trust—and even fewer who listen with real insight. Mark Thompson is that rare adviser we can call day or night. *CEO Ready* captures the broad perspective he's gained from working with entrepreneurs and leaders around the world—precisely when judgment matters most."

—**JASON EICHENHOLZ,** founder and CEO, Relativity Networks; cofounder and CTO, Luminar Technologies

"As someone who has hired CEOs, served as one, and coached those in or preparing to step into the role, I can say unequivocally: *CEO Ready* is not just a playbook for ambitious executives—it's a boardroom asset. Mark Thompson and Byron Loflin offer something rare: a brutally honest, deeply human, and rigorously practical guide to navigating the most complex promotion in business. This book belongs in the hands of anyone serious about building future-ready leadership—for themselves or their organization."

—**MARK PARSELLS,** former President, Citibank Online; three-time FinTech Chair and CEO; Board Director; and CEO coach

"I love Mark's lifelong dedication to helping leaders and his commitment to the principles of working together. *CEO Ready* helps leaders prepare for higher levels of responsibility and the privilege of leadership."

—**ALAN MULALLY,** former President and CEO, Ford Motor Company; former President and CEO, Boeing Commercial Airplanes

CEO READY

**Mark Thompson
Byron Loflin**

CEO READY

What You Need to Know
to *Earn the Job*—
and *Keep the Job*

HARVARD BUSINESS REVIEW PRESS • BOSTON, MASSACHUSETTS

HBR Press Quantity Sales Discounts

Harvard Business Review Press titles are available at significant quantity discounts when purchased in bulk for leadership development programs, client gifts, or sales promotions. Opportunities to co-brand copies with your logo or messaging are also available. For details and discount information for both print and ebook formats, contact booksales@hbr.org or visit www.hbr.org/bulksales.

Copyright 2025 Mark Thompson and Byron Loflin

All rights reserved

Printed in the United Kingdom by TJ Books, Padstow, Cornwall

10 9 8 7 6 5 4 3 2

No part of this publication may be reproduced, stored in or introduced into a retrieval system, or transmitted, in any form, or by any means (electronic, mechanical, photocopying, recording, or otherwise), without the prior permission of the publisher. Requests for permission should be directed to permissions@harvardbusiness.org, or mailed to Permissions, Harvard Business School Publishing, 60 Harvard Way, Boston, Massachusetts 02163.

The web addresses referenced in this book were live and correct at the time of the book's publication but may be subject to change.

Library of Congress Cataloging-in-Publication Data

Names: Thompson, Mark (Executive coach) author | Loflin, Byron author
Title: CEO ready : what you need to know to earn the job—and keep the job / by Mark Thompson and Byron Loflin.
Description: Boston, Massachusetts : Harvard Business Review Press, [2025] | Includes bibliographical references and index.
Identifiers: LCCN 2025020967 (print) | LCCN 2025020968 (ebook) | ISBN 9798892791687 hardcover | ISBN 9798892791694 epub
Subjects: LCSH: Chief executive officers | Executive ability | Management
Classification: LCC HD38.2 .T4735 2025 (print) | LCC HD38.2 (ebook) | DDC 658.4/2—dc23/eng/20250814
LC record available at https://lccn.loc.gov/2025020967
LC ebook record available at https://lccn.loc.gov/2025020968

ISBN: 979-8-89279-168-7
eISBN: 979-8-89279-169-4

From Mark Thompson:
To my lady, Dr. Bonita Thompson, and my amazing daughter, Vanessa—whose love, wisdom, and unwavering support inspire me every day.

From Byron Loflin:
To Anne, Megan, Michael, Kate, Tucker, Rhodes, Keats, Millie, Shaye, and Ginny—each of you motivates my commitment to the leadership excellence journey.

Contents

Foreword, by Marshall Goldsmith   ix
What Got You Here, Got You Halfway There

1   The Hard Truth about Your Candidacy   1
You're the best at what you do, but the odds are against you.

2   Earn Readiness Twice   11
First you must get qualified. Then you must be selected. Here's how to work on both.

3   The Number One Stakeholder: You   23
Get to know your blind spots and fears, then learn to manage them.

4   Win the Board's Trust   47
Help directors know you are the best candidate for the job.

5   Prepare to Move from Peer to Chief   73
C-suite colleagues can't get you the job, but they can kill your chances.

6   Partner with Your Predecessor   93
Smooth the existential transition for the incumbent CEO and discover what's next.

Contents

7 Engage with the Owners — 113
Your candidacy depends on what your shareholders value.

8 Embrace the Scrutiny — 137
Learn to live under the microscope of assessors and consultants who've never had the job.

9 Honor Culture, Comfort Customers, and Manage Celebrity — 159
Employees and customers must believe you're ready.

Conclusion — 185
Permission to be happy: What anchors you, what fuels you, what lights your sky.

Appendix A — 205
CEO candidate assessments that you can anticipate

Appendix B — 209
Assessment frameworks

Appendix C — 217
Recruiting firm assessments

Notes — 233
Index — 239
About the Authors — 251

Foreword

What Got You Here, Got You Halfway There

Congratulations, you've just landed on the shortlist to become CEO! You have every reason to imagine you're the obvious choice to be selected. You're picturing yourself standing on the one-yard line in the Super Bowl of corporate leadership, and you're absolutely certain you've heard the board and current CEO talk about your achievements in such glowing terms that they've implied you've basically scored already. You might even feel their chummy warmth over intimate dinners with your board members lauding your progress. You're confident that you're reaching an all-powerful place with ultimate control to finally do what you've always known is right and to do it your way.

Well, let me pop that balloon. That is not how this works. Here's the problem: in your current role, you actually do not have as much visibility as you think about what the incumbent CEO and board of directors are planning regarding who will become the next CEO—no matter what you may have heard. Becoming CEO is not about achieving *your* definition of the most qualified candidate. It's about building the confidence of the decision-makers based on *their* criteria, not yours. It's the role of the board to hire and fire the CEO, and each member has their own selection criteria that will shift many times before the new leader is selected. Think of this as a Shakespearean drama complicated by many influencers inside and outside your company with their own conflicting motivations.

The good news is that Mark and Byron are the two most experienced copilots to help you find your way. As the world's number one CEO coach, Mark has insights that have shaped the careers of over eighty leaders, guiding them from the C-suite to roles as presidents, CEOs, and chairs. I have had the distinct privilege of being Mark's partner and mentor for the past twenty-five years, watching with pride and feeling the honor of passing the baton as he has grown into the most successful CEO-readiness coach in history and a Thinkers50 and Global Gurus hall-of-fame coaching legend. Mark is the world authority in helping leaders take it to the next level. He has guided more leaders to ascend to top positions than anyone else in our field.

At Nasdaq's Center for Board Excellence, Byron Loflin has created the world's best evaluation process for directors. So, what you're getting with this book is the dream team: while Mark coaches CEOs, Byron advises the boards of directors—the two ultimate decision-makers who will choose the next chief executive. From their unique perspective in the boardroom, they've created a playbook that is more than just a guide to becoming CEO; it is a comprehensive resource for anyone aspiring to get promoted. With Mark and Byron's combined expertise, you are in the best possible hands to prepare for and succeed in the biggest job of your life.

—Marshall Goldsmith,
World's #1 Leadership Thinker

CEO READY

1

The Hard Truth about Your Candidacy

*You're the best at what you do,
but the odds are against you*

You're the one.

You're one of the best at what you do. Your boss has told you you're on the fast track. Maybe a board member whispered to you that when the time comes—and it's coming soon—to bring on a new CEO, you're the top candidate. At many board dinners, members have shared a knowing smile and a wink; undoubtedly you've got the inside track, you're the favorite. The point is, you're the one. If all goes to plan, and why wouldn't it, you're the next CEO. So, you feel no compelling reason in your overbooked day to actually build a CEO-strategic plan for this life-changing opportunity; there's no obvious threat that would shift your view that you're clearly the most qualified to win the job.

But here's the hard reality of being in your position. Your definition of who deserves it doesn't mean much. No matter how certain a metaphor they used to pump you up, the odds are against you. Remember that. Even though you have a long record of delivering amazing results, the odds are against you. When it's time for the board members to make their final decision, you'll find there are a lot more players they're considering who are not obvious, and plenty of people vying to steal bases on you. The clubhouse isn't full yet, even if you're the leader there. You are not alone in this competition. With the stakes so great, the board has a fiduciary duty to systematically consider a host of world-class external candidates that at first appear as more attractive (outsiders you don't know) and, perhaps to your surprise, several internal candidates besides you (even though that might strike you as absurd). And no matter what a few people may have told you, other very important stakeholders who influence the selection of the CEO have already signaled the same message to other candidates.

Part of the problem is that your board is not aware of *all* you are doing in every aspect of your role and would be capable of accomplishing as CEO. They know you from a narrower job. Yes, you've done well in your swim lane, and you feel good about your relationships with several directors, but you may not necessarily have the reputation or context to excite directors with whom you've not made deep enough connections in the context of this succession process. So, what you must recognize is that the board is facing a complicated decision that will be made by a complicated collection of decision-makers with conflicting metrics, opinions, and agendas, and you won't have enough access or visibility into their selection process.

And despite the votes of confidence you have gotten, you're not as ready as you think you are; we rarely meet candidates who are, and we've met thousands of candidates.

This is the reality of your candidacy. We want to help you win despite it.

Collectively we have coached more than two hundred executives who have been selected by their board members to become CEOs. We can help you prepare to be a great CEO either in your current organization or elsewhere.

To get there, we must prepare you for the unintentional *Game of Thrones* journey you will go through as a CEO candidate, which is both crucial to getting the job and, to date, frustratingly underserved. Little of what has been written previously about CEO readiness covers the personal toll of taking the baton of leadership and the emotions involved for all parties. Leadership selection and succession planning are usually presented as a dry, check-the-boxes manifestos during which seemingly robotic executives are only concerned with jargony attributes like strategic fit, core competencies, track records, cultural alignment, value creation, empathy with an edge, and building long-term shareholder value. That's great, but half the story.

The literature on the CEO selection process generally ignores the fact that all the stakeholders involved are human beings. They are overachievers like you with extensive, but wildly varying career experiences that impact and narrow their point of view. Most important, every person involved has a strikingly different level of self-interest, ego, or (heaven forbid) feelings. For that reason, you can't count on CEO succession being an entirely methodical process that yields the best candidate—or that it's impersonal, objective, unfettered by market conditions, and unaffected by geopolitics or industry crises. It's not.

Know Your Customers (or Jurors)

Every one of the seven stakeholders who weigh in on whether to choose you as CEO defines success in shockingly different ways. As we introduce you to each of these stakeholder groups in this book, we insist that you think of each as a *customer* and sit with every one of them to learn their individual story, because they have no obligation to buy into your objective. As with any big customer, this is not about you, exactly. It's about what's going on in their lives and their perceptions of you and the organization that will impact their view of your candidacy and their verdict about whether you're the one. We've seen an executive's candidacy shift from worst to first in a single quarter. If you're serious about this, you will need a strategic plan that forces as much scenario analysis into your preparation as you would invest in any other major project that will come under the deep scrutiny of your current CEO and board of directors.

But that's not usually how candidates approach their candidacy as CEO. Because you're human and generally fair yourself, you will go into the process thinking that merit will win the day. So many of the hopeful CEO candidates we've coached start our engagement with them by saying something like, "I don't need to market myself. They know who I am," or "They are well aware of what I bring to the table."

Bad strategy. Assume people don't know. Assume it's only one factor of many. Assume what you bring to the table is table stakes, not the thing that puts you over the top. When Enrique Lores was among several candidates for the role of chief executive at Hewlett-Packard, an HP board member described him to Mark as an unlikely candidate before Lores ascended to the top job. The director said Lores was extremely bright, gifted, and inspiring, with both technical and leadership skills and a proven business track record globally within the company, but that assessment of him also fit the profile for at least two other executives under consideration, one insider and one outsider. "I'd put him among the most elite in the world, but third place in this contest," the director said. That was a full year before the board saw everything necessary that he needed to do to win the entire board's approval. In this case, the most qualified person got the job. But you can't count on that, nor is the most qualified person in first place in this race at the beginning.

You may feel your skills and experience are self-evident, or that your CEO, peers, and certain board members will make a compelling case on your behalf. Maybe they will. But the boards we work with are under great pressure to choose the right CEO, and the failure rate is at record levels. There is so much at stake for their organizations—and for each of their reputations—that they usually feel compelled to fuel a high-stakes internal succession contest as well as launch an extensive search for external candidates. You will compete with people you've grown up with in your company, along with a cadre of outside world-class executives you might never have expected to be rivals. You'll also continue to go through wave after wave of assessment and vetting that is unlike any you've ever been through before.

We know you *deserve* the top job, but in our extensive experience, the only certainty about CEO succession is that you never truly know for sure who's getting the job. We've been surprised any number of times working with candidates. In practice, the process of who gets hired is influenced as much by emotions and timing as by logic. By now, we hope it's sinking in as you read our cautionary message that you've got to be strategic and calibrate for internal power plays, unspoken director grudges, biases, and behind-the-scenes board relationships with people you've never met. Some contenders also wrestle with conflict from qualified and perhaps jealous peers, C-suite executives who are also intensely vying for the same coveted position.

At other times, unqualified candidates sabotage their more qualified peers, as they are certain, in their own minds, that they could realistically be the CEO, when objectively they haven't the slightest chance to be chosen. Worse yet, the less-than-best candidate wins the favor of the incumbent CEO, who unwittingly prefers a nonthreatening and weaker "mini-me" version of themselves because they aren't ultimately willing to face the existential reality of departing the biggest job of their lives. It is difficult for a successful founder, for example, to let their baby go. They fret about the future of their company, and they worry about their own futures.

The Boomerang CEO

Any or all of these can sway promotion choices in unexpected directions. As a CEO candidate, your prospects might be interrupted by the boomerang CEO phenomenon—where legendary executives return to lead their former companies when the old model is struggling. High-profile examples include Howard Schultz, whose presence has long defined Starbucks's brand identity, stepped back into the CEO role not once but three times. Under Schultz's influence, Starbucks appointed two internal executives (Orin Smith and Kevin Johnson) and three external CEOs (Jim Donald, Laxman Narasimhan, and now Brian Niccol, who ultimately was recruited from his turnaround success at Chipotle). But, as with all returning CEOs, it consistently signals critical moments of course correction for the company. Bob Iger's unexpected second tenure at Disney, Michael Dell's return in 2007, and Jack Dorsey's two stints as Twitter's CEO further illustrate the trend.

The ongoing appeal of bringing back founding leadership or celebrity CEOs appears in the news every day, from Sam Altman's dramatic ouster and reinstatement at OpenAI and Kevin Plank's return to Under Armour. This recurring phenomenon underscores a deeper insight about how you must prepare for your candidacy as CEO: when organizations face identity drift, culture breakdown, or strategic paralysis, it's often the founding DNA that stakeholders look to for realignment, even when the board would intellectually prefer fresh new thinking from an experienced candidate like you. Have you considered how you will develop the skills and narrative to fill those needs? Founders and iconic leaders bring not just operational know-how, but emotional resonance, narrative control, and symbolic authority. They calm markets, reengage employees, and in the best cases, restart stalled innovation. But that innovation is only rarely reignited fully by a longtime founder. These boomerang moments reflect the value of deep trust, mission continuity, and executive presence at times that you as a CEO candidate must build when the company's future feels uncertain. In today's boardrooms, the call to bring back a known leader often isn't just nostalgic, it's strategic. So as a CEO candidate, you will have to show that you can define a better future path at the same time that you build on and provide a safe bridge from the past. Intellectually, the board knows that your organization needs fresh thinking and direction that is different from the past. That's why you deserve consideration for the role, but that's also why other outside candidates can seem so appealing.

In some cases, the former founder and chief executive returns with a renewed sense of purpose and a much better selection process for inside candidates, as founder and CEO Michael Bloomberg landed back at his namesake, Bloomberg, then promoted inside candidate Vlad Kliatchko as CEO of Bloomberg LP in August 2023. Prior to becoming CEO, Kliatchko served as Bloomberg's chief product officer, overseeing the development and management of the company's products.

The good news for you as a candidate is that the boards that we coach tell us they will do everything possible to avoid that boomerang, as it tends to destabilize stakeholders and accentuates leadership turbulence in an organization. Instead, most founders and incumbent CEOs prefer to invest in inside leaders like you who have the advantage of experience and context managing through the many chapters of the company's evolution. Netflix promoted from within when it elevated two longtime executives, Ted Sarandos and Greg Peters, to co-CEO, marking a carefully orchestrated leadership transition from founder Reed Hastings, who had been CEO for more than twenty years. Both leaders had been with Netflix for over a decade and played pivotal roles in transformative moments, including the bold and controversial decision to separate the company's well-established DVD-by-mail business from its then-nascent streaming platform. They also helped build one of the world's largest film production enterprises. These moves, once criticized as risky and premature, were defining, existential, strategic pivots that reshaped the company from the inside out and transformed their industry. That's our hope for you.

Filling the shoes of a highly effective, larger-than-life leader is no small feat. We're proud to report that we help great executives do that every year. By investing in a long-term CEO transition strategy, charismatic founders and CEOs like Chuck Surack of instrument distribution giant Sweetwater Sound and his board selected longtime digital insider Mike Clem—who invested in executive coaching with Mark for well over a year before the handoff. He is the now-beloved CEO of that company. U.S. Venture chair and former CEO John Schmidt set a long-term plan with the board that led to the appointment of Eric Kessenich, who had historically led one of the company's most successful divisions. At American icon Kraft Heinz, Chairman and CEO Miguel Patricio transformed the company and—with the support of a board that includes three members of Berkshire Hathaway, including Greg Abel, Warren Buffett's handpicked successor—promoted Carlos Abrams-Rivera to become CEO. Each candidate embraced and managed the complexities. But you have to know what to look for. When you're in the running as a candidate for CEO, you must deftly manage perceptions and relationships amid the unpredictable internal and external elements at play, in addition to rigorously evaluating your formal skills and organizational strategy if you are selected.

The CEO Journey: More Grand Prix Than Mount Everest

Consultants who've never walked the CEO path often frame it as scaling Everest, where the focus is avoiding a plunge off the mountain. While sounding courageous, that's the wrong focus—and a strategic mistake to see your candidacy that way. Boards and founders like Michael Dell are wary of that self-absorbed mindset. As Dell—who returned to the CEO role twice—told Mark, boards watch for candidates who act as if becoming CEO were a one-time summit to plant a flag for personal glory. With over four hundred companies launched under the Virgin brand, Richard Branson has recruited scores of CEOs, telling Mark that the best candidates approach it like winning the Formula One championship season after season—and this may be your penultimate race. Victory comes from expanding your skills, not just surviving the climb—learning lap after lap, quarter after quarter—and building a high-performance team to deliver faster and smarter. The technical difficulty of this "race" is set by seven stakeholders at the heart of the CEO selection process. Each of them matters in the final decision—some more than others—but the complexities surrounding the selection process are rarely discussed because they involve myriad human fears and political considerations that evolve in intimate private negotiations among these seven key decision-makers. We'll not only introduce you to these stakeholders in the coming chapters, but will help you learn what they really value, respect, and admire in the leader they perceive that they want to select for the next CEO. We will share their nuanced, secret handshakes and code language necessary to win their hearts and minds.

This playbook will improve your chances of getting the top job through the often multiyear, multifaceted CEO selection process. In the following pages, we will delve deeply into the thoughts, feelings, and expectations of each of the core stakeholder individuals and groups. We'll examine who they are and how you can best partner with them to enhance your chances of getting selected for the job and, to your surprise and others, becoming more qualified to succeed with the company and the board.

Most executives who want to become CEO will never win the job. Each of the seven stakeholders who make the ultimate choice has a story to tell—and we'll share many—to provide clarity about how to be a worthy frontrunner, but more important, to help you create a vision in which the stakeholders can see you in the job. They must be able to visualize building a long-term relationship with you that makes your candidacy a more obvious choice as their partner at the company. In each chapter, we'll break down a list of tools and practices to turn into action. As an experienced executive, you know some stakeholders much better than others, particularly those in the roles that you may have held yourself or worked with extensively in the past.

In this book, we will share how great CEOs earn the job and keep it by identifying their gaps as a candidate and filling them one by one. For that reason, we recommend that you read this book straight through because the road map you seek is not obvious. You have already been successful in your role by the old definition of what that means; that is why you are on the short list for the corner office. But you don't know what you don't know about who and what lies ahead.

We always tell candidates: you cannot rely on your noteworthy accomplishments to win hearts and minds, or on consistent transparency about an often-contentious process run by the decision-makers. Nor can you count on the current state of your business or stable market conditions to support what your board may think or be forced to rethink about the qualifications of a CEO for your company in an era of disruption. So don't leave this process to chance. With the tools and advice we provide here, we're giving you a leg up in the process against all odds.

Let's get started. For now, forget about how much you deserve the job. As you'll see in the next chapter, becoming a CEO requires that you prove you're ready *twice*.

Five Hard Questions You Must Ask Yourself before the Race Even Starts

Because being the favorite doesn't mean you're the final choice

1. **Do you understand how the CEO decision will be made and who's shaping it?** Succession decisions are rarely as formal or fair as they seem. Do you know what the board members value, who influences them, and what the current CEO is—or isn't—saying about you?

2. **Are you being typecast by your current role? What can you do to shift that image?** You are excellent at what you do, but boards promote who they *see* as ready for more. Have you made yourself visible in the right ways?

3. **Are you respected for your judgment or just liked for your performance?** Being popular doesn't win the CEO job. Are you seen as someone who can make hard calls, manage complexity, and hold others accountable when it really counts?

4. **Do you know how you're perceived and who's helping you see your blind spots?** Have you invited honest, tough feedback from those who will tell you the truth, not just cheer you on?

5. **Are you building relationships that matter to the process or waiting to be discovered?** Boards don't promote résumés; they promote people they trust. Are you creating meaningful, visible moments that shape how decision-makers experience your leadership?

2

Earn Readiness Twice

First you must get qualified.
Then you must be selected.
Here's how to work on both

Shooting for the CEO role demands a profound reset of your understanding of your strengths and, perhaps more importantly, the skills you have yet to acquire and may be surprised that you need in order to be CEO ready. When Cristiano Amon, now the CEO of Qualcomm, was among the inside candidates for the role, Mark had the privilege of partnering with him as the CEO coach, interviewing the entire board, peers, direct reports, and a few customers. But Amon himself offered the biggest insights. He shared his sense of humility, vulnerability, and driving ambition with striking clarity when reflecting on advice he was given early in his career: "The most important thing for you to know is the distance between your areas of competence and your areas of incompetence, and this is how you manage your career. You go all the way to that line, and you stay there until you can push the line forward" with new skills, hard-won experience, and a better team around you.[1] This is not about lacking confidence; it is about recognizing where you excel, but also what you need to learn and where you need to rely on the expertise of others. Amon continued, "If you're still the same executive you were a year ago, I'm not sure you deserve the next promotion."

Our best, most successful, and longest-lasting CEOs share this realistic, lifelong learning point of view, and boards are impressed by that unique combination of behaviors when they witness how you show up for board meetings where you're now being considered a CEO candidate. You'll give the board a new lens for looking at you beyond your current role as a chief financial officer (CFO) or division president or other prior C-suite role. But, remember, boards will instantly and easily sniff out false modesty from all the candidates in the running because every board member is also well rehearsed at spinning a good yarn.

As a former CEO himself at Palo Alto Networks, Qualcomm Chairman Mark McLaughlin told Mark that "you learn quickly as the next leader of the enterprise that you still have much, much, more yet to learn than you expected, no matter how well prepared you thought you were to become CEO. And that's intensified by everyone's expectations that you as an executive will get better every quarter, because the bar goes up for the company every year." You must disrupt yourself before others do.

Cut from the same cloth as Amon and McLaughlin is Corie Barry, the current CEO at Best Buy. She was a finance expert who was tasked to lead bold strategic growth initiatives by her legendary boss, former CEO Hubert Joly, who transformed Best Buy when the big-box retail consumer electronics company was on the brink and the founding team was departing.

But when Barry was first approached to throw her hat into the ring for the CEO job, she turned the offer down. She sent a seven-page memo to Joly, detailing her reservations about being ready and wanting to take the job. Her remarkable self-awareness now serves as a Harvard case study. Joly was prescient, attributing Barry's response to authenticity, humility, and humanity. He applauded her courage and doubled down on talking to her. Why? As Joly told us, Barry was extraordinarily gifted and had an exceptional character combined with an impressive ability to learn and grow. When it comes to taking the leap from the C-suite to CEO, it's easy to underestimate how much there is to learn. "It's simply not like any other job," Joly said. When he first took the role, he announced to the executive team, "I'm Hubert Joly, and I need help!"[2] He institutionalized an ethos of being coachable and getting coaching because "everybody has gaps, and everyone is working on something." Few will admit that, especially when they're being courted for the role. It can feel like sabotaging your candidacy.

As we coach future CEOs and conduct 360-degree assessments with their stakeholders, we find that the overwhelming majority are elite executives, checking the boxes on accomplishments and intellectual capacity. Almost every one of these candidates is perceived as being extremely bright. These people also have a history of achieving big results. If they didn't, why would they even be considered? Each one is also extremely dedicated and vigorously committed to the success of their organization. They care about their company and its customers.

The question is whether you have the courage and humility to intentionally explore what you may not know about customers, employees, or shareholders, indeed, every stakeholder that you have never known as deeply as you know your own division or function. What we don't see often enough is what Amon and Barry recognized in themselves that had served them so well in taking this critical leap to CEO. Both were experienced executives who had to shift from the C-suite by not assuming omniscient understanding of the entire business, including areas of the organization not frequently within their view.

Candidates often think of their credentials and accomplishments as easily transferrable to the parts of the business they didn't need to know earlier in their careers. Any candidate faces that when first entering the C-suite from their prior senior roles. When Mark was promoted to his first C-level job as the company's initial chief customer experience officer, he needed to align teams across many silos at the Charles Schwab Corporation. He was flattered that he was reporting to namesake CEO Chuck Schwab and mistook his appointment as a mandate from the famous founder. He assumed what he knew about marketing and user experience to be portable across all the functions and departments necessary to rally the entire company around the clientele. He thought of human resources and legal as overbearing gatekeepers and dismissed his peers in the C-suite as competitors for budget and resources. His arrogance led to an initial train wreck and service outages in the early days of Schwab.com, the world's first online stock trading and investment platform. He was lucky to get a second chance and became a lifelong learner.

When entering the C-suite—and particularly as a pre-CEO candidate—the only assumption you need to make is to assume a new level of humility. You need to go through a complete reexamination of your understanding of the business, now seen through a broader lens. It takes even greater courage to reexamine your behaviors as a leader and a human being when you think you already know how others perceive you. Most executives are surprised when they learn how others perceive them in the 360-degrees we conduct. As former Baxter CEO Harry Kraemer—now everybody's favorite business school professor at Northwestern—is widely quoted for saying: "I'm surprised you're surprised." Don't let yourself "get caught off guard by how you think your stakeholders *should* perceive you. Go find out what's actionable about the feedback" so you can qualify and be selected as the next CEO.

At this level, most requests for CEO coaching focus on helping the candidate develop two skills. The first is *strategic scope*. This is an ability to demonstrate to the board and your incumbent CEO that you have the ability to see the entire range of the functions of the company with both technical understanding and equal appreciation for those other functional roles' contribution to the overall organization, not just valuing your own expert function as the most important part of the company. If you, as a candidate, currently run a division, you should no longer be competing with the other divisions or criticizing staff functions or headquarters. Earlier in your career you may have engaged in that behavior because you were busy promoting the accomplishments of your individual department or division. That was your focus in those roles when you did not have the broader scope of accountability for the entire enterprise. You no longer can indulge in looking at your responsibility with a narrow scope; your board is counting on you seeing the bigger picture.

The second skill we're asked to help candidates develop is what the board recognizes as *leadership agility*, which we would define as four crucial behaviors.

Show confident humility

Here a growth mindset meets true curiosity to learn and grow your own skills and relationships rather than fall back on tried-and-true experience and old frameworks as the world and markets change daily.

Humility at the elite executive level is a learned skill and practice, but is often assumed to be a natural talent, as if a miracle happened that leaves the rest of us guessing. Often humility is confused with low confidence, but it's not that. Cristiano Amon and Corie Barry have very high confidence, like most high achievers.

"Gold medalists who have won in more than one Olympic Games describe humility as urgent curiosity and boundless ambition," Sarah Hirshland, CEO of the United States Olympic & Paralympic Committee, told Mark. As Mark's CEO coaching client, she applied this principle to herself as a new first-time CEO. "What looks to others like humility is actually a discipline," Hirshland says, "a framework and growth mindset that provides a more reliable way to de-risk your next bold move. Once you've set a world record, do you think more athletes or fewer competitors will come to beat you? The conditions and rules of the game are changing continuously, so you've got to gather intelligence that increases your prospects for consistently winning the game."

It's better to think of humility as an epiphany in which winners commit to a discipline that was acquired through nasty setbacks, but more importantly an insistence on finding a way to win again. "Whether it's painful losses that make you finally willing to debrief why you failed, or a realistic desire to repeat a gold medal, your training is never ending," says Hirshland. "It's easy to lose that healthy fear and curiosity when you're winning!"

Even worse is when you've been flattered with promotions and attention for your candidacy as the next CEO. Humility clearly is a matter of practice that leaders rehearse to identify growth opportunities; it's your chance to discover what you don't know before, during, and after you become CEO. For most highly ambitious, habitually successful executives, this skill must be reacquired after all the learning that has led to this moment of candidacy as the next CEO. You're never done learning.

Accelerate talent

"To be a great CEO, you've got to love discovering and investing in great people," says Frank Blake, chairman of Delta and former Home Depot

CEO. "The job of a leader is to recruit and develop other leaders," he adds, paraphrasing Peter Drucker, the father of management science. Whether you index toward introversion or extroversion, the best business leaders love developing people and teams in your organization. A talent accelerator never pretends to be the smartest person in the room and instead has a propensity for actively sparking and nurturing the potential in others, driving rapid skill development and career progression in many of the same ways that an individual exhibits confident humility.

Be a chief engagement officer

Best Buy's Joly loves to describe the CEO role as a "chief *energizing* officer." He said, "A leader who sparks a celebration of customers and employees and reignites the best attributes of the organization's culture and heritage and empowers the team drives the changes necessary to 'create the magic' for the next chapter." Joly thinks of the CEO as the chief *engagement* officer who "finds, attracts, and develops leaders who can form a high-performance team. Because they have excelled with their own energy, expertise, and experience, your role as CEO becomes less cheerleader (as it has been at lower levels of management) and more about busting internal and external barriers and giving them support to make decisions and drive for results."

Your role as a CEO candidate is the sum of chief culture curator, chief engagement officer, and courageous communicator. You must demonstrate a willingness to engage all stakeholders despite increasing tribalism and divisiveness in the media when you become CEO for the first time. Our CEO coaching clients frequently experience surprising scrutiny and an uncomfortably cultish curiosity surrounding them as they take office. The role is seen as lofty, romanticized, and yet often demonized—both celebrated and reviled in society. We dedicate much of chapter 9 to this discussion, as the CEO role combines the joyful celebration of your organization's history and culture while defining a new vision to embrace future challenges. At the same time, every successful CEO and executive team is now a target, assuming new dangers. Consider that a part of your CEO candidacy also has implications for physical safety or harassment on any media platform that may attempt to ensnare your role as a lightning rod for controversy.

Be a chief evidence officer

We describe this as a behavior, not just a technical skill, because the candidate's best frame of mind is one that encourages differing opinions, draws out the best ideas, and elevates the role of evidence that helps the organization discover actionable and measurable data from all levels, rather than your own natural biases and ungrounded assertions. There is a noisy tornado of data and opinions swirling and limited time and capital, so every board and CEO is looking for better discipline to manage and drive change and transformation.

Amy C. Edmondson, the Novartis Professor of Leadership and Management at Harvard Business School, is renowned for her pioneering research on *psychological safety*, a concept she introduced in the 1990s to describe environments where individuals feel safe to express ideas, questions, concerns, or mistakes without fear of negative consequences. She told Mark that her popular notion of "psychologic safety is too often hijacked by a tendency for people to avoid courageous conversations and settle for 'niceness' that could result in complacency or failure of the organizational goals." Her intention is for leaders to encourage and require teams to bring you bad news and build an avalanche of evidence. The "safety" part is the discipline not to be trigger-happy, shooting the messenger and evoking hostile opinions and biases. High-performance teams encourage accountability for bringing the whole story and seeking help in working together to find solutions.

You Must Qualify Twice—Be Skilled and Be Selected

With many years of experience in so many executive roles—from chief evidence officer to chief engagement officer—most CEO candidates don't realize that they still must qualify twice more in significant ways for the board and their boss to be confident they're ready for the top job. The successful candidates follow a two-step playbook: first, they focused on the new additional and often nuanced skills to get qualified (that we've been discussing), and second, they had the discipline and humility to know they needed to become more obvious as the right choice to get selected by the seven stakeholders who are judge and jury in this contest. As you think about making the leap to a chief executive's job, let politicking and posturing give way to humility and determined self-improvement. That's what caught the board's attention about Barry and Amon and ultimately won over any lingering skeptics.

In this regard, behaviors matter much more than you may assume. Indeed, your behavioral agility doesn't matter a *little* more at the CEO level than it does in your prior role; it matters *much* more. CEOs today need to walk the talk to a far more complex variety of stakeholders who must see you flourish in a nearly impossible breadth of behaviors, as fluent with your empathy and vulnerability as you are with your bold vision and ambition. The board must witness you as having courage to command when necessary but choosing to coach and collaborate with the team most of the time. Your every move is under a microscope.

Introducing the Seven Judges

As in any competition, when you seek to become a CEO, judges will evaluate your efforts. You need to prove your readiness twice to these stakeholders. Based on our experience, we believe seven key stakeholders define your candidacy. These individuals and groups wield the most influence on the final decision. Each will assess in their own way whether you are qualified, and together they will determine whether the board and the current CEO will select you or not. No one of them alone can get you the job, but each can impact or undermine your chances. In the coming chapters, we'll delve into the psyche and expectations of each stakeholder group, what they are looking for, and how to better connect with them.

1. *You.* While it's natural to assume you're going to take a run at becoming a CEO—and that others will be the judge of your candidacy—you should pause to evaluate your fears, blind spots,

and delusions of grandeur. In the next chapter, we'll share how most candidates second-guess every decision they make. They "should" on themselves: "I should do this," "I should have done that." When they realize they face competition from extraordinary external candidates, some start to unravel or overanalyze signals from their boss or other stakeholders. We will help you work through skill gaps and think clearly about promoting yourself as a potential successor, all while addressing fears and uncertainty.

2. *The board of directors.* The board has the ultimate authority and responsibility to hire and fire CEOs. That's its primary job. Increasingly, it is also redefining the role for the new CEO, not based on past successes or in the image of the last leader, but to lead future growth in the face of new opportunities and increasingly complex uncertainties. Boards face complicated challenges, including time constraints, limited insight into the candidates, and internal politics filtered to them by myriad executives' agendas. While the incumbent CEO's vote might be the most influential, the board makes the final call on who is selected.

3. *C-suite peers.* Fellow executives usually feel uncertain about a peer becoming their boss. They wonder how the new CEO's appointment will impact their future careers, especially if they have competed for the same job. Others will wonder if the new peer-turned-CEO really appreciates their value and will keep them on or support their work. C-suite peers rarely select the next CEO, but they can ruin your chances. They may have connections with other influencers that can help or hurt your candidacy.

4. *The current CEO.* The incumbent CEO will suggest a few potential successors who have the greatest potential to create value for the next phase in the company's history. But after dedicating a lifetime to becoming CEO, rarely does the incumbent have a complete exit strategy or even know exactly what to look for in a replacement. As a result, some CEOs can unintentionally slow or block the process of succession.

5. *Owners.* Wall Street, analysts, large shareholders, and the court of public opinion regarding stock price and company valuation all wield increasingly game-changing influence that impacts the future candidacy of CEOs and boards through powerful new levels of scrutiny, risk, and shareholder activism.

6. *Recruiters and assessors.* Boards commonly expand their talent search by hiring recruiting and assessment firms to evaluate inside candidates and vet outsiders as a comparison. This discovery process adds to the competition and expands the set of variables the board may consider in a selection process that is not going to be transparent to all the candidates.

7. *Direct reports, employees, and the customers they serve.* Employees at all levels represent the future of your company's ability to create value for customers as well as your organization's long-term legacy. The people who work for you today can't directly recommend you for CEO, but they can kill your candidacy with bad reviews. Are you spending quality time developing the people below you? Do they respect you? Do you understand their concerns? Do you speak their language?

As you consider these seven stakeholders, ask yourself: "As a candidate, what key relationships are most critical for me to ensure that I can get more qualified and eventually be selected to lead our company?" Make a list of names and their core needs and concerns. If you don't know some of the stakeholders, get to know them and build a relationship. Find out what drives them. Learn what they think of the organization's strengths and opportunity gaps. Find out what they think of you.

As you start gathering this information, recognize that every one of the people you meet has benefited from and become biased by their extraordinary career experiences; some might be acting on incomplete data, while others might just have differing opinions. Look for clear patterns. If one stakeholder has an issue, it may be their problem, not yours. If several have the same issue with you, then it may be a pattern. In every case, it's still your problem.

In this book, we will share tools you can use to get objective feedback from all stakeholders, so you will have complete visibility into what you're up against. Barry, Amon, and Joly engaged in 360-degree evaluations throughout their careers, and you probably have had a quite few at this point in your trajectory. Making sure that you engage in frequent feedback can illuminate broad perceptions about you, so that you can be more strategic about becoming qualified and ultimately selected in the eyes of the decision-makers. Most senior executives have had personality tests and business scenario tests long before they became candidates for CEO; that will greatly intensify now. We will share with you how to factor that feedback into your strategy and preparations as a CEO candidate.

While the assessments don't determine the CEO decision, again, they can undermine your chances because they stop far short of shining light on the historical biases and experiences of the board about the entire process and exposure to other candidates who are competing with you. We will share the criteria under which the board will determine whether it believes you have the skills and whether you're the best to be selected.

As you train to win the race for CEO, these varied audiences will be watching your every stride. The stakeholders care more about your performance than the people in the stands watching their home country's Olympic athletes, because they all have something at stake in your candidacy. Owners will be gauging your words to make sure that they will get a return on their invested dollars and wondering if you can keep delivering. Employees will be critically reviewing your actions to make sure that your deeds match your words and see whether they have a future under your leadership. Peers will want assurances that you will have their backs and will promote their contributions. All the while, competitors will be looking on for any signs of weakness and hoping that as a CEO, you will be a dud.

Your goal as you work with stakeholders is to create a readiness plan for yourself that builds on your abilities as a leader, provides an elegant exit from your last role, improves your chances for a more exciting and successful future ascent to CEO for your organization, and provides the best possible legacy for the company.

So, let's get CEO ready!

Your CEO Readiness Pulse Check

Five questions to answer to become CEO ready

1. **Are you relentlessly learning what you don't yet know about the business?** Have you shown the humility to explore unfamiliar functions and the discipline to do it with curiosity instead of entitlement?

2. **Are you leading—and being seen—as a CEO-caliber enterprise thinker?** Have you demonstrated strategic scope, not just operational excellence? Are you helping others experience your leadership across silos, in board settings, and through cross-functional impact?

3. **Have you earned the trust of every stakeholder, especially the ones who don't report to you?** Boards, peers, owners, and customers are watching how you listen, learn, and lead. Are your behaviors reinforcing trust or quietly eroding it?

4. **Can you model confident humility? Are you ambitious but coachable, visionary but real?** The best CEOs aren't know-it-alls. They're learn-it-alls. Are you investing in feedback, coaching, and self-reflection to grow before the job becomes yours?

5. **Are you growing leaders behind you or just building your own case to move up?** Boards don't just want strong successors; they want succession builders. Are you actively developing talent and signaling that you can build an organization that endures?

3

The Number One Stakeholder: You

Get to know your blind spots and fears, then learn to manage them

When thinking about the seven key stakeholders that you need to work with to become CEO ready, remember *you* are the first one you must understand better. There's no point reading about the rest unless you're *all in* yourself. You're number one.

This comes down to addressing your blind spots and fears as you become a candidate for the CEO job. Directors often tell us they are surprised by how few CEO candidates are aware of their own strengths and weaknesses and what they need to work on to prepare for this unique role. Former candidates often tell us how surprised they are, in retrospect, about what was making them fearful about taking the top job. This is not to say fears aren't warranted; some are. But you need to be aware of them in order to deal with them.

As a way to help a CEO candidate address their first stakeholder—themselves—Byron encourages executives to imagine where they are and what they're doing ten years from now. If they were able to sit down and have a cup of coffee with their future selves a decade into the future, what would they say they've found most rewarding during those years?

Michelle Seitz is the former chair and CEO of Russell Investments, which manages $300 billion in assets. She says, "Self-awareness is a lifelong journey. I think it's key to anyone trying to bring their best self to the table. I've sought out a lot of advice along the way. It is incredibly important to be curious about other people, curious about yourself, and looking for people that genuinely want to give you feedback to make you better at what you do and how you can have a positive impact in your sphere of the world. Never become too full of yourself or too insecure to take constructive, candid feedback. That has been a critical part of my journey."

This kind of self-awareness is also what she is looking for in CEO candidates. Can you look at yourself realistically and take others' input? If you don't have curiosity about what you might be overlooking in this process, and if you don't harbor doubts about your status as heir apparent, it means you're not preparing yourself properly for the race. As coaches, we will encourage your concerns, not dissuade you of them. Most of you harbor fears or emotions that can be surprisingly rational and helpful when you use them to create action plans to overcome them. If you pause and reflect, you will find and define most of your fears almost instantly. Fear can catch your attention in a good way. While it's challenging to separate the root cause, thank goodness you have some fears as a candidate, because you're likely to take them more seriously amid your overbooked day and set a course of action to address them.

"Why should I be CEO?" asked Arthur Levinson, as he reflected on an offer to become leader of Genentech. Levinson is a great example of addressing the first key stakeholder: yourself. Just as Corrie Barry eschewed her CEO candidacy at Best Buy and then focused on making strides to become a great one, Levinson's first response was also to think of reasons he wasn't qualified. That's a healthy approach.

"Will I still recognize myself when my [scientific] mission gets swallowed by corporate priorities?" he wondered. Not only would Levinson eventually accept the challenge, but during his fourteen years as CEO, his leadership helped accelerate his original objective to find new therapies, including those that save eyesight, reduce heart attacks, relieve asthma, and curb the development of psoriasis and a host of specific breast and intestinal cancers. During his tenure, Genentech generated a tenfold increase in the company's market value, which is, among many measures, the penultimate measure on which a board judges a CEO's fiduciary duty to the shareholders of a public company.

But at the time, despite his status as a brilliant R&D leader and research scientist at the company that had launched and defined the entire biotech industry, he paused when approached to be a CEO candidate. Levinson considered what this role would challenge him to do—shift from his scientific role—and what his prospects might be in this unique and peculiar new role. Initially, he determined that he was *not* CEO ready. From our experience, his clear assessment substantially improved his prospects for not just being an effective CEO but going from good to great.

As a CEO coach, Mark argues that the doubts, fears, and courageous humility you will read about in Levinson's journey—and many candidates like him—represent exactly the right mindset to start your next stage of evolution to become not just chief executive, but an extraordinary one. Levinson learned to understand his blind spots and fears, and it wasn't until he could find exciting ways to manage them that he became CEO ready.

Let's look at the top nine blind spots and fears that are typical of the highest achievers, a few of which may resonate with you as you become a CEO candidate.

1. Overestimating Your Status as Heir Apparent

The biggest derailer CEOs face is not any particular fear but, rather, failing to feel any fear. As a CEO candidate, fear is your friend when it forces you to identify objectively what your concern is or what you need to learn that will help you become CEO. The most common misperception that CEO candidates experience is the opposite: they assume their prior experience that got them promoted to the job just below CEO will also get them promoted to the top job. You might think you've heard the decision-makers say you already have the job. After all, when you think about the results you've delivered, you believe you deserve it. It's your job to assume that it's not true. Imagine yourself as a great candidate that the board and incumbent CEO has cast into a much more opaque, complex, and often changing decision-making process, no matter what signals you're getting about your candidacy.

Let's take the example of Steve Hasker, who was an inside candidate for the top job at Nielsen. He admits he didn't take the candidacy process seriously enough. He wasn't CEO ready. "If I'd thought about it logically and looked at where I was and what I'd achieved and my readiness for the role, I would have concluded there was nothing certain about it. I think there are lots of people in that category; they wrongly assume that they have the full picture and hear what they want to hear," Hasker said.

Hasker, who now is CEO at Thomson Reuters, told us he first interviewed for this role with a handful of board members, including Ed Clark, former CEO of TD Bank Group. "I saw in Ed someone from whom I could learn a tremendous amount. And I got a feeling halfway through the first interview that he was open-minded about my candidacy."

Since you are on the elite short list as a CEO candidate, you have already been flattered by board members and the incumbent CEO. Earlier we cautioned you not to count on that well-intentioned narrative. It's true that you have a great track record, but you are never the only choice, because it's the board's fiduciary duty to widen the net. And more important—and even harder for most candidates to believe—you are not necessarily the best choice or favorite. Do not think of this as either a pure meritocracy or a totally clear process in terms of what the directors are looking for. What the board and incumbent CEO are doing when they tell you're the right choice is appropriately keeping you motivated, because you *might* be the right one.

2. Miscalculating Your Authority

Another crucial blind spot to watch for is the belief that your candidacy comes with an omnipotent mandate. This perspective is natural for anyone tasked to be the spoiler, to fix things and tune them up with a hammer. You're the bad cop getting stuff done, and your boss, the CEO, plays the good cop motivating the entire company. Consider how that's often the case for many C-suite roles, particularly a COO. In this example, John Smith took over at a $83 billion global manufacturing company when the CEO stepped away for health reasons. He was an obvious and easy choice. The COO had been running operations for five years and had deep experience, including a stint as president at other industry companies.

While Smith drove significant commercial successes in his new post as CEO, his habitual hatchet wielding strained relationships with the board and partnership dynamics with the company's biggest manufacturing partner at the time. These stakeholders—the board, the investors, and the big client—are every CEO's biggest customers. They have the impression that all of you in the C-suite work for them, and you must honor and patiently listen and respond to their perceptions, fears, needs, and delusions. Smith did not notice his former boss's deferential behavior as CEO when he was working with them because Smith was tasked with a very different and essential mission: to squeeze every ounce of productivity from the operations. To him, the board and owners were wrong about their take on the situation; he didn't think they were in the right position to know what they were talking about. But the board and owners still believed they were in charge and discounted this seemingly arrogant new CEO who they felt was bullying authority to drive results. Smith had not demonstrated to them that, while it was Smith's call, he did understand their point of view. If they had felt he heard them, it would have stitched the widening rift. At the time, he thought the board meeting was a waste of precious time.

As a candidate, it is shockingly hard to fully recognize that you might misinterpret how your prior role as COO, CFO, or any senior C-suite leader—in which you were tasked with the hardest choices and given relative permission to behave in a nearly autocratic style—may lead you to miscalculate your approach. As a CEO, you actually have less authority to behave that way, except in the most extraordinary crises. For the most part, you must inspire, influence, and recruit hearts and motivate a broader array of people. The board and the owners always have more authority than you do as CEO.

What got you here will kill you there

With tragic irony, leadership behaviors that got you promoted to your current job will get you fired as CEO. The most insidious derailer for many candidates is accidentally demonstrating in the selection process a sense of entitled authority that you'll get the job without needing improvement. This next step is really a giant leap you can't fully imagine yet, and for that reason, the board would rather you think of yourself as a work in progress and a bit of a fixer-upper. That's what concerns your board and CEO—not a need for you to be perfect; that's definitely not true. Quite the contrary, they're concerned about an executive's delusion in thinking that they've arrived and the journey to the corner office is another rung on the ladder to put them on top of the company. It's not an end point—not the pinnacle of authority; it's a new starting line to make the case that you are a really fast learner. You're a candidate because you demonstrated great talent and results in the past, but it behooves you to admit you're on a very different growth trajectory.

That's what happened with Smith, who continued to play his old ultra-tough COO role as CEO, staying in character with what had always worked, showing up like the police. He was unintentionally overconfident that all the dues he had paid over the years, along with his track record of prosecuting hard-won successes in the same fashion, finally had earned him the right to a less encumbered path ahead as CEO. It would be fair for him to expect that, after all the positive reinforcement from the board and prior CEO, what got him here would get him there. Any reasonable candidate could easily suspect they should do the same. But that's not how this works.

With his urgency, edge, and sharp elbows necessary in that old role, Smith betrayed the most common blind spot of all CEO candidates—that he'd finally been authorized to do his job with full, unfettered, unedited authority. As he peered into his boss's office, all he thought he saw was great power, where the buck stopped, and he wildly overestimated and exaggerated the independence and authority in the role. He thought he knew the stakeholders because he had worked with them for years; he did not fully realize that he was going from having one boss—the incumbent CEO—to a dozen people on the board, with different expectations of his role. Particularly if you're heavily exposed in interacting with the board and other key stakeholders as a COO, president, CFO, or whatever role, you're unwittingly getting caught in the stakeholder role trap too.

You will become disoriented, since so many routine board meetings, executive sessions, late dinners, and other meaningful contacts with all the stakeholders in the selection process have given you the impression that you are doing great, which you probably are in your current job. But your great relationship with them and their accolades for your authoritative performance are in the context of the COO, CFO, or president role and doesn't mean they think you should just take those traits to the CEO job. They know that job is different. Most C-level candidates misunderstand the intimacy of the relationship they've built with stakeholders as a signal to "keep doing what they're doing." But the relationship will change, and the one you have now with the board and the owners doesn't translate into what they expect of you when you become CEO.

When you arrive in the big chair, you need to see the shift away from being the sheriff. Smith needed to adjust his leadership style after decades of doing it differently. He was disconnected from the reality of the breadth and depth of the stakeholder relations, which made him appear to be out of touch with the tensions with employees and industry.

He also didn't realize that what his former boss did as CEO interacting with the media was harder than it looked. In his COO role, he had not faced this level and sophistication of scrutiny, which couldn't be met with authority. This was his first real experience being exposed to the nuances of public criticism. He didn't take that skill gap seriously enough; after all, how hard could talking to the press be? His naively stubborn overconfidence about the importance of developing his media communications as another skill to master before becoming CEO led to several trainwrecks, followed by his resignation.

3. Ignoring Inner Signals

"You've got everyone 'should-ing' all over you," Deanna Mulligan said, laughing about what happens when you're considered for the CEO job.

"Your colleagues, friends, and family all have a vision for you, but unfortunately it's not exactly yours." As she pondered exiting as chief executive of Guardian Life, which had $90 billion in assets under management, all her loving critics "weighed in knowing absolutely what's best for me. Some may feel it's a morality play to do whatever they have in mind for you, based on who you are, what you've done, or where you're from." But, she said, that's their vision. "Those are *their* shoulds and should-nots. Don't should on yourself!"

When Mark was considering accepting an appointment to become chief executive of the CEO Academy, he was amazed how clear his loving critics were about what *he* should do and how he had an obligation, with his extensive business experience, to pay it forward for the next generation.

Mulligan likewise says her community of well-meaning fellow leaders pressed her endlessly, even after she retired, to take on new board roles, philanthropic projects, and another CEO gig, unintentionally "shaming me to step up and represent all women." This pressure intensified after she retired from Guardian in 2020. She was an extremely hardworking and successful executive who earned a break if she wanted it. She had done a lot of good, not only for the organizations she worked for but for nonprofits she volunteered with and for her entire community. She wrote books and sat on prominent boards including Vanguard, DuPont, Arch Capital Group, New York–Presbyterian Hospital, and many others.

Is it fair for others to push you to do more? The point for you as a CEO candidate is to realize that many will tell you what you should do and should want, but you need to want it, too, especially the CEO job. Don't tune out your dissenting inner voice even when everyone around you is telling you you'd be crazy to pass it up.

Mulligan had a powerful epiphany that Mark shares with every chief executive who is considering their pre- and post-CEO opportunities: "If you're busy doing everything for everyone else, you won't have time to figure out the right thing for you when the right thing comes along!" Mulligan said. "It took a while to get clear about what mattered most to me," because ironically so many people piled on with what they insisted should be her reality.

Therapist Nancy Colier addresses the concept of "shoulds" in her *HuffPost* article "Are Your 'Shoulds' Really Helping You?" As the author of several books addressing the burden and overload that women executives experience—pressured by work and family—she encourages readers to become aware of their use of the word "should" and to question its validity by asking, "What is happening?" This practice aims to shift the focus from imposed expectations to the reality of the present moment. Colier wrote, "Because so much of our behavior is driven by 'should,' we are losing our ability to distinguish what we really 'want.' We have been taught what we 'should' want, but no longer know what we *actually want*, and often confuse the two. Out of touch with our own 'wanting,' we have lost a sense of intimacy with ourselves. We know who we are supposed to be, but not who we are."[1] Don't take any promotion or opportunity without reviewing your options and distancing yourself from well-meaning onlookers. Carve out time in your overwhelmingly busy schedule to set a plan for your CEO candidacy—if that's the role that you're choosing to pursue next—and make that choice based on some thoughtful introspection.

Interestingly, when Mulligan finally freed herself from obligations and embraced guiltless permission not to do what others felt she should, she found the next best adventure of her career. As she hated the outside pressure, she also found retirement unsatisfying under those conditions. Today Mulligan is leading a new project that never was on anyone's "should" list. Certainly, it was never a goal or obligation in her mind to launch a startup, but it is now a new kind of thrill for her. Based on her insurance knowledge and gravitas, she's building one of the world's most innovative technology-based insurance startups as its new chief executive.

4. Behaving Badly If You're Passed Over (Again)

A valid fear you might feel (though too few candidates actually believe it) is that you won't get the job. This becomes real most often if you've been passed over before. If you do the math, not everyone who aspires to be CEO will get the job at your company. Our job is to help you to be brilliantly prepared at your present firm or at the next company. When you become CEO ready, you become more valuable and marketable in your next role here or somewhere else. There is no downside to preparation; you just get better and better. But at your level of accomplishment, you're in a small, elite community where key influencers in your future career moves may observe what happens next. You must be honest with yourself that you may get passed over in the current selection process despite being the best candidate. It happens a lot, and with the world watching. We recommend that you make peace with the reality that you do not control the ultimate outcome and it's in your best interest to react extremely graciously to whatever happens. Here's why.

Steve Hasker, current CEO of Thomson Reuters, was disappointed when he did not become CEO at Nielsen. You need to watch your behavior when this happens because it could determine whether you are passed over a second or third time. Lucky for Hasker, his friend Sean Bratches called him after. Bratches had missed out on the job of running ESPN and told Hasker that people would be watching his every move now to see how he took the news. "So, I didn't blink, I didn't complain, I supported the other guy. I just went forward to keep learning what it meant to be a CEO, to acquire the skills necessary."

A year later, the phone rang with the opportunity for Hasker to run Creative Artists Agency and, soon after that, to become CEO at Thomson Reuters. When you become CEO ready with class and grace, you can be CEO ready anywhere.

5. Fearing Not Being Enough

At Harvard Business School, now-senior lecturer Hubert Joly (former Best Buy and Carlson Companies CEO) says that among the three most common fears that he sees in the younger executives early in their careers is "impostor syndrome" or not being qualified for the job. Prominent figures like billionaire Facebook COO Sheryl Sandberg have publicly shared their own impostor syndrome experiences. Sandberg suggested to Mark that the best way to begin to overcome it is to first realize that you are not alone with that feeling. About a quarter of our

CEO candidates have felt it at some point in their careers. Researchers estimate that 70 percent of the general population has experienced impostor syndrome.

"Leaders often focus on their perceived deficits rather than their proven capabilities, creating a vicious cycle of self-doubt," Ram Charan and coauthors note in *The Leadership Pipeline: How to Build the Leadership-Powered Company*. Being CEO created "another order of magnitude of chaos even after my experiences running the largest division of the company and then even serving as COO," Eric Kessenich said of his first year as the CEO of U.S. Venture, where he recruited a few mentors and advisers like Mark. He said, "Fortunately what seemed like overpreparing hardly covered what I needed to learn, and the extra focus and training soaked up all that nervous energy not assuming that I knew what I knew!"

Tennis player Venus Williams told Mark that he was among *four* of her coaches. Mark helped her think about scaling her leadership team during the pandemic at EleVen and V Starr, companies she had created. The other coaches helped with her physical conditioning, nutrition, and other essentials. The best athletes are attuned to getting the help they need from the right advisers in each season of their leadership, just as you are as a CEO candidate. Nobody does it alone, and nobody can take you the whole way. The wisest coaches don't try to convince you you're perfectly qualified, only that feeling like an impostor is to be expected and dealt with simply by acknowledging that you have gaps. We're talking about gaps in knowledge and experience, fears and phobias that are rarely cured but usually brilliantly managed by high achievers. You've got all those issues, and that's OK, because all the other elite candidates do, too. The board doesn't expect to find a perfect superhero to replace the outgoing boss. Every candidate will have talents and skills that are underdeveloped or that the board perceives are not entirely on target for this situation; every choice of the decision-makers will involve trade-offs. If the board brings in someone from the outside, that person may not know your industry or business like an insider. If the board chooses someone from the inside, whether it's you or one of your peers, that person is going to have significant experience gaps in parts of the business they haven't worked in. This book is not about how you can overcome these very real fears but rather how to address what you can control—like your skills—and make peace with the fact that you may not be *everything*, but you're probably enough. You're not an impostor.

Mark's mentors at Stanford, Jerry Porras and Jim Collins, coauthors of the business classic *Built to Last*, told him that the fears should lead to humility. And, as noted in chapter 2, humility is not lack of confidence, but a huge dose of curiosity and courage to address what you fear. When Porras and Mark wrote the sequel, *Success Built to Last: Creating a Life That Matters*, they met with two hundred leaders at the World Economic Forum who had thrived for at least twenty years. What they had in common—including CEOs, Nobel laureates, Academy Award winners—was that they were like Olympians shooting for their second Olympics. They were living the true definition of humility, not a lack of confidence but a brutally frank and accurate self-assessment of their current situation. They showed curiosity, willingness, and even urgency to acknowledge and address limitations. Collins, in *Good to Great*, describes humility in leadership as a blend of "personal humility" and "professional will," emphasizing that great leaders are both confident in their abilities and grounded in their recognition of the team's contributions.[2] If you decide, after your self-assessment, this is something you really want to commit yourself to learning, then we will help you get there.

6. Fearing Failure in the Shadow of Giants

Both new and experienced CEO candidates share the particularly intense and valid fear of stepping into the shadow of a larger-than-life founder or predecessor. Best Buy stood on precipice of disaster when Hubert Joly, now a larger-than-life CEO hero, turned the company around; Corie Barry had to replace him. To be clear, Joly is the first to tell you the transformation occurred with the help of the Best Buy team that Joly led and empowered, and his successor Barry was on that courageous team. But Joly was still a very hard act to follow. Barry did what we'd advise any successor to a legend should do—don't imitate, don't try to replicate, address your gaps, get prepared, and do it your way, while honoring the legacy of who came before.

Imagine the pressure on Tim Cook as he took Apple's reins when Steve Jobs stepped aside. When Mark met Cook at the World Economic Forum, Cook shared that he had worried about the transition and what Jobs still meant to the company. Cook's performance had been exemplary at Apple—as yours has been, no doubt—but Jobs's image still defined the Apple brand. It's fair to say that Jobs's ongoing health issues related to his battle with a rare form of pancreatic cancer, which he had been managing since his diagnosis in 2004, gave him what Marshall Goldsmith calls "temporary sanity," realizing that he wanted Apple to prosper as he faced a real existential crisis. Except for Cook, Jobs had not been great at building a pipeline of leadership talent or handing over the reins until he was fifty-six, when he anointed Cook. Jobs died later that year. Cook, who had been Apple's COO, already was effectively running Apple and demonstrating his capability to survive his boss's mercurial nature, balance the needs of the board, and reassure the Apple community that he shared a deep understanding of Apple's culture.

But customers and investors still worried whether he could continue to instill the soul of Apple with the artistic sensibilities of Jobs. Crucially, Cook invested in and supported the team of people who preserved those sensibilities rather than try to remake the place in his own likeness. As a CEO candidate, this is usually your best approach as you manage the fear of succeeding a legend: don't completely reinvent yourself in the other person's persona. No one expects you to duplicate your predecessor. You must assess and acquire the necessary added operating skills along with the broad strategic view that encompasses the entire company and then build the necessary relationships so the board recognizes and selects you.

The lesson for you as a CEO candidate is that Steve Jobs and his board were watching Cook to see if he could *replace*, not *replicate* the founder. Not being identical to your predecessor is something that you should worry about briefly, only so you can channel that energy toward understanding how you can develop in the new role and perhaps expand your self-concept of what makes you a good leader. As a candidate,

Five Favorite Warren Buffett Role Models for CEO Candidates

It wasn't just Apple's board or investors who noticed Tim Cook's extraordinary preparation for leadership. "Nobody but Steve could have created Apple, but nobody but Tim could have developed it as he has," Warren Buffett famously remarked, adding that "Tim Cook has made more money for Berkshire Hathaway than I have"—a rare and extraordinary acknowledgment from the world's most admired investor.[a] "Tim Cook is one of the best managers in the world, and he's a terrific human being on top of that." Under Cook, Apple became Berkshire's most profitable equity investment—a testament to quiet leadership, long-term thinking, and operational precision. This kind of deliberate, steady stewardship is a hallmark of the CEOs Buffett holds in highest regard.

Also among Buffett's favorite role models is Kathryn Farmer, CEO of BNSF Railway. When Buffett acquired BNSF for $44 billion in 2010, he wasn't just buying railroad track—he was investing in a leadership model that would endure. Farmer, the first woman to lead a Class I railroad, embodies that model with operational excellence and unshakable resolve. "She possesses all of the qualities that make us excited about the future," Buffett said.[b] He still holds a controlling interest in the company through Berkshire Hathaway.

Cook demonstrated to Jobs and the board that he was willing to preserve the best of Apple's brand sensibilities. But Cook succeeded where other CEO succession candidates failed by leveraging skills that Apple needed and that he had: his prodigious operational expertise and ability to scale Apple's global supply chain. At the same time, the board did not expect Jobs's visionary style but rather Cook's own definition of the future of Apple. The strategy worked brilliantly, and Cook was the first CEO to preside over the world's first company to exceed a trillion-dollar market capitalization and today a tenfold increase over what Apple was valued when Jobs departed.

Charles Schwab also earned Buffett's admiration by democratizing investing and staying relentlessly focused on the customer. "I've admired Chuck Schwab for a long time," Buffett wrote. "When you read his [story], you'll understand why" Schwab's emphasis on access, transparency, and integrity reshaped the financial services industry—and offered a master class in customer-led growth.[c]

Buffett's respect also extended to the fiercely principled Rose Blumkin, the legendary founder of Nebraska Furniture Mart. "I'd rather wrestle grizzlies than compete with Mrs. B and her progeny," he said. Her unshakable credo—"Sell cheap, tell the truth, don't cheat nobody"—captures Buffett's belief in ethics as the foundation of sustainable success.

And finally there is Greg Abel, Buffett's handpicked successor whom he praised at Berkshire Hathaway for his operational fluency and character, saying: "He's a straight shooter. He's smart, and he understands operations better than I do."

a. Warren Buffett, "Berkshire Hathaway Annual Shareholder Meeting," Omaha, NE, May 3, 2025.

b. Rob Lenihan, "Buffett's BNSF Unit Names First Female CEO of Major Railroad," TheStreet, September 15, 2020, https://www.thestreet.com/investing/bnsf-railway-warren-buffett-chief-executive.

c. Charles Schwab, *Invested: Changing Forever the Way Americans Invest* (New York: Crown Currency, 2019).

As an aspiring CEO possibly replacing a beloved or remarkably successful one like Warren Buffett, Greg Abel became an obvious, well-tested choice. As a CEO candidate, the pattern here is that you need to build your skills as a great operator of the business and seek to position yourself in a role where those skills can be tested in public, rather than worrying too much about looking like your predecessor. Develop a clear and fresh vision that ideally builds on the prior point of view with clearly measurable progress about where the world and your industry are heading. Stay attuned to changing customer preferences, competitors' strengths, and emerging technological advancements. Build a strategic perspective grounded in both data and intuition and prepare to articulate how your vision aligns with the company's next series of goals and opportunities.

Carlos Abrams-Rivera did this to prepare himself at iconic brand Kraft Heinz. Abrams-Rivera wanted to honor his extraordinary predecessor, Miguel Patricio, who had transformed the business. Even now, as nonexecutive chairman, Patricio continues to be loved as a gregarious and genuine extrovert who has earned great affection from the board, employees, and all of Kraft Heinz stakeholders.

Like most aspiring CEOs we have coached, Abrams-Rivera had proven himself as head of the largest division. He was known in the industry as a great business operator, strategist, and a leader of people. Fortunately, as a CEO candidate, he built relationships with the board, confirming his reputation as a no-nonsense, straight-shooting leader who based decisions on evidence. Like many great division business operators who become effective CEOs, Abrams-Rivera has a rare combination of conviction, analysis, and a lack of pretention that comes off to some as reassuring and capable, and yet also reserved, even introverted. In what is a great act of courage and confidence for any CEO candidate, Abrams-Rivera didn't assume that he could lead exactly as he had done so effectively for decades in his previous roles. In preparing for this role, he listened differently as a CEO candidate in one-on-one meetings with the board, each member of the executive team, and vendors and suppliers—finding a new level of intimacy to learn what they thought he needed to ignite those relationships culturally at Kraft Heinz.

Abrams-Rivera brought his genuine humility to the process. He asked deep questions of stakeholders, showed a willingness to develop himself, and shared personal stories of his background for the first time in his career, which included his upbringing in Puerto Rico, that bridged the natural distance between his more introverted personality and his extroverted predecessor. He didn't try to be just like his predecessor but rather dug deeper to show stakeholders the foundation on which he built his character and conviction: his sincere dedication to honor the Kraft Heinz legacy while bringing his own style. "I understood there were a lot of things about the job I wouldn't know and that all the stakeholders deserved to be heard and figure out who I am," he says. "But you must be public about that. You need to prepare for the position with the mentality that, as much as you have prepared your whole life for a job like this, there's still a lot to learn. Whatever you have done before, you are not fully prepared without engaging everyone."

The point here is that the board and your boss—and your entire company—want a CEO candidate who can bridge the culture because, not despite, who you are. By focusing on how you can grow as a person and a professional—understanding the company's trajectory, addressing evolving customer needs, and rallying stakeholders—you can chart your own path, even in the shadow of giants.

7. Fearing Loss of Yourself

Arthur Levinson could have easily been one of those gifted scientists never to know he could also become a great CEO, one so good that Steve Jobs would recruit him eventually to become chair of Apple, where he remains today. Levinson is like inventors whose primary emotional connections professionally are to what they've accomplished as scientists, so he pumped the brakes when asked to run the company. Levinson never imagined himself as CEO. Most experts in most fields don't have that aspiration and never choose it, or find a CEO replacement quickly when initially feeling the pressure or necessity to take the job. There's nothing wrong with that. We too often herald the CEO's role as "a prize to be won rather than a job to be done," says collaboration expert Bonita Thompson. As coaches, we only wish for you to be the best at what you love most. Any other path is suboptimal for your life and your organization.

Nevertheless, colleagues and loved ones will encourage you to take the CEO job if offered no matter what, as we noted earlier. Levinson was against what at first appeared to him a seductive distraction from his life's purpose and identity. He was an impassioned scientist whose mission was to directly touch therapies that were inches from curing terrible diseases. Most experts in most fields never choose to become CEO, and most who aspire for that job are passed over. He had no interest in getting sucked into the bothersome politics of shareholder meetings.

Levinson joined Genentech in 1980 just four years after the world-changing idea of the biotech industry was launched by founders Robert

Swanson, a venture capitalist who became a first-time CEO there, and Herbert Boyer, a biochemist who codeveloped recombinant DNA technology, foundational to modern biotechnology. Scientists like Boyer or Levinson wouldn't have relished the idea of leaving the lab to engage in the business and media controversies that swirled around the fledging biotech industry. Daniel Goleman and coauthors discuss this in *Primal Leadership: Unleashing the Power of Emotional Intelligence*, observing that "the weight of conflicts within the organization, particularly among C-suite leaders themselves, can feel overwhelming" as a distraction from the bigger mission.[3]

Levinson's fears of facing a massive distraction from his mission were not butterflies or impostor syndrome; he genuinely had something better to do for himself and humanity by obsessing over molecules to cure cancer. For fifteen years, he had been parochially running R&D with his scientific tribe.

As the board intensified its recruitment of Levinson, his fears of the political intrigue that can come with being a manager were not to be underestimated. His concerns—just as you might be feeling with your candidacy—pointed to the need for the additional due diligence research you must do. In his case, the emotions warning Levinson were the real risks of failing the company at an existential crossroads. At Genentech, the board members believed he was the best candidate for that moment for two special reasons. They recognized Levinson's high integrity and credibility in the industry, and his lack of the most common unintentional hubris of leadership. This is as relevant for you as it was for Levinson in shifting his identity as a scientist to take the CEO job and making the right calculations about risk.

8. Fearing Loss of the Noble Cause

Two decades after building his career as a breakthrough research scientist, Levinson's thoughts about not wanting the CEO job were rational. He was at Genentech, after all, to develop therapies that could change lives. It was his noble calling. Giving that up to run the company must have felt like giving up the calling.

But Levinson's wife reminded him that his gravitas as a scientist was exactly what the company needed at that moment in the company's history, despite the perceptions that his leadership and operating experience might be underdeveloped. He had demonstrated skill in different organizational and strategic settings, albeit at a smaller scale—he had run R&D with a team—and his integrity and credibility were beyond reproach. Levinson realized he could learn what he didn't know about operating, scaling, and envisioning a business beyond the intermediate steps he'd learned running R&D.

Many candidates who may feel inadequate are making a clear observation about how much it's worth to them (or not). They are considering what appear to be additional hundred-hour weeks, shunning an opportunity for the CEO role because it requires leaving behind parts of their professional identity or long-held beliefs that have been a source of motivation and passion, along with confidence, comfort, and stability. Robert S. Kaplan and David Norton explain in their book *Strategy Maps: Converting Intangible Assets into Tangible Outcomes*, "Concerns about losing autonomy or becoming overburdened by the responsibilities of the CEO position are prevalent among the highest achievers."[4] This fear reflects the tension between staying true to one's objectives and being consumed by the relentless demands of the role. Hubert Joly, in *The Heart of Business: Leadership Principles for the Next Era of Capitalism*, emphasizes this point, noting, "Leaders fear that the constant demands of the role will strip them of the ability to manage their time and their most meaningful priorities effectively."[5]

But Levinson discovered that at this next level, a key part of overcoming his fear of losing identity or his original personal mission was to recognize he could serve his cause even better if he helped build Genentech in this next phase of its growth. He made the choice to recruit, train, trust, and empower others to inherit his current role. Levinson led with the expectation that you need great leaders under you so that you and your board are more confident about you vacating your current seat to become CEO. Levinson found that by investing in and growing others, he could in fact shift his own identity and accelerate his company's original mission.

You have been selected to the short list of contenders for your company's CEO role because you have a solid history with your company, like

Levinson. In fact, Levinson had lived every moment of the launch of an entirely new industry. He came to realize new meaning in how being CEO could put Genentech in the best position to have the biggest impact on his dream to find disease cures that were finally within reach. It was a company that he loved and, eventually, a job that he would come to love.

Levinson turned down the opportunity to be chairman at Apple at first, too. Again, he didn't feel qualified or confident for good reasons. By that time, his role as CEO of Genentech was more than a full-time gig; he was not enthusiastic about joining high-profile boards. To some it might seem sexy, or a feather in the cap. To him, it was, again, a distraction from his cause. His prescient wife, again, pointed out his organizational leadership mojo and his success leading a technology company. Levinson eventually overcame the fear and realized the value of his experience managing his wildly complicated, heavily regulated biotech firm gave him more than adequate experience to be a disciplined, evidence-based mentor to Steve Jobs. When Art Levinson became CEO of Genentech in 1995, the company's market capitalization was approximately $4 billion. Levinson retired as CEO after fourteen years, having sold the company to its largest partner. The deal was valued at $46.8 billion. Today, he's CEO of Calico, a Google Alphabet company that focuses on health and longevity research, and he remains independent chairman of the Apple board.

You obviously don't have to be a board member or a CEO to still have massive influence in your industry, your business, and even management of your vision. Most high achievers don't take the job. Genentech cofounder Herbert Boyer is an inventor of an entire industry and never aspired to the CEO role. Levinson did not have to make the choice to become CEO, and neither do you. But we encourage you to remain open to it even if your initial fears suggest such a role might somehow conflict with your initial passions at work.

9. Fearing Destruction of a Great Brand's Legacy

By the time you're being considered for CEO, you've had to face hard choices, like layoffs and restructurings, and many of you have already taken massive risks and made mistakes. As you think about the CEO role, you may worry that these mistakes will have profoundly negative consequences for a vast number of people and even a brand's legacy.

It's OK if you don't want this responsibility and better if you know that now. You must consider and address this fear in the selection process.

"It's frankly a horrible job—I wouldn't want it," says Nicholas Bloom, a Stanford University professor who studies CEOs. "Being a CEO of a big company is a hundred-hour-a-week job. It consumes your life. It consumes your weekend. It's super stressful. Sure, there are enormous perks, but it's also all-encompassing."[6] Many CEO candidates fear becoming disconnected or lonely at the top, leading to emotional and professional struggles. Building a health plan and practice with your family, developing strong peer networks, and seeking mentorship can mitigate this issue.

High achievers often fear that failure as a CEO will also jeopardize their reputation and career. Failure as a CEO is often seen as a reflection of one's entire professional identity, making the stakes feel impossibly high. "Every public failure feels magnified in the CEO role, where even small missteps can seem catastrophic," Eric Weiner observes in *The Geography of Genius: A Search for the World's Most Creative Places from Ancient Athens to Silicon Valley*.[7]

The worry is grounded in reality. The S&P 500 typically sees twenty to twenty-five iconic brands disappear from the index despite long histories of market dominance. General Electric, RadioShack, and BlackBerry were all once fixtures in the S&P 500's top tier. Even Silicon Valley chip pioneer Intel was removed from the Dow Jones Industrial Average—a gravely symbolic shift in its tech leadership. Others like Sears, Eastman Kodak, and Bed Bath & Beyond also failed to adapt and ultimately exited the index. If you were in charge of such a company at the end of its run, you'd find it hard to recover.

We're not going to tell you there's no reason to fear this. There is. You must consider the brutal truth. Are you prepared for managing and dealing with this fear, or is the time not right for you to be CEO ready?

Get Yourself a Truth Teller

To address your blind spots and fears as the first stakeholder in the process, don't try to do this alone. Leadership is already a lonely enough place. Engage with other leaders, peers, truth tellers, and loving critics. In this process of striving for the biggest job of your life, you may be beset by fears and fantasies, "shoulds" and "should nots." Seek out someone to be a sounding board as you consider options and to hold you accountable without judgment. To avoid drifting on goals, procrastination, and denial, Marshall Goldsmith and Mark Thompson have served as each other's accountability coach for many years. They check in daily in a half-hour ritual to update progress on goals, fitness, relationships, happiness, and meaning. As Goldsmith once famously wrote, "What got you here won't get you there," unless you're willing to get help and take advice. It's a practice that never ends—a journey, not a destination.

Your coach is not there to dismiss your fears or entirely diminish your hubris; we want you to use those contradictory emotions as tests of your true convictions and intrinsic beliefs so you can make a better choice about how to get prepared or whether you want to become CEO ready.

Understand your blind spots and embrace your fears to raise your awareness of what you need to address with your coach. Use every shred of insight not as an order to follow but as input to escalate your preparation for the job. Then you'll be ready to address the second stakeholders: the board of directors, whose primary charter is to hire and fire CEOs. They have the authority and responsibility to select you, or not.

Your CEO Readiness Pulse Check

Five questions you must answer to become CEO ready

1. **Are you brave enough to question whether you even want the job?** With colleagues, mentors, and family all cheering you on, don't "should" on yourself. Have you created space to ask what you want and whether this role aligns with your values, energy, and vision for the next chapter of your life?

2. **Are you using your fears as fuel or letting them quietly control your decisions?** Have you named the doubts—fear of failing, of not being enough, of losing your identity—that often live beneath your ambition? Great candidates face these fears early and turn them into focused action.

3. **Are you mistaking familiarity for readiness?** Just because you've been told you're "next in line" doesn't mean you're prepared or that the board is convinced. Have you built a compelling case for the CEO you're becoming, not just the role you've mastered?

4. **Do you appear to others to be overconfident, assuming you've got the job?** Are you clinging to the habits and authority that worked in your last role? If the board sniffs a sense of entitlement, it may see a blind spot in you where self-awareness should be.

5. **Do the people who matter most see your growth or just your résumé?** Are you actively seeking feedback and investing in the development you still need or relying on your past performance to speak for a role that demands reinvention?

4

Win the Board's Trust

Help directors know you are the best candidate for the job

"The search for a successor can often become a Shakespearean event with intrigue and all sorts of drama," observes David Lawrence, founder and chief collaborative officer at RANE Network, underscoring the gravity you face as a candidate during CEO succession planning. The process demands readiness for a wide-ranging assessment—covering your skills, strategic thinking, ability to inspire, and fit within the company's culture. Most critically, it gives you the opportunity to articulate how your leadership can advance both your career and the company's future in an unpredictable world.

Lawrence brings decades of experience to this strategic conversation at the intersection of law, regulation, risk management, and corporate governance. A former associate general counsel and managing director at Goldman Sachs, he has advised *Fortune* 100 boards, investors, and C-suite leaders on leadership, compliance, and succession. "Every company is different. Every company does have a unique culture, whether they want to admit it or not. And so finding the right person is not a one-size-fits-all process," he explains.

As a CEO candidate, you must recognize the burden of stewardship boards carry. "The board really has a fiduciary obligation to investors, of course, but no less to the people who work there, as well as the alumni of the company, customers, and clients," Lawrence notes. "Getting it right means taking in information from a wide variety of sources." The right or wrong choice carries significant long-term reputational implications.

Winning the board's trust means helping directors make fully informed decisions—with no surprises from any source, including the evaluation of open-sourced or social media content. "Diligence today is a full 360-degree exercise. It's not just about easily accessed data; this isn't about red or green lights—it's about scrutinizing historical statements, even those made casually or years ago, through a lens of potential risk," says Lawrence. Remember Faulkner: "The past is never dead. It's not even past."[1]

Due diligence now extends far beyond litigation and settlements, even those under confidentiality agreements, and includes medical or psychological history. Many boards also draw insights from the political world—how candidates have been vetted, how allegations were addressed, and how omissions shaped public perception. Boards want a clear, complete, and unflinching picture—one that withstands scrutiny and fosters trust.

Boards also conduct their own independent diligence beyond what the search firm provides. As a candidate, you must cultivate relationships with each board member, knowing every one of them will form their own judgment. Ensure every element of your story is accurate and aligned with how you want to be perceived. Assume that anything overstated or omitted will be tested—and eventually revealed. Boards are looking for clarity, credibility, and completeness.

Surprises are the enemy of boardroom trust. In today's transparent world, hidden issues can surface quickly. Lawrence emphasizes it's "imperative to know if there [is] anything out there that could cause legal, regulatory, investor, financial, or reputational exposure." The worst-case scenario? "After an announcement has been made, or somebody's actually been in a position for a few years, certain revelations come to light."

Warren Buffett's careful succession planning at Berkshire Hathaway offers a world-class example: "Buffett understood his obligation to his investors; he and Munger were very methodical and careful," says Lawrence. Greg Abel, the incoming CEO, was observed and vetted over time. He represents continuity with Berkshire's culture and the capacity to adapt its legacy in service of shareholders amid change.

Another critical insight: "The office that candidates often run for is not the office that they get." Just as in politics, the real demands of leadership often diverge from expectations. Events like pandemics, cyberattacks, and geopolitical unrest demand leaders who can pivot swiftly, mobilize teams, and bring in outside expertise. Lawrence recalls, "When 9/11 hit New York and Washington, DC, the leadership inside companies was absolutely critical—to investors, to clients, to suppliers." In such moments, the ability to engage board expertise and inspire confidence becomes essential.

From a practical standpoint, be prepared for questions about your strategic plans—immediate and long-term. Lawrence frames the mindset: "This is now *your* company. Tell me on day one what you're doing—the first hundred days. And the next hundred. And the next hundred. Recognizing that events may supersede that are exogenous." Even longtime insiders must treat the process as "virtually a de novo one." Familiarity doesn't excuse scrutiny; presumed competency is not enough.

As a candidate, you must also interpret and present your leadership experience with precision. Examine your statements and accomplishments to ensure they reflect your authentic track record and align with the organization's strategic priorities. Ultimately, boards are judging not only IQ or business acumen, but emotional intelligence and the ability to lead through ambiguity. Comprehensive preparation—and a visible commitment to readiness—can significantly elevate your standing as a candidate.

Fears and Blind Spots of the Board That's Choosing You

At Nasdaq's Center for Board Excellence, founder and head Byron Loflin (and one of the authors) has facilitated board and CEO assessments for over fifteen years. During assessment interviews, he's asked over ten thousand questions, probing the real hopes, hesitations, and hidden concerns directors carry into CEO succession decisions.

"I've seen many CEOs who love their jobs—and a few too many who hide how much they *hate* it," one director confided to Byron. "You have to understand whether this high-potential executive is the *real deal*—we must determine whether this is just advanced salesmanship by an experienced executive or whether they're pursuing the CEO role as a life-or-death calling based on long-term passion. Is this really just the next rung on a ladder for them?"

Many directors quietly admit they wish for more time with internal candidates—people like you. Far from being distant or disinterested, they welcome outreach and are hungry for it. One director bluntly shared with Byron: "I need to know enough about the candidate to feel confident they're doing the right things when no one is around, so they have the full confidence to do the right things when everyone is watching." What the board is searching for are signals of your intrinsic character—integrity, maturity, and internal compass. And because so few directors get to see you in action in the real world outside the boardroom, your signals must be intentional and consistent. In your pursuit of being CEO ready, recognize that, if chosen, you predominantly set the tone of integrity for the organization.

Ironically, while CEOs and executive teams often feel they spend too much time preparing for board meetings, Byron has never heard a director complain about being overinformed by a CEO or about meeting CEO candidates too often. Particularly if you are the internal candidate, you already spend considerable amounts of time with your board at meetings, presenting reports, hashing out plans, then laughing over dinner. With all the complexity of your day job—and now the preparations we're urging you to make as a candidate—you think that's plenty. The last thing you expect to hear from us is that your relationship with the board is inadequate.

Quite the contrary, most incumbent CEOs and CEO candidates fret about how much extra time they must spend preparing for and running board meetings. Ironically, what takes a lot of time and commitment for you and your CEO does not usually feel like a lot of time to the directors. They only see you four to eight times a year. That's not enough time to create an excessive amount of trust and comfort in times of stress. Only 15 percent of CEOs report they are "always" vulnerable with their board during high-stakes strategic decisions, according to executive search firm Spencer Stuart.[2] As a candidate, watch how that lack of psychological safety plays out in meetings; it reveals the tightrope your boss is navigating and the one you'll be expected to cross next when you're interviewed as a CEO candidate.

Many directors emphasize to Byron that a standout CEO trait is "active listening." CEOs (and their most promising potential successors) are people who "have built a reputation for absorbing board feedback and responding—not always immediately, but always with prudence and purpose."

The best CEO candidates and incumbent CEOs "invite open dialogue. Curiosity is a key that unlocks critical thinking. And critical thinking fosters balance and understanding," another board member told Byron, offering a simple but profound signal of leadership potential: in this director's view, curiosity isn't a soft skill; it's a sign that you're open to "good governance, to real debate, and to partnering with the board as collaborators, not just evaluators."

But many directors also express frustration about a lack of transparency in succession conversations between the CEO, the board, and the potential candidates. As one director put it, "What irritates me is a senior executive who practices mushroom management—leaves you in the dark and then throws crap on you. We get it—your role is wicked hard. We know that talent, risk, and strategy (TSR) can be moving targets in volatile times. But we're partners, not passengers. Don't surprise us." How you show up under pressure from the board signals how you'll behave under pressure in the real world.

What's Measured Improves

A theme that Byron hears in every board meeting is the importance of management-specific key performance indicators that help board members identify and assess future CEO candidates. One of Byron's longtime director colleagues regularly asks the CEO and her potential successors a pointed question, usually at least twice a year: "Investors expect a CEO to take the lead and clearly communicate a measurable path. As Peter Drucker said, 'What's measured improves.' So tell me: How will you lead the company toward its future with clearly defined milestones? Without getting overly philosophical, I'm looking for a candidate who can authentically communicate both realism and vision."

The point is, as one senior board member told Byron, "Running a large public company—or any complex organization—is holistic." It's not just about one product or division, as it might have been in your last job. It's about how the parts work in concert. "It's not about knowing all the answers; the next CEO must seek wise counsel, not just run the show."

In this regard, another director described a rising candidate with admiration: "I think she's going to be a fantastic CEO. She's the opposite of some guy essentially with lots of hand-waving about making progress, revealing that 'we're lost, but we're making good time.' As an executive, I think she's focused, she communicates clearly, delivers the numbers, and there's no bullshit. You always know where she stands, and that gives our board confidence."

Since the opacity of the board's selection process is affected by limited exposure, inconsistent access, or shifting opinions or rumors about your readiness as a candidate, the process can feel unfair. That's likely unintentional, but that might be the challenge you're facing. However, an accelerating trend among boards is that when they realize the succession process is episodic, inconsistent, or inadequate, some are taking more aggressive command as independent directors advocate for acceleration of CEO succession, just as an external activist investor would. As one disappointed governance and nominating chair shared with Byron, "The current management team has not driven or communicated a clear strategy. A lack of strategy makes a CEO a prisoner of events. Our prior CEO wasn't a strategist, so he needed to have or hire one, but since he ultimately didn't, we concluded that we needed a new CEO."

For that reason, as a candidate you need to be disciplined about becoming CEO ready, even if your board is not, because in the cases where the CEO or board hasn't settled on a transparent plan and consistent process, the chances of a sudden "fire drill" CEO transition isn't fiction; it's front-page news. A record number of CEOs were pushed out in recent years largely due to performance failures, policy violations, or misconduct, but also due to resistance to building a team. Even high-performing companies can find themselves in crisis when the board and CEO fall out of sync on strategy and succession.

Every Board Member Has a Rich History

To better understand how each board member approaches their role in your CEO candidacy, it's crucial to learn about their personal and professional history that brought them to the boardroom. The average tenure for S&P 500 board directors is approximately 7.8 years, while the average CEO tenure is around 7.4 years, with internal hires tending to stay longer than external ones.[3]

In his role as founder and head of Nasdaq's global board advisory practice, Byron routinely conducts board evaluations, just as Mark does as a CEO coach leading 360-degree reviews in which he talks to every board member and executive leadership team member. During each process, we get a very clear picture of what matters to them. You need to spend time learning each individual's biographical history to understand the source of their scar tissue and the crises they've managed, averted, or created over the years. As you visit with board members, ask questions that build relationships with them and how their experiences can contribute to your leadership development. Seek to understand the board's journey and how the existing board was selected. Watch carefully during board meetings to evaluate each member's hot buttons and how each serves and influences.

Hopefully it's obvious that directors are human beings, but we don't stop often enough to think about them as volunteers. While they appear to be relatively well paid, they see themselves in a generous pay-it-forward opportunity, because most don't need the money. What they seek is what we all want as people: to be relevant, to add value, and to be seen as contributing to discussions with insights that positively affect both you and the shareholder. They also, like anyone, want to be loved, admired, and respected by their colleagues and you. They may show off for each other and for your CEO, but some go to great efforts to subdue their emotions.

In a rather more colorful metaphor, the general counsel and corporate secretary of one of America's best-known brands commented, "Board members are like rescue dogs, because they're all survivors!" Board members earn their seats through experience and skill. Like rescue dogs, they are trained that timing and toughness are essential for success. Information must be processed quickly and decisively. They've not only faced trauma from wounds acquired while running companies, they've defeated it. They all need you to be a great candidate because they are anxious to successfully finish this risky but tedious process of CEO succession. The better boards are stewards of corporate continuity looking for a CEO candidate who will lead the pack quickly, competently, and without drama or trauma—or as our corporate counsel friend says, "not driving us off a cliff or into the hands of wolves!"

If you aspire for the top job, a good place to start is by getting to know your board and committee chairs. Know their roles and why they have their jobs. This will help you better understand the board's leadership dynamics and their present approach to succession. The nomination and governance committee, for example, oversees board performance evaluations, board succession, and often CEO succession planning.

Know the trends in directors' positions on what they consider makes a good CEO candidate. Effective boards revisit the criteria at least annually and perhaps more often if they see dramatic changes in the industry, threats from competitors, regulatory drama, or geopolitics, and then review them again before they begin a search. Criteria may include factors such as capability in strategic thinking, a track record of delivering results, the ability to develop other leaders, knowledge of the industry, an ability to motivate and engage large teams, and breadth and depth of experience in making big decisions.

You Don't Know Them; They Don't Trust You Yet

Whether you are an internal or external candidate, winning the board members' trust is paramount, and they don't know you in the context of a CEO. You do not yet have a relationship with the board, as the chief executive does, so you need to move in that direction to enable the board to see you in a broader context of expertise and leadership. Until now, even if you're sitting shoulder to shoulder with your current CEO and you already wield a very expansive role—like chief operating officer, chief financial officer, or president—most board members still do not yet imagine you as their equal. Unlike the CEO, they do not yet see you as a commanding presence in the boardroom who could get them fired. No matter how big your job or impact on the company, you don't have that penultimate power, and everyone knows it. No decision is your final decision and the buck doesn't stop with you—not yet. When you consider that power dynamic, you really don't know who you're dealing with here, because in their minds, you're running a specific operation, not driving the whole company.

Complicating matters further, you're not just trying to win the board's enthusiasm that you are capable of something bigger than your current role; you need to watch carefully the board's evolving relationship with your boss, the current CEO. That dynamic is under pressure in many companies. Only 22 percent of CEOs say they receive effective support from their board, while 43 percent of directors believe they're providing it.[4] As a candidate, you may witness these disconnects firsthand in meetings where your boss is forced to navigate competing opinions, vague feedback, or minimal alignment. Observing these moments is an education: they show you how fractured the board-CEO relationship can be and what kind of leader you'll need to become to bridge that gap, not widen it.

Board Relationship Management

In the context of your current role as an operations chief, finance chief, or other C-level job that has put you into the CEO succession limelight, you need to consider how to find opportunities for more frequent engagement with the board on different terms and at a different intensity than you're used to. Take a bigger role with the board. The most effective CEOs utilize the board as a mentor not only for themselves but for the C-level candidates like you. The benefit of this expanded relationship works both ways, for you and the directors who want to know more about each other. CEO Bruce Van Saun built a robust governance structure at Citizens Financial Group through effective board utilization: "Board members should be encouraged and granted free access to visit company sites and personnel. We have five board/top executive mentoring relationships in place, plus another thirty execs who have three-to-four-person group meetings with directors around the gaps in the two-day board and committee meeting schedule."

High-performing board members are in great demand. Ideally, but not always, they arrive well-read (or at least have done the homework) and ready to engage. Nevertheless, during most succession processes, they probably have not spent enough time really thinking about you or your career. At Hewlett-Packard, CEO Enrique Lores instituted a program of director mentorships with individual C-suite team members that rotates each with a different board member. If your management team and board doesn't interact like this, it's worth planting seeds to do that with your boss and board.

Twelve Jurors, But a Few Swing Votes

The 1957 film *Twelve Angry Men* highlights how each juror's perspective, bias, and arguments shape a final decision. During our engagements with CEOs and boards, we see the same dynamic play out. The board members are your jurors deliberating your fate, weighing evidence, emotions, and ethical considerations. Board members engage in intense discussions, evaluating candidates' qualifications, leadership styles, and strategic visions. In both scenarios, a single voice—whether a persuasive board member or a determined juror like Henry Fonda's character—can shift opinions, challenge assumptions, and steer the group toward selecting you or someone else. The process is not just about logically who seems best, but also about how they perceive you will build stakeholder excitement in the company's future.

First you need to identify who will be the biggest influencers in the final vote on your candidacy. From a corporate governance standpoint, the process is led by your board chair or the chair of your governance and nominating committee (although often the board leans on the internal CEO to guide this process). One of the two may or may not be among the most influential board members in the decision-making process. Try to identify those who are skeptical and build your rapport with them; a director who develops a strong negative bias against you can get you eliminated from the short list easier than a supporter can keep you on it. Any doubts about you are hard to overcome, but you should anticipate them.

A board veteran and former chair and CEO of Ball Corporation, John Hayes frames succession in deeply personal terms: "Leadership is about getting people to do things they couldn't otherwise do on their own. But if overused and you're not self-aware, your superpowers become liabilities. My advice? Help the board see how you bring people along—not through fear, but through belief."

As a CEO candidate, start learning these board dynamics early from your boss and your peers in the C-suite who might have wider visibility into the board's thinking and about your candidacy. Van Saun says, "I think the chief human resource officer is an integral part of the compensation and human resource board committee meetings, but should attend the full board meetings periodically for topics such as talent management; leadership succession; compensation, retention, recruiting strategies; and organizational health or culture reviews. In general, I have my top execs attend only the portion of the meetings relevant to them."

As you prepare for meetings with the board, remember that being a director is a surprisingly tough role, particularly for experienced former or present CEOs who are unaccustomed to holding back because they had power, commanded attention, and created impact in their day jobs, things that are less prevalent in their role as a board member. As a CEO candidate, you can benefit from having empathy for that shift in position and help them feel a deeper connection with those historic roles as your mentor.

We cannot overemphasize how much you will differentiate yourself from the pack of competitor candidates by making it obvious that you understand how they feel undervalued. This must be authentic. We are not suggesting fake salesmanship, since the board is watching for that. The board can smell that a mile away. As Marshall Goldsmith famously quips, "It's not that we hate suck-ups; it's that we hate bad ones." Do not patronize, flatter, or ingratiate yourself with the board. You must win hearts and minds through deeper understanding of each member of your board—their experience, their pain, and their insights. They are your customer. As Peter Drucker insisted, your directors "do not have to buy, but you do have to sell."

CEO as Biggest Enterprise Risk

The drama of CEO selection—so many failures, many quite public—has left boards examining options for improved processes. Since publishing its enterprise risk management (ERM) framework in 2004, COSO and the Treadway Commission have been examining ERM with a goal of categorizing and clarifying risk within the corporation. Previously, ERM was presumed the purview of finance, audit, safety, and other logistical departments. Now the incumbent CEO and CEO candidates are seen as the biggest single risk and responsibility of the board of directors. Choosing who will lead the company is primary; there is no close second. Whereas ERM in general is not the directors' responsibility to manage, it is their job to strategically monitor it, which means as a candidate, you are a risk they are monitoring. Bill George's 2024 article "Why Boeing's Problems with the 737 MAX Began More Than 25 Years Ago" makes this exact case. He recounts actions by a series of CEOs at Boeing who led the organization away from a focus on aviation excellence to a focus on maximizing short-term earnings. "The Boeing board, which is composed of exceptional individuals, failed to preserve Boeing's culture and reputation," he wrote.[5]

The board is taking a risk to its reputation should things go wrong with you or any other candidate. We encourage you to engage in projects that highlight your abilities not just in vision and strategy, but also in core operational areas like risk management assessments of company strategy.

Look to Instill Confidence, Accountability, and Trust

Many high-performing CEOs are leaders who instill confidence, invite accountability, and build their vision on trust. These three characteristics play a dominant role in boardroom strategy discussions, including CEO succession. Imagine that you've just presented a plan for the next year to the board. As you exit the boardroom, you are asked these questions:

- Do you feel that your presentation was well received?
- A presentation outline was in their preparatory reading; did they seem to have read it?
- Did the board ask insightful questions?
- Do you have more confidence in the board after this presentation?
- Do you sense that the board has more confidence in you?

If you are answering no to these questions, it might signal that you have not established credibility with your board and you have work to do. As you communicate confidence in your leadership, the board should reciprocate confidence in you as a leader.

Wanting the CEO job requires ego. Being great at the job requires humility. Evaluate your leadership style to consider whether the way you're showing up builds credibility. Despite twenty-four years in C-suite positions at Texas Children's Hospital, Michelle Riley-Brown (now CEO of Children's National Hospital) told us, "I'd say the biggest surprise in moving to a CEO's role was the level of board engagement and how to win their confidence. They're interacting and engaging with you every day, and it's a delicate balance to weigh the board's expectations and the operational demands of the organization. The board was a big reason for me taking this role at Children's National. The board and CEO relationship is integral and so important to the success of any CEO that you have to be comfortable with the board members—especially the board chair—their philosophy, and how you will work together."

Riley-Brown told us that her new board did its due diligence interviews to ensure that not only would she be a good fit in the existing mission-driven culture, but also that she had the skills to help move the organization toward a new future that it envisioned. "I met with Horacio

Rozanski [CEO of Booz Allen], who is our board chair. Immediately we had this very authentic, real conversation. We talked about strategy, we talked about operations, and he got a real sense of my leadership style." While Rozanski is only one vote, his early read as board chair carried influence. Riley-Brown instilled deep confidence and trust. That candid exchange served as a critical inflection point: a clear, early signal to the rest of the board that Riley-Brown was not only prepared, but also deeply attuned to the organization's evolving needs. Her ability to connect substantively in that one-on-one meeting helped catalyze broader trust and alignment across the board.

But as Riley-Brown warns, the process can't just be about the organization wanting you and your unique skills; you have to want the organization as well: "It has to be a good fit for both. So beyond traditional interviews and the panels and the presentations, I toured the campus and met candidly with senior leaders to get a sense of the culture. That two-way exchange with the board was fundamental to the decision-making process. It allowed me to feel comfortable and to understand the organization more completely."

Your Board Sees Your Business at a Crossroads

Ironically, the other major surprise that we frequently hear about from CEO candidates is that boards today universally think the next leader is someone who not only needs to build off the foundation of the existing business—to cherish it—but must also urgently change it to drive a new transformational strategy for the future.

"Every board believes that your company is at a crossroads!" said Jim Citrin, leading CEO placement expert at Spencer Stuart. "When talking to the board as an inside candidate, you must make the existential case: we're at a crossroads, and here's what I would do that I believe is right to evaluate and address the coming challenges and opportunities. No board will ever disagree with that point of view." If you, as the internal candidate, and even the leading candidate, give a historical message of doing business as usual, you're *not* going to win the position. To compete with outsiders, you need to give the board your proactive approach as an insider to addressing the business's changing and highly disruptive environment.

Steve Hasker, CEO of Thomson Reuters, agrees. "I've not met a board member in the last year or two who says, 'We're just fine.'" Fast-paced change through technologies like generative AI is going to be as big or bigger than the advent of a PC on every desk, the internet, and cloud-based computing. So, anyone applying for the top job in for the next few years must communicate and demonstrate adaptation to transformational change and an agile sense of disruption.

As you advocate for transformation in front of the board, be careful not to unwittingly trash the prior CEO—especially if you served under them. It's a delicate balance: the board wants to hear your vision for necessary change, but they'll also be thinking, "If you were so convinced this direction is critical, why haven't you done more about it already?" The best CEO candidates can thread that needle. They acknowledge their role in the current state while showing how they'll lead differently in the top job: "While I've worked to drive results in my current role, if chosen as CEO, I'll be in a position to evolve the strategy further and take the company in a bolder direction."

Headwinds for the External and Internal CEO Candidates

Let's pull the curtain back a little further on the process of how boards make their final choice for CEO as they compare internal candidates with external executives. The Conference Board found that 77 percent of new S&P 500 CEOs in 2024 were promoted internally, compared with 74 percent the year prior, reflecting boards' growing preference for candidates who are already culturally aligned, organizationally embedded, and strategically informed.[6] These internal leaders are perceived as lower risk, particularly when continuity and performance stability are top priorities.

But internal candidates also face a terrible headwind. "They suffer from the curse of familiarity," Jim Citrin mused. Too often, board members assume that an external candidate will be more innovative and bring more experience versus the internal executive who the board has seen grow up in a narrower role at the company. Citrin has worked on 850 top succession assignments, from Bob Iger to Roger Goodell. "The advice I give an internal candidate is, even if you believe your board knows you, assume they don't. Tell them your story. What was your journey? Discuss turning points. And then in terms of the bias that some directors have with the 'grass-is-greener' outside candidate, play to your natural advantages as an internal candidate by underscoring your deep knowledge of the company. Articulate your vision for the degree of change necessary. Be the change agent internally based on your knowledge."

Sometimes recent events or trends just catch on, and you should try to be aware of them, Citrin said. "I'm just finishing a large company's CEO succession right now—with an internal candidate and an external candidate," he told us. "The internal is not getting it because he didn't have any experience in capital allocation, which is the buzzword that boards are using for essentially being strategic, doing M&A, and investing. The external candidate has a lot of capital allocation experience. So, in retrospect, the internal guy should have argued for at least a year or two in advance to generate the experience to do that, even if it was on a project basis. The board wants to know that the internal candidates have done something enterprisewide that has some kind of investor relations aspect to it."

From the board's point of view, here are factors in favor of choosing internal candidates:

- *Knowledge of the company, its culture, and how it operates.* An insider is already up to speed on the culture that made the company successful and trusted by internal stakeholders, so it's easier to maintain momentum.

- *A proven track record.* The board has seen what internal candidates have done, and how, and who they worked with to get it done.

- *Continuity.* Hiring an insider as CEO allows for a smooth transition and for maintenance of current projects and goals.

- *Stronger morale and loyalty among employees.* When employees see one of their associates rise through the ranks, they feel the company cares about its own.

- *Lower risk.* If the company and a prospective candidate have been performing at a consistently high level, a contingency of board members will likely prefer the stability of an internal candidate.

External candidates have factors in their favor, too:

- *Fresh and broad experience.* An outside candidate may bring new and innovative ideas that can help the company adapt to changes in its market or industry. They may have led a noteworthy prior transformation, and change is captivating to see with all the public fanfare and success but without all the messy sausage-making details required to accomplish it.

- *Absence of ready internal candidates.* If the top execs under the CEO aren't deemed ready, the board may feel it has no other choice but to seek an outsider.

- *Different skills and experience.* An outside candidate may lead the organization in a new direction or navigate through a specific challenge.

- *Objectivity.* An outside candidate may be viewed as more neutral and capable of honestly assessing the business than an internal candidate; the board may feel choosing someone from the outside may make the selection process seem fairer and more transparent.

- *Lack of internal politics.* An outside candidate, unencumbered by the history of maneuvering and power plays, might be perceived as better able to make decisions based on what is best for the organization rather than on personal relationships or agendas.

- *Signal to Wall Street that overdue transformational change is coming.* New technologies or contexts may demand a hard pivot the board doesn't think can come from within.

As either type of candidate, you want to be mindful of what the other type has going for them and think about ways to address those yourself. As an internal candidate, note too that external candidates may also face challenges that work in your favor:

- *Lack of organizational knowledge.* They will not have the same level of understanding of the organization's culture, history, and operations as an internally promoted CEO.
- *Difficulty building relationships with key talent.* An external successor may have a harder time gaining the trust of employees, stakeholders, and other key parties.
- *Different leadership style.* A new style might create a culture clash and make it harder for the new CEO to lead effectively.
- *Difficulty aligning with the organization's strategy and culture.* They may have a harder time aligning personal goals and strategies with those of the organization.
- *Unrealistic expectations.* The board of directors, investors, and employees may have such high expectations that the new CEO is almost doomed from the first day in the office.

When you're pursuing the CEO role—or even preparing for the day that opportunity arises—it's essential to understand what best practices look like from the board's perspective. Your ability to build authentic relationships with directors and demonstrate alignment with their expectations will shape how ready you appear. And once you secure the role, you're immediately responsible for shaping the leadership pipeline behind you. Developing future talent, broadening opportunities for high-potential leaders, and collaborating with the board on evolving succession criteria all become part of your job from day one. Succession doesn't end with your appointment—it begins again with your leadership.

Table 4-1 outlines how boards distinguish CEO-ready organizations from those that fall short. As a CEO candidate, it gives you a window into the kinds of organizational behaviors and cultural practices boards associate with long-term leadership success—and shows where your influence can begin, even before you step into the top job.

TABLE 4-1

CEO-ready organizations from the board's perspective

CEO-ready organizations	Non-CEO-ready organizations
Develop a culture of succession planning at all levels, coach direct reports, and hold skip-level meetings to identify talent	Limit C-suite executives' access to directors, stifling potential successors' ability to gain visibility relationships with the board
Identify and develop a large succession pipeline for the board to consider; identify talent that could succeed the CEO	Refuse succession-planning-process transparency, including criteria and requirements for advancement
Mentor potential successors and make coaching opportunities available to *all* high-potential and high-impact leaders	Confide only in a small inner circle of trusted advisers, limiting the pool of potential successors
Expand the options for the C-suite team to acquire the skills and visibility to be worthy as the CEO's successor	Limit and firewall opportunities for C-suite executives to gain the necessary experience to become CEO ready
Build a cohesive leadership team and pipeline that will support the next CEO, regardless of who is selected	Refrain from involving the board in the succession-planning process, limiting directors' ability to provide input
Invite feedback from leaders about how to improve the succession-planning process	Demonstrate an inability to objectively evaluate candidates without bias

Create the Best-Prepared Pitch to the Board

When Andy Reid showed up to interview for the Philadelphia Eagles' head coaching vacancy in 1999, he brought a loose-leaf binder with him. Several inches thick, it was stuffed with detailed information about everything he planned to do to build a Super Bowl–winning organization. It even got into details like how players should dress when traveling.[7] Eagles owner Jeffrey Lurie and team president Joe Banner were impressed. They hired the forty-year-old Reid—who at the time was the Green Bay Packers' quarterbacks coach—even though he had no experience as a head coach or even as an offensive coordinator. Reid spent fourteen seasons with the Philadelphia Eagles and, as of this writing, eleven seasons as head coach of the Kansas City Chiefs. At the time of publication, he ranked fourth in NFL history with 258 regular-season wins and second with 26 postseason victories. His teams have claimed three Super Bowl titles.

The loose-leaf binder was an important symbol to those choosing their leader. It symbolized Reid's knack for organization, his amazing attention to detail, and his ability to master that which he can control. Most importantly, it showed he had a vision for the future of the organization.

As you prepare for your board interviews as CEO candidate, consider that the board wants to see you as a critical thinker and either the company's chief strategist or someone who understands strategy and how each decision will fit into the company's strategic direction. As such, the directors are going to ask you tough questions. Smart directors will push you to examine your weaknesses and reevaluate your strengths. Prepare to engage with them authentically.

The following examples are the types of questions and prompts you should expect, and some thoughts as you consider possible responses.

- *How will you grow the business and build investor engagement? If economic conditions negatively affect financial results, describe your approach to delivering bad news to your stakeholders.*

Few actions or messages strengthen a business leader's position more than instilling investor support. When all is operating as expected and goals are being achieved, the team and players (employees, stakeholders) gain faith in the coach (the CEO). Now imagine that a top customer goes bankrupt. During economic turmoil, stakeholders turn to the leader. Preparedness can't prevent the possible, but it can give a message of confidence, particularly to investors, employees, and especially to your board. Watch how your boss communicates with key stakeholders and anticipate directors' questions on how you will navigate stormy waters if given the role. Articulate how you will balance transparency and diplomacy with the investor community during challenging times.

- *Talk about an opportunity you've had to manage a crisis alone (or did you always have help from above?). How did you take initiative to solve a big problem?*

The board will want to know how you solicited input from your team and other trusted counselors, considered various directions, and pressed ahead without too much delay. Be ready to talk about other options you could have chosen and why you decided on the course you did. Consider your skill and agility to exercise prudent, decisive leadership.

- *How do you demonstrate decisiveness under pressure—especially when the stakes are high and the data is incomplete?* As Elena Lytkina Botelho and her coauthors observed in Harvard Business Review, "high-performing CEOs do not necessarily stand out for making great decisions all the time; rather, they stand out for being more decisive."[8]

This research shows that high-performing CEOs make decisions earlier, faster, and with greater conviction. And they do so consistently, even when dealing with ambiguity, incomplete information, and unfamiliar domains. "In our data, people who were described as 'decisive' were 12 times more likely to be high-performing CEOs," Botelho noted.

- *How will you shift your bias from your vertical or department orientation so that you're now representing all parts of the business?*

This shift necessitates a deliberate and expansive approach. Be ready to share how you have already fostered a culture of collaboration with other divisions and departments, with examples, and how you have ensured that open communication and cross-functional initiatives have thrived under your watch. Be able to describe a real plan for how, after you take the reins, you will embrace broader perspectives and encourage interdepartmental synergy, creating a cohesive organization where innovation can flourish. Your commitment to representing all facets of the business will underscore your dedication to driving collective success for a truly unified vision.

- *How will you work smoothly with peers, especially other C-level peers, who see you as a competitor for this top job?*

The board will want to know of your conviction to demonstrating humility, actively listening to peers, and recognizing the expertise of others, and how you will develop a plan to break down any perceived barriers between silos and cultivate a culture of cooperation, enabling C-suite team members to become valued allies to each other. Talk about how you will leverage your personal strengths to enable others to join with you to move the organization forward with unity and purpose.

- *You have a reputation for having too many yes-folks under you. How would you overcome that to pick the strongest team?*

As directors dig into backgrounds, candidates frequently get asked this question or similar ones that levy judgment on you or your performance. It can be surprising and spur an emotional response. Resist the urge to combat the premise—they've done their homework, and perception is reality—and address the concern authentically. Show how you value constructive dissent. Share an instance of how you listened to someone who disagreed with you and changed your mind. Be ready with an example of how you encouraged your team to share their opinions and the good that resulted from the exchange of ideas.

- *Eight years ago, you helmed that disastrous project that saw three high potentials quit. Also, there was the incident at the off-site three years ago that required considerable work to fix. How can we be sure we're not in for more of that?*

"Another disadvantage the internal candidate must address," says Jim Citrin, "is that they have twenty years of stuff they've said or done that can be dredged up, and they can get killed on that." He advises candidates to be clear and honest. "When the board asks if you have any concerns or any questions for us, you say, 'I'd love to share something where I thought I was managing in a very inspirational way, and I realized now in retrospect, I didn't. I said this, and this is what I meant.' You can get a do-over if you come clean. It's like the hero's journey. It's not that the guy is flawless; it's the fact that he admits the flaw and steps into it. That's a very strong, powerful, confident way to help set it right."

Prepare to ace these questions and similar ones. And know that, even still, you may not get the job.

Why the Board May Not Select You for the Job

Even after preparing all their working lives to become CEOs, most candidates will not be selected. There is, after all, only one slot per company, and a lot of people want it. Based on our experience, here are the most common reasons candidates are not selected in terms of board perception:

- *Lack of leadership skills.* Candidates may be perceived as not having the necessary abilities in areas such as decision-making, communication, or relationship building.
- *Lack of strategic thinking.* Candidates may be seen as unable to align their vision with a company's bigger goals and objectives.
- *Lack of Wall Street appeal.* Those who win the CEO's job must be able to think like an investor but, more importantly, seem attractive to the Street by having the kind of vision, experience, and style necessary to supercharge growth. It's a delicate balance between delivering on quarter-by-quarter challenges while planning for the long term. Often, candidates are seen as good at one view, but not the other.
- *Lack of collaborative skills.* A candidate may not be seen as sufficiently transparent or a good team player. The candidate may have struggled to build effective relationships with colleagues around the organization.
- *Limited industry or functional knowledge.* Some executives, though skilled in their area of expertise, may not have developed enough knowledge in other functional areas. Some may lack a depth of industry experience, simply by not being in the industry as long as others.
- *Insufficient results or performance.* While most executives in the CEO pipeline have a strong track record of delivering results, some may have hit a tough spot of performance during their tenure, giving them a black spot on their record that may make it difficult for them to advance.
- *Lack of flexibility and adaptability.* Executives who are not selected may be seen as unable to adapt to changing circumstances or resistant to new ideas and ways of doing things.

- *Personal or professional issues.* These issues may include such proclivities as "telling the world how smart we are," "withholding information," "not listening," and "failing to give proper recognition." (Please refer to Marshall Goldsmith's list of twenty bad habits in his classic book *What Got You Here Won't Get You There.*)

Aspiring to become a CEO demands more than ambition; it requires integrity and a proactive, deliberate approach that integrates personal development with a nuanced understanding of board dynamics. As a CEO-ready candidate, you must master leadership intricacies and demonstrate your ability to navigate the emotional, psychological, and strategic considerations that inform board decisions.

Your CEO Readiness Pulse Check

Five questions you must answer to become CEO ready

1. **Are you the safest—and strongest—bet the board can make?** Selecting the CEO is the biggest risk the board will ever take at your company; CEO succession is the board's most consequential decision, destabilizing or stabilizing everyone. Have you shown that you're the visible, trusted, strategic leader who can steady the ship and steer aggressively into uncertainty?

2. **Have you reintroduced yourself as the future, not just the familiar?** Internal candidates must overcome the curse of familiarity. Is the board still seeing you in your current role, or have you reframed your story to show how you will lead transformation, not just continuity?

3. **Do you act like you're always being evaluated, because you are?** Even when there's no formal plan in motion, the board is assessing you in every interaction. Are you showing up with presence, curiosity, and maturity, even when no one says it's an audition?

4. **Can you speak to the board's sense of urgency without panic or denial?** Most boards feel their company is at a crossroads, even when things look good on paper. Can you offer a bold, optimistic vision for what comes next, one that honors the past but isn't trapped by it?

5. **Are you operating at CEO altitude or just waiting your turn?** Tenure is not a strategy. The board is looking for cross-functional fluency, enterprise-level thinking, and leadership presence. Are you already acting like a CEO today or just hoping to grow into it tomorrow?

5

Prepare to Move from Peer to Chief

C-suite colleagues can't get you the job, but they can kill your chances

Inevitably, your peers in the C-suite, the third set of stakeholders you need to address to be CEO ready, will face uncertainties about one of their own becoming chief. Your colleagues will wonder how your promotion will impact their future careers—no matter how much they express support to you directly—especially if they compete with you to become the new boss. They will worry you may show bias for your previous division or department. If you are running a division of the company or are the CFO, they already have had moments of frustration with you and your team. They have been both your partner on certain projects and your rival for resources, attention, and opportunities. What will be different now? How much worse might that be?

Your relationship with peers is crucial to your success as a candidate and as CEO. As you attempt to move from peer to chief, you must change your mindset, treat your peers with dignity, and provide support. Your peers are deeply influential players in your candidacy despite their lack of formal power. They don't make the final decision, but they do influence it. We've seen boards get spooked by candidate peers who threaten to bolt if a certain peer gets the job. The candidates who succeed typically have spent time, long before the formal process of selection starts, building their skills, interacting with a broad range of colleagues, and recognizing and encouraging their special expertise and mission-critical contributions to the success of the company.

The months or years leading up to the final selection of a new CEO provide a unique opportunity for you to learn about and celebrate those who, you hope, soon will become direct reports. Remember that you want those colleagues to stay with you after you get the job. They are your allies in building a bright future together. You can't do the job effectively if you're building an entirely new leadership team the moment you get the job. Your former peers represent your company's long-term legacy as well as its ability to create value for employees and customers. No organization is better than its vice president level. That means that in addition to your current division or department responsibilities, it's time to start inspiring your peers and celebrating them and their employees in every corner of the company and working and communicating with them in ways you haven't before.

Greg Case, CEO of Aon, says he "explicitly expects leaders to spend one day a week helping colleagues outside of their own areas to succeed."[1] That should be considered a minimum outreach for someone who wants to be CEO.

Mike Clem, who was promoted from chief technology officer to CEO at Sweetwater Sound, the world's biggest instrument retailer, told us, "If I had to do it over again, I would have invested more time earlier in developing a broader set of relationships across the company." Clem, like most candidates for CEO, was so busy in his specific area of responsibility that his long days at the office were already overbooked. If you don't think you have the time, make the time. Deprioritize something else. It's that important. Take a hard look at your schedule and prioritize building these relationships over some other activities. "So much of this job is about relationships across the company," Clem says.

It's taken a year of thoughtful, patient coaching and relationship building for Clem to feel he's fully activated and inspired his original team of peers, particularly because he was stepping in for a founding CEO after decades of his predecessor's charismatic leadership. "I could have done more to develop those relationships with a different point of view before I got into this seat," he reflects. "We will succeed or fail by our ability to work together and communicate effectively together. A lot of that is tied to relationships with people who wished they'd get this job." Today, his team and employee engagement scores are the highest ever.

If you want your peers to support you, then be the kind of peer they will respect and admire. Reach out regularly, Clem says, "to make sure you're operating on the same wavelength and with the same set of priorities. Reinforce to them that you have their backs and will support their decision-making."

Ask Yourself: Are You Someone Who *This* Executive Team Will Follow?

As potential candidates in the C-suite vie for the big job, they will probably try to spend an inordinate amount of time with the current CEO. This is natural. As a succession candidate, you do need to work closely with the person in the job you want. But you also need to fight the urge to rely too heavily on them for advice in lieu of spending time with peers. After all, that soon-to-be-former CEO is going to be leaving, whereas you want many of your key peers to remain. Many times, particularly if you are a new CEO coming from outside the company, the senior leadership team assumes you're bringing in your tried-and-true buddies from your prior leadership roles elsewhere. This is not how most candidates have been thinking until now. You must demonstrate in tangible ways in front of your peers (if you're an insider or if you're interviewing as an outsider) that you value their opinions as much as the current CEO's. Respect the past but look to the future.

The challenge here is balance. You, of course, must keep your own goals and what you want to achieve if you become CEO front of mind. But it's equally important to invest time to understand what's going on in the worlds of other people. To influence an entire organization, you need to step outside your own concerns and goals so that you can understand what truly concerns and motivates others.

All people feel the need to be heard and understood. Some of us assume that when we acquire power, we should assert our point of view

Ten Ways to Work with Peers in Order to Be CEO Ready

- **Actively seek their input.** Ask for insights on key decisions and challenges. Make it clear that you value their expertise, not just the CEO's.

- **Acknowledge and celebrate wins.** Publicly recognize contributions in meetings and communications to reinforce a culture of shared success.

- **Support their initiatives.** Help them achieve their goals, rather than just focusing on your own.

- **Facilitate cross-departmental collaboration.** Organize strategic discussions and problem-solving sessions that encourage teamwork across functions.

- **Be a resource, not just a competitor.** Offer mentorship and support, demonstrating that your leadership is about collective success, not just personal ambition.

- **Handle disagreements with respect and diplomacy.** Navigate differences with grace, ensuring that debates strengthen relationships rather than create divisions.

- **Demonstrate a future-oriented vision.** Share your perspective on where the company needs to go and how peers will play a key role in getting there.

- **Engage in peer coaching.** Initiate knowledge-sharing sessions where executives can learn from one another's experiences, creating a culture of trust.

- **Be visible and approachable.** Make time for informal check-ins to deepen relationships outside of formal settings.

- **Elevate their voices.** In leadership discussions, advocate for peers' ideas and perspectives.

ahead of everyone else's. As a C-level executive, you would naturally expect your peers to also have the level of confidence and swagger that they don't need your support. As a leader and as a peer at the top of the company, your task is to draw out other people's beliefs, assumptions, and goals so that you can include their perception of reality in your calculations of what it will take to execute strategy. This will also enable you to find ways to help them to achieve their personal best as you work together toward common goals.

So, as you accelerate your preparation to evolve from peer to chief, reflect on the following four questions:

- *Do I believe I can lead this team of senior leaders and this company to their next chapter of greatness?* If your honest answer right now is no, then take time to assess what's holding you back. Is their lack of experience or yours undermining confidence? Is fear of making the wrong decisions or uncertainty about how your peers perceive you hindering you? Confidence isn't just a feeling; it's built through preparation and deepening relationships with those you aim to lead. Start by seeking direct feedback from trusted colleagues, identifying skill gaps. You still have gaps when it comes to understanding their function with depth and full respect.

- *Do I have a commitment to improve and learn every day, valuing the opinions of others and including my team in the journey?* If your honest answer right now is "Not really," then consider how that mindset is affecting your leadership potential. Have you really been demonstrating an openness to feedback, or have you been relying too much on what worked in the past or the hidden agenda, as you compete with peers for resources and the attention of the CEO? Do you engage with peers as collaborators or competitors? It's OK for the real answer to be the latter. But the CEO that your board wants you to become will need to shift to asking supportive and thoughtful questions, seeking diverse perspectives, and creating an environment where your peers feel heard and valued, because their buy-in will be crucial when you step into the top role.

- *Do I have the humility to know that epic success is only achievable through my team's efforts?* If your honest answer right now is "Not really," ask yourself: Do you instinctively take credit, or do you actively elevate those around you? Are you more focused on proving yourself than promoting your peers as a leadership team that thrives together? Leadership isn't about proving you're the smartest person in the room; it's about making the room smarter. If you want to earn your peers' trust, start by recognizing their contributions publicly, asking for help when needed, and demonstrating that you're invested in collective success, not just personal achievement.

- *What would help my peers feel ready to recommend me as CEO?* Instead of assuming they already see you as the natural choice, take an intentional approach. Ask trusted and untrusted colleagues for honest feedback on how they perceive your leadership style and what they'd need to feel confident in your ability to lead them. Remember, you don't have to take anyone's advice, but you do have to make it clear that you heard and understood them (even if you disagree). They will be skeptical, looking for signs that you're not prioritizing their concerns. Understanding their expectations allows you to actively shape your leadership presence in a way that earns their trust and support.

Let's consider the last question in more detail. Your peers will want you to be someone who consciously seeks out their views, who is able to withhold judgment when listening to a teammate, and who is able to navigate between their own perception of reality and what others are seeing and saying. That means you need to focus less on being right and telling people what is right, and more on discovering what we collectively believe to be right. This won't always be easy. There's a burdensome weight that about eight out of ten CEO candidates carry around: they need to prove they're right. And frankly, you don't get to be in the running for a CEO slot if you haven't been right a lot. Yet a big part of this shift is that, as a CEO, you know on a good day you may only know about 20 percent of the answers you need. You can't be right as much as you're used to. The bigger the job gets, the less you'll be sure about, and the more you will need others to contribute.

The best CEO candidates demonstrate empathy so that they can see things from the perspective of those at all levels, not just their own. This ability to perceive the point of view of stakeholders is essential in understanding and engaging them and invaluable in crafting the collaboration that will be essential to you for getting the job and succeeding in the job.

Compete While Courting

When you are in a very tight race with other elite internal and external CEO candidates, you'll need to show tangible ways that you've acquired the respect of your colleagues to the board and to the current CEO, even those you're competing against. Additionally, the board and the CEO will be assessing your continued capacity to keep the hearts and minds of those in the C-suite by demonstrating your teamwork with, and genuine enthusiasm for, your peers. They want to know that those you'll oversee will be willing to partner with you to run the company, even sometimes in the case your peers lose out to you for their top job.

That means you'll have to spend time now to understand the differences between your peers' various points of view and the languages they speak—marketing, strategy, finance, operations, supply chain, and so on. And yes, show new levels of understanding and support for human resources, compliance, and legal—groups you may have treated as a thorn in your side, gatekeepers who you may have perceived occasionally made it harder for you to execute. There is, for instance, a big difference between the point of view and language of the chief legal officer and that of the chief revenue officer. The same is true for the differences between the worlds of a chief human resources officer and the head of operations. You have had the luxury in the past of not seeing them as your team the same way you view your department or division. That changes now.

Mark McLaughlin, former CEO of Palo Alto Networks and chairman of Qualcomm, shared a critical insight with Mark about these challenges: "One of the biggest concerns for a board is what happens to the leadership team once a new CEO is chosen. One of my colleagues shared the common story of two top candidates who were the two general managers—each leading half the company. The rest of their peers were caught in the middle. No matter who we picked, half the team would have to adjust to a leader from 'the other side.' That kind of uncertainty can be unsettling."

He emphasized how crucial peer feedback was in shaping that selection process. If the two could not reconcile, or if one of the two could not rise above the fray, then the board would have to select an outside candidate as the next CEO.

McLaughlin continued: "These were long-term executives who genuinely wanted the best for the company. That's not always the case, but as a CEO candidate, we are going to assume that you do. The problem is that, behind the scenes, the two sides shared honest concerns; some mentioned that one candidate had a 'good heart,' while others worried whether he had the right strategic vision. Their insights were invaluable, and I used their concerns to coach both candidates along the way. Because they felt heard, they stood behind the leader we ultimately chose."

To prepare for and demonstrate leadership as the CEO candidate of choice, McLaughlin says, "Never forget—your peers have worked just as hard as you to get where they are. They're ambitious, driven by impact, and obsessed with big, audacious goals. People who chase big numbers never stop competing; it's in their DNA. So, when you become the boss, your job isn't just to lead; it's to inspire these leaders to win. Because at that level, it's not about you anymore."

The final selection for the CEO's job often comes down to the board's belief that not all of your peers will bail the moment you become their boss, even those competing with you for the job. While the board and your boss realize that some change is likely and some is necessary, they don't want your promotion to clear-cut the culture or cause a mass exodus.

So, ask yourself again: *Are you the type of person your colleagues would be willing to work for?* If your peers think you are arrogant because you make every interaction a contest, if you display an obvious lack of interest in recognizing their distinctive contributions, or if you show an unwillingness to evaluate their point of view with empathy and understanding, then you're going to lose their support. That can cost you the job.

It's no longer about you becoming the top player on the team—you're becoming head coach. Those are different jobs, and any sports fan knows the best athletes don't always make the best coaches. Successful coaches are the motivators and visionaries; their players will follow them.

As people like Virgin's Sir Richard Branson assess CEO candidates, they often ask a candidate's peers to describe how a potential successor is good or bad at developing collaborative, win-win relationships with them. Most owners and board members will be sensitive to political motivations. They understand that some of the people they interview will believe they are more qualified than you. Those peers may not feel motivated to make you look good. Don't worry about that. Board members will take such comments in stride. But if they sense a theme recurring with many of the executives they speak with, whether they have been your rivals or not, then alarm bells will sound.

Developing an understanding of the language and perspective of your peers isn't easy, but it's crucial. As a serial entrepreneur who's relied on recruiting professional management to his ventures, Branson emphasizes that a CEO candidate's ability to demonstrate empathy and genuine excitement for their peers' expertise is among the top traits he looks for in a leader. Given that Virgin oversees more than four hundred companies, and Branson maintains relationships with all of them, his insight carries weight. Mark hosted Branson at the World Business Forum in New York, where the legendary entrepreneur said that "as a CEO candidate, you're making a serious shift from what made you successful in all your previous roles. Although you and some of your peers may now be co-competitors in the CEO succession plan, it won't help your candidacy if you behave like an opponent. No matter how qualified you are," Branson explained, "you'll be more effective as a leader if you invest time and effort inspiring employees' trust as a supportive colleague rather than a rival." (See table 5-1.)

Assume Everyone in the C-Suite Thinks They Have a Shot at the CEO's Job

During this process, you'll find that more executives believe they are in the running for the CEO role than those who have a real chance. That

TABLE 5-1

How to win the hearts and minds of peers who will become direct reports

Listen and learn their language	Engage in their world	Find opportunities to be of service	Communicate in ways that resonate with them	Build personal relationships, not just professional ones	Test and adapt your approach
Shadow key executives in different functions to see how they operate and what challenges they face.	**Read what they read.** Subscribe to the trade journals, reports, and market analysis they use for insights.	**Offer strategic support**—identify ways your function can help solve their biggest challenges.	**Adapt your messaging.** Frame initiatives in terms of their impact on your peers' goals and challenges.	**Schedule informal check-ins** to connect outside of high-pressure work discussions.	**Regularly ask for feedback** on how you engage with them and adjust based on what you learn.
Join team meetings as an observer to understand the mindset and priorities of their function.	**Attend their industry conferences** to understand their external pressures.	**Celebrate their wins publicly** in leadership meetings, internal communications, or town halls.	**Use their terminology** in conversations and presentations to build credibility and demonstrate understanding.	**Find common ground** through shared interests such as family or hobbies outside of work.	**Bridge gaps with skeptics** who are showing resistance to the idea of you as leader.
Be genuinely curious; seek to learn their pain points and what excites them.	**Understand their key performance indicators**—know what drives them and what obstacles hinder their performance.	**Facilitate cross-functional collaboration**, ensuring their expertise is recognized and leveraged effectively.	**Avoid one-size-fits-all communication**—use high-level overviews with those who need topline understanding and deep dives with those doing analysis.	**Seek their mentorship and insights** as part of a continuous learning mindset.	**Check your impact**—if your peers start seeking your input proactively, it's a sign you've earned their trust.
Keep a notebook or digital log of key phrases, industry terms, and repeated themes from conversations with peers.					

means there'll be more internal competition, unspoken tensions, and even blind spots among the leadership team to deal with than is logical, since so many more people are jockeying for position than are actually under consideration.

At one *Fortune* 500 company we worked with, the board had privately narrowed the search down to two candidates, yet at least five members of the C-suite believed they were still in serious contention. Why? Because the board and the current CEO had a vested interest in having everyone engaged and committed to keeping the lights on and trains running. They didn't want top talent to disengage, leave, or become disruptive while they were making their decision.

When the process of selection begins, every small signal is amplified as a sign that someone's in the running, whether it's a passing comment from the CEO about someone's "great leadership potential," or a board member saying, "We're really impressed with what you've built," or simply inclusion in high-level strategy discussions. These moments, while valuable for learning new insights and doing your job, can also fuel unrealistic hopes. Mark has seen executives spend months preparing for interviews they were never going to get; they are blindsided and devastated when they aren't even on the final list.

The lesson here is to *never* assume that you're the front-runner just because you've received praise or feel valued. The best thing you can do is seek direct feedback, understand where you truly stand, and prepare assiduously by using this playbook. Focus on proving your impact in ways that make you indispensable and capable of bringing your peers along—whether or not you get the job.

When too many executive team members think they're in the running to become CEO, we also see *sneaky peer syndrome*. We faced this situation recently when we were coaching one CEO candidate who told us a peer had approached him to express support. The peer said he had no interest in the job because he was getting too old. At the same time, our client learned that this supportive peer had also informed the current CEO of our client's faults and lack of readiness for the big job. This Machiavelli suggested that he become CEO for a few years until our candidate was up to the task. As we explained to the current CEO, if that guy got the job, he would never leave.

We acknowledge that the CEO candidacy process puts you in the awkward place of actually being in a competition with your peers without appearing so. Almost none of the jockeying will be discussed, and the decision-makers will be annoyed to hear anyone describe it as competition or that any office politics are involved. People will pretend to do what's best for the company, even when they are in it for themselves. The way to manage this palace intrigue is to focus only on what you can control. Be the best version of yourself and stay out of the politics. Don't form dark alliances; don't bad-mouth anyone. And don't get cocky. When you've become CEO ready, you're investing in becoming a better, more worthy leader and broadening your options for future career moves.

We've seen so many promising candidates miss their shot. We watched the heir apparent at one of the world's largest pharmaceutical companies brag so much about what he was going to do when he took over that the current CEO pivoted away from him. The candidate literally talked himself out of being considered for the job. Be humble. Be open. And don't assume anything, despite what you've been promised.

Learn Productive Disagreement and Get Coaching

Being a team player doesn't mean that you must become passive or overly agreeable. That's not the goal. Peers want their potential boss to be able to disagree, debate, and work through tough issues *with* them. Remember to prosecute the issues, not the people behind them. Fight over the right path ahead, not whose idea it was. Your boss and board respect leaders who stand their ground when necessary, assertively pursuing the objectives and being frank about the issues so that the company can win customers and the team can succeed.

When you disagree in a meeting, be direct and provide reasoning, saying something like, "I disagree because of [specific evidence]." Back up your position with facts, because without evidence, it's just an opinion.

You shouldn't avoid conflict but approach it with a learning mindset. If you have an issue with a team member, address it directly and promptly. Don't let tensions simmer or escalate through side conversations. And most importantly, don't use the CEO as a proxy—meaning, don't run to the CEO expecting them to handle interpersonal issues on your behalf. Instead, speak to the person face-to-face and resolve the conflict professionally.

Additionally, remember that anyone you have met who undermines colleagues behind their backs is also undermining you. They're playing all sides. You can count on that. Instead, role-model the opposite behavior. We've worked with enough executives to know that you, like all execs, have some work to do in improving your peer relationships. We also know from experience that you, like most execs, are sincerely motivated to grow, and that with luck and grace on your part, your peers will give you a fair chance to do so.

If those assumptions about you are accurate, then it's time to get coaching to emphasize that learning is a lifelong process. At this level, learning becomes public and also essential. One of the most exceptional CEOs we have coached is a leader we'll call Mary, known for her rare ability to balance strategic brilliance with deep emotional intelligence. She's also excellent at productive disagreement, sometimes even when it has a sharp edge. One of Mary's most revealing moments of leadership came during an interaction with a division president we'll call Rob. Mary had high hopes for Rob as a potential successor.

Mary had asked us to coach Rob, recognizing his extraordinary business acumen but also his blind spots when it came to people. Executives and peers saw Rob as a strategic genius, someone who could cut through complexity with ease, but also someone who lacked tact and emotional awareness. His off-the-cuff remarks, meant to be witty or sharp, often cut deeper than he realized, leaving colleagues feeling undervalued and dismissed.

After one team meeting, Mary pulled Rob aside and gave him direct feedback. His peers had shared concerns about his behavior, noting that his sarcastic quips and dismissive tone created tension. Rather than absorbing the message and reflecting on it, Rob bristled. His face tightened, his posture stiffened, and he dug in his heels.

"These comments are so picky," he said, rolling his eyes. "Does this mean I have to watch everything I say and worry about how I act in every meeting for the rest of my career?" His frustration was palpable;

he saw himself as a high performer, and to him, this kind of scrutiny felt unnecessary and stifling.

Mary didn't miss a beat. She locked eyes with him and fired back: "Welcome to my world! If you ever want to become a CEO, get used to it. People are going to be listening to what you say—and watching how you act—in every meeting for the rest of your career. You should be thankful that you are getting honest feedback, and that you are being given the opportunity to learn from it!"

Her words landed like a thunderclap, cutting through Rob's defensiveness. This wasn't nitpicking. This was leadership. The higher you climb, the more people scrutinize not just what you say, but how you say it, how you react, and what that signals about your leadership style, especially with those who used to be your peers.

Take Mary's words as a lesson. Your peers are watching. They are measuring how well you listen, adapt, and evolve, because one day, they may be asked if they will follow your lead. Their feedback isn't a nuisance; it's a window into how you are perceived. It tells you what they need from you as a leader, what they expect, and what will make you effective in their eyes.

If you're aiming for the CEO role, this isn't a burden—it's the job. It's inevitable that you will have things to work on to become ready to be a CEO. Your peers don't expect you to have already fully developed all the skills you will need. What they will want to know is that you are striving to become the best version of yourself, both for their benefit and for the benefit of the organization.

How do you follow up on your request for their help with your own leadership development? In ongoing dialogues with stakeholders, reiterate the specific areas where you're trying to improve and ask for advice. The asking part of follow-up may sound something like this: "Last month I told you that I wanted to become a more effective listener when I interact with my team and during our executive team meetings. Based on my behavior in the past month, what suggestions would you have for me? Do you see anything that could help me become a better listener next month?"

As you regularly work to improve, the decision-makers will see that you're increasingly ready to be a CEO.

Build a Team

Your board will want to see that you can build strong teams with your peers and that you have a deep bench of talent under you, said Harry Kraemer, former CEO of Baxter International Inc.—today a $16 billion global medical devices, pharmaceuticals, and biotechnology company. He's now admired as an author and business school professor at Northwestern University. "My view in each job at Baxter was to develop the people under me in the best way possible. If I created an environment where the best people wanted to work for me, I knew I was going to do phenomenally well. But let's say I'm a vice president and there are six of us, and only two executive vice presidents. If I wake up one morning and I say, 'I want that bigger job.' Well, the day it becomes about me, it's no longer about my team."

Kraemer was appointed as CFO of Baxter at age thirty-six; he said there were suddenly ten other folks who could have been chosen for the job who now worked for him. "I could have gone in thinking: 'I'm going to show these guys why the CEO picked the right guy.' Instead, I decided I would treat each of them the way I would want to be treated. I met each alone. I told them I was aware they were equally or more qualified. I said, 'The way I'm going to work is this: If we have a big issue, I will make the final decision. But I will never, repeat never, make a decision without your input if you've got some input for me. And if I make a decision different than what you are recommending, I'll always let you why.'"

Kraemer offered genuine, ongoing support for his new teammates in their careers. "I told them, 'I've never been in a job more than a few years at Baxter, and I'll do everything I can to help you be well qualified as a successor, if you want.' Also, I explained that I was chosen because, rather than just being in finance jobs, I ran a couple of divisions and then came back to finance. I could help them find a way to prepare better, perhaps move to run a division or do an international stint. Finally, I said, 'If you say that by the time I'm out of this job, it'll be too late for you, I'll help you get a job elsewhere. I have headhunters call me every week.' They all decided to stay." And Kraemer's team was so supportive that he became the unanimous choice of the board to take over as CEO at age forty-two. He was doing everything we've talked about in this chapter, even before he was a CEO candidate.

The best CEO candidates we've worked with typically have a short list of "must-have" characteristics they see as important for the leaders of their teams. For example, Gail Kelly, former CEO of Australian multinational banking and financial services firm Westpac, offers her list: "Enthusiasm, smarts, flexibility, and results orientation, coupled with clear alignment with the company values."[2]

Brad Smith, former CEO at Intuit, adds, "Thirty percent of my time was in coaching and growing talent. [I did that in] town halls, skip levels with ten to twelve employees at a time, one-on-one sessions, coaching sessions."[3] His outreach demonstrates a constant search for potential leaders, both internal and external—a real commitment to developing a bench.

Cristiano Amon, president and CEO of Qualcomm, told us about his shift from running the largest division to thinking more about the expansive role that he would take on as chief executive. At every increasing level of senior executive responsibility, you become less and less the expert, and by the time you're CEO, you had better become proficient at finding experts, not being one. Amon engaged Mark for coaching when he was tapped as a CEO candidate. He commented, "You are leading people who know better and more than you do." At least, that should be your ambition: to improve your team so that a "rising tide of talent" lifts all parts of your division.

Amon told us about an internal executive he was coaching for a potential higher-level role. The executive was good in sales but not in engineering. He needed to hire people with skills he didn't have, Amon says, but that challenged him. "The problem is that most of us are attracted to and hire people that are just like us." The leader Amon was coaching didn't need another person just like himself. "I'm very proud of my leaders who can do a self-assessment of what they understand and what they don't and then surround themselves with people who can do those things better," Amon says. "For me, a big sign of maturity is understanding your blind spots. Once you understand that, there's no limit for you." Amon offers this advice: your new superpower must become the ability to identify experts who are *not like you*.

How to Build a High-Performance Team That Includes Your Successor

Here's a practical guide to building a high-performing team that's ready to take your job so that you're ready for the next one—the chief executive.

- **Define the leadership competencies needed for success.** Align these with the company's values, culture, and strategic goals so you build a team that thrives in the right environment.
- **Identify high-potential leaders.** Use formal talent-review processes to evaluate emerging leaders and match them against the company's long-term vision.
- **Invest in leadership development.** Provide high-potential talent with training, mentorship, coaching, and stretch assignments that help them grow.
- **Test leadership skills over time.** Monitor key performance indicators and strategic outcomes to ensure future leaders are developing the competencies needed for success.
- **Expose key talent to different parts of the business.** Use job rotations, cross-functional projects, and secondments—temporary assignments in different departments or organizations—to broaden their understanding of the company.
- **Create a leadership culture.** Encourage leaders to take risks, learn from failure, get coaching, and continuously develop their skills while modeling these behaviors yourself.
- **Assess team dynamics.** Have members confidentially rate their current level of teamwork and desired level of teamwork to identify alignment gaps.
- **Identify key behavioral changes.** Ask each team member to pinpoint two behaviors that, if improved, could enhance team collaboration.

(continued)

- **Prioritize the most important behaviors.** Through discussion and consensus, focus on one key behavior for the entire team to work on together.

- **Facilitate one-on-one dialogues.** Encourage team members to offer feedback and suggest additional areas of improvement to their peers.

- **Commit to personal behavior change.** Each team member should choose and announce a personal behavior they will work on improving. When the boss gets a coach, then coaching is more quickly embraced by the whole team.

- **Hold monthly feedback sessions.** Establish a habit of continuous improvement by gathering peer feedback on team effectiveness.

- **Measure progress through mini surveys.** Every six months, collect confidential feedback to track improvements in leadership behaviors.

- **Analyze and adjust.** Discuss progress, reinforce improvements, and ensure sustained behavioral change.

- **Maintain accountability.** Conduct regular check-ins and, after a year, assess whether further team-building efforts are necessary.

Ultimately, treating your peers with the respect they deserve will help you get the job and leave the job gracefully and effectively. As soon as you're CEO, you'll be thinking about your successor, and that job becomes easier if you've spent a good amount of your time as a leader helping your former peers—key stakeholders in becoming CEO ready—grow.

A structured approach to leadership development keeps the team focused on meaningful behavioral changes, avoiding pointless meetings and empty initiatives when the time comes for everyone to move up in the succession process. It ensures consistent feedback, regular follow-up, and accountability, driving continuous improvement rather than sporadic, once-a-year feedback cycles.

Most importantly, this approach shifts the focus from fixing others to modeling self-improvement—a principle that strengthens teamwork and inspires leadership at every level. By implementing this process now, you build a high-performance team that delivers results and positions you as the natural choice as the next chief executive.

Start today. The best CEO candidates build strong alliances with their peers on the executive team, and they build strong people under them so that their board and incumbent CEO have the confidence to promote you, knowing your past role is in good hands. In the next chapter we'll talk about how you can partner with your boss—your predecessor and the current CEO—so that they're ready to help you become the most likely successor.

Your CEO Readiness Pulse Check

Five questions you must answer to move from peer to chief

1. **Would your peers genuinely want to work for you or just tolerate it?** Have you built the credibility, empathy, and emotional intelligence that make your leadership feel like a promotion for the team, not just for yourself?

2. **Are you investing time now to understand how each of your peers sees the world?** Do you know their language, their pressure points, and what success looks like from their perspective, not just your own?

3. **Can you balance competition with collaboration without hiding your ambition?** Are you proving you can lead assertively while still lifting others up, even those you're competing against for the top job?

4. **Are you modeling the kind of humility and curiosity you want your future team to show?** If your peers were asked privately, would they say you elevate others, seek feedback, and lead with shared purpose—or that you're more focused on your own rise?

5. **Are you building a team strong enough to make your promotion safe for the business?** If you were selected as CEO tomorrow, would your division thrive without you? Are you preparing your successor as seriously as you hope your predecessor is preparing you?

6

Partner with Your Predecessor

Smooth the existential transition for the incumbent CEO and discover what's next

Many CEO candidates we work with chuckle at our warning to be extra sensitive to the feelings of the incumbent CEO. They can't imagine their current leader would feel queasy about the transition. CEOs tend to engender deference, and most CEO candidates see the boss as more powerful and larger than life than bosses see themselves. We have learned that the complexity of that viewpoint deserves examination because, even for those CEOs who confidently initiate the succession process and plan for it years in advance, the transition can feel existentially threatening. Many feel the weight of an impending end to the greatest, most important part of their career and maybe their life. Sounds melodramatic, but transition day is an abrupt end to a lifetime of achievement. At least, that's how it feels for your boss.

Guardian Life CEO Deanna Mulligan partnered with her board of directors as they led the succession planning process a few years before her departure as part of a ten-year successful run—an intentional plan set when she first became CEO. Even though the process was successful and rewarding, it also involved moments that felt deeply emotional. They started considering CEO candidates in a twenty-four-month cycle "because that's what world-class companies do—we develop great talent! The project is about investing in the future and reducing the risk of instability or emergencies that you so commonly read about with CEO replacement," she told us.

"I knew it was healthy for the company's long-term success to have a leadership development pipeline. It's what I wanted to do with my full heart and soul. I had always been clear about that when I started in the job: I had successfully grown the company and was delivering on my corporate targets and leadership goals." It was an exciting collaboration as the board and CEO worked together to build a strong pipeline and identify the most promising final successor. When the best candidate was chosen, "We were thrilled! Mission accomplished!"

My Last Day Felt Like Cutting Off an Arm

Mulligan swore to herself, "I'll never look back. *But it was like cutting off an arm!*" She found it difficult to reconcile the fact that "the greatest impact I've ever had might be over. I'm unlikely to ever run a company of that size and scope, and that has great meaning after my career building toward that objective."

Fortunately, Mulligan's impact is far from over. As CEO coaches, we hope that your boss will see future opportunities as new adventures—ones they're uniquely privileged to explore due to their extraordinary experience. Mulligan wrote a book, expanded her board memberships, taught business courses, and advised private equity firms. And now she's reinventing the life insurance industry as the CEO of a disruptive startup. Meaningful, but not at all the same. Radically different and exciting after her last gig. Still, in the moment of that first transition, none of this had come to pass, and Mulligan felt the difficulty of letting go.

CEO candidates routinely witness their hero—their boss, who is currently a successful, powerful CEO—feel vulnerable, occasionally panicky. A few bosses become downright irrational near the end. As a candidate, you may not see that the outgoing CEO is struggling with stepping out of the role. Whether you notice your CEO's stress or not, don't overestimate their confidence and stability in weathering the emotional transition. Every human being, particularly those in power, feels the impact of losing a position of influence. It's an act of generosity to do what's right for your company and for the next generation of leaders. But every CEO, no matter how experienced or accomplished, wants to feel valued on the way out. Many CEOs remain as chair, which means their role may shift rather than disappear entirely, making your ability to navigate this transition even more critical.

A CEO-ready candidate should make managing this transition *with* the incumbent CEO—the fourth stakeholder in the succession process— part of their plan as they are being considered for selection. There are several ways to accomplish this.

Encourage Nominating and Governance Committee Participation

Once, the incumbent CEO was the main driver of the transition, making this relationship, and this particularly fraught moment for your boss, even trickier. They still hold great sway over the process, but increasingly boards are inserting themselves. You should advocate for that as a way to mitigate emotion and personalities muddying the transition.

In US corporate governance, the responsibility for CEO succession planning is increasingly assigned to independent directors, particularly those serving on the board's nominating or governance committee. Their responsibilities are well beyond just CEO succession, but it's a key responsibility for this committee, typically outlined in the company's bylaws or the committee's charter. By entrusting CEO succession planning to independent directors, companies aim to promote effective governance and ensure leadership continuity.[1] This shift aims to ensure an unbiased and objective approach to leadership transitions, and it helps prevent short-term, reactionary decisions.[2]

An increasing number of companies like Hewlett-Packard and Apple have institutionalized the succession process as a long-term leadership development program so that there are always internal executives in the pipeline. That's good news for you as a candidate because you'll know where you stand and what to do to develop the skills and visibility you need. Your HR department, CEO, and board have a steady stream of deliverable key performance indicators guiding the progress of the leadership development of candidates, driven by the nominating and governance committee, not always the current CEO.

A notable example is the Walt Disney Company. Following challenges with previous succession plans and pressures from activist investors, Disney's board entrusted the CEO selection process to an independent board member with substantial gravitas. In this case, James Gorman, who became chairman of Disney's board in January 2025, is leading the succession planning committee. Gorman's extensive experience, including his tenure as CEO and chairman of Morgan Stanley, positioned him well to guide Disney through this critical transition.[3]

Research indicates that companies where independent directors lead succession planning are more likely to treat CEO succession as a top priority. According to a report by Heidrick & Struggles, 44 percent of such companies prioritize CEO succession planning, compared to 29 percent where the CEO or another executive director leads the process.[4]

Still, in every case the current CEO will be deeply involved. Delegating formal authority to a committee does not relieve you, as a candidate, from actively engaging with the outgoing CEO. You should be prepared to invest significant time in managing the transition—including attentively monitoring the CEO's behavior and emotions for signs that they may not be ready to let go.

Expect Emotional Distress or Resistance

Prepare for the possibility that your predecessor will not step aside gracefully, even if they profess a desire to do so. Even CEOs who have announced their departure may change their mind. At one company, Mark was recruited by the incumbent CEO and his board chief human resources officer to groom a CEO candidate who was the obvious heir apparent. The retiring CEO had celebrated his farewell in public, cleared out his office, and handed over his keys. Yet, over the holidays, with time to reflect, the CEO panicked. He started calling board members, insisting his replacement wasn't ready and demanding that the assessment firm come to reevaluate the candidate's readiness. The directors stood firm, telling him, "It's you who's not ready." They told him he was loved and admired and would make a great chairman of the board. But the transition plan for the CEO candidate continued as scheduled. A year into his new role as chairman, he's thriving, and the new CEO is getting applause despite a much more difficult economic environment.

If your CEO starts showing signs of reluctance or erratic behavior, don't take it personally. Acknowledge their emotions but stay the course. The best approach is to be patient and enthusiastically support your boss. Trust the process. It is absolutely vital for you to try to be empathetic with the departing chief during this process and not show impatience or frustration or anger over any second thoughts.

A growing body of research shows that CEOs today are managing far more than just the normal myriad challenges that may be affecting their consistency of behavior and temper; they're constantly reacting to increasing real-time volatility, often under immense psychological strain. Harvard professor and former Harvard Business School dean Nitin Nohria found in a study with Michael Porter that CEOs spend 36 percent of their time reacting to unfolding events, rather than proactively leading strategy.[5] He argues that this reactive burden—combined with emotional fatigue—can make succession feel not just like a professional shift, but a personal unraveling.

Nohria encourages leaders to distinguish between different types of incoming challenges:

- *Normal noise* refers to the small stuff—the kind of daily flare-ups that are unlikely to grow. Think of a one-off complaint from a major shareholder, a temporary system glitch, or grumbling from a frustrated team that doesn't go anywhere. These moments are easy to overreact to, but smart leaders don't. Instead, they note the issue, delegate appropriately, and keep their focus on what matters most. The point isn't to ignore it; it's to not let it hijack your agenda.

- *Clarion calls*, on the other hand, are the big ones—loud and sustained. These are major regulatory threats, activist investor movements, or sudden, game-changing competitive moves. You can't wait these out. They demand your direct attention, strategic clarity, and executive presence. These are the moments that test whether you can pivot fast, rally your team, and lead under pressure. Drop everything and lead.

- *Whisper warnings* are the trickiest to spot. They start small—a comment in an exit interview, a pattern of product complaints, a few high-potential people quietly checking out. On their own, these may not seem urgent. But if left unexamined, they often grow into crises. This is where great leaders earn their reputation—not by reacting to problems after they escalate, but by anticipating issues, asking the right questions early, and stepping in before trouble takes root. Ignore the whispers and you may find yourself blindsided.

- *Siren songs* are the seductive distractions. They're loud and dramatic—headlines, social media uproar, political noise. They demand attention, but not necessarily action. The danger is that they *feel* like clarion calls when they're really just temporary turbulence. Strong leaders don't chase every shiny object. They resist the urge to react, stay focused on long-term priorities, and protect their organization from spinning its wheels.

As a CEO candidate, you can help your outgoing chief executive mitigate the overwhelming siren songs by stepping up to help with as many of the distractions as possible that feel urgent but will fade. And don't let them miss the whisper warnings, the quiet signals that something deeper is at stake.

For you as the potential successor, that means becoming a calm presence in already overbooked life and career. Be someone who can help the current CEO process those signals without amplifying stress. That may require resisting the temptation to fix everything and instead becoming the one who listens to what isn't being said.

Understand the Stated Perceptions and Resistance

A CEO's job is not just what they do; it becomes part of who they are, and they struggle to imagine themselves without that level of influence.

For some, it's hard to leave if things are good because they're finally seeing the fruits of their hard work. No one wants to quit when they feel on top of their game. On the other hand, it's hard to leave when things are bad because they don't want to leave the company in a bad spot; they want to stay and turn it around. No one wants to be remembered as the person who dropped the baton. Good times or bad, it's just hard to let go.

CEO candidates underestimate these feelings and should anticipate the possibility of resistance to leave and be prepared to deal with the resulting reasons. Many CEOs postpone their exit, using justifications like:

- My successor isn't ready yet.
- The organization needs me now more than ever during this period of change.
- It's just not the right time to leave.
- The employees, customers, and shareholders won't stand for it.
- The board wants me to stick around.
- I need to work through the merger or latest transformation.
- I'm planning to leave after the next year or two (or some noncommittal period).

What they are really saying is they feel like they're losing part of their identity as a CEO—or losing organizational influence that they worked a lifetime to achieve.

As a CEO candidate, you can't change how someone feels, but you do have a distinct advantage if you choose to slow down and think strategically. You are an experienced executive, so you have considerable context for many (but not all) of the pressures that your boss is facing. You routinely need to win the hearts and minds of critical senior stakeholders—like big customers, investors, and board members. Now you need to exercise an odd shift to a new level of compassion for your boss. The CEO is still the boss, not your equal, of course, but transitions for people at any level are torturous.

Redefine Your Support without Being Judgmental

You might think that the CEO is having trouble letting go because the job is luxurious and they like wielding power. You might covet that privileged place that you imagine the boss holds. Stop thinking that way. By now we hope we've clarified that the CEO role does not give unlimited agency or omnipotence. The CEO role is more difficult than you know, and you might not believe that it could be harder than your job. You're close enough to see what the job is while far enough away to wrongly presume you're doing all the heavy lifting while the CEO just leads. Don't mistake the front row in the theater as clarity for what's happening backstage. Shift your confidence to focus on learning what's really happening in your boss's life and what the job really entails. You need to observe the nuance and subtle leadership burdens that the CEO endures.

Since the CEO is your boss, you've likely been looking at them in somewhat judgmental and possibly superficial ways because of his positional power and relative celebrity. As Steve Jobs's health continued to fade, Tim Cook would take long walks with him or sit with him during treatment. During those hours of silence and moments of conversation, the real flashes of insight ignited in Cook, taking his relationship to the next level of intimacy and developing a different level of empathy. In 2009, Cook even offered a portion of his liver to Jobs, as they shared a rare blood type, but Jobs declined the offer.[6] This gesture underscores their personal and professional bond during that challenging period. We're not suggesting that you donate body parts during this CEO mission, but as a CEO candidate you must embrace a deeper reality of the human you're partnering with.

Mark also had the opportunity to reconnect with Jobs in the hospital. He'd met him at Pixar and at Stanford, and even before that at Homestead High School. In Jobs's later days, it was finally obvious to Mark that everyone needed to stop confusing the man with the legend. Only when he was sick did the history of Jobs's life and work emerge in ways that his management team could fully embrace and internalize to carry the Apple torch forward. As a CEO candidate, you need to acknowledge your boss's accomplishments and challenges for what they really are, not what you wish they were or what you assume it *must* be like in the corner office. Seek to understand how to rise to the struggles they face.

Every CEO wants to leave on a high note, be remembered for their achievements, and have the world know what they sacrificed. It's ideal when the succession plan is a part of the company's overall ongoing strategy so that you and the CEO build toward a crescendo of transition, but if that doesn't exist at your company, you need to reach out and demonstrate your prowess as a CEO candidate.

Don't Be Overlooked as a Candidate

Microsoft nearly missed its most transformative leader in the noise of transition. Satya Nadella—now widely credited with reinventing the company into a $3 trillion powerhouse—was almost passed over for the CEO role. Why? His defining traits—empathy, humor, and humility—stood in stark contrast to Microsoft's historically aggressive, often cutthroat, culture. Founder Bill Gates later admitted he wasn't initially sure Nadella had the edge to lead. Nor did Nadella's immediate predecessor, Steve Ballmer, whose bombastic leadership style had long set the tone. Compared to that legacy, Nadella's quieter, more collaborative approach didn't fit the familiar mold.

One of the smartest decisions Nadella made as a CEO candidate was to build a strong, respectful connection with Ballmer. Rather than distancing himself or posturing as a radical departure, Nadella opened his heart and mind to understand his predecessor's perspective. He worked to see Microsoft through Ballmer's lens—to grasp what had inspired loyalty among leaders and employees, even amid a culture in need of renewal. That genuine curiosity gave Nadella access not only to insights into the company's challenges and opportunities, but also to Ballmer's trust.

This approach shaped Nadella's eventual success. His collaborative nature—once considered a liability—proved to be exactly what Microsoft needed for its next chapter. As *Fortune* reported, he managed to refresh the culture and reignite innovation without blowing up the business.[7] That ability to build bridges across past, present, and future is now one of the most sought-after traits in CEO succession.

As a CEO candidate, you are likely to face a formidable dual mandate, to prove to the board that you can deliver on two fronts that often feel in conflict. First, you must lead the company through transformation—driving innovation and growth in volatile conditions. At the same time, you must honor, harvest, and renew the cultural foundation that made the company great. Nadella chose not to treat this as a paradox. Instead, he demonstrated that sustainable innovation and cultural continuity can—and must—coexist in the most effective leadership transitions.

Behavioral psychologist Eric Fazen, quoted in the same *Fortune* article, underscored that "self-awareness" was the top predictor of success in high-impact leaders. "Are we resisting this candidate because they're wrong for the role—or because they challenge our assumptions of what a leader should look like?" he asks. The lesson: Don't try to mimic your predecessor or fit a mold. Lead from your truest and highest value; go deeper into understanding your predecessors so that you and they can feel more comfortable selecting you. Help the board and your boss see what the company truly needs next, not just what feels familiar.

As a CEO candidate, you must take similar steps before your appointment is finalized. Nadella spent months aligning with the board, his boss, and leadership on the company's challenges, future direction, and key priorities. He actively sought input from key executives and employees, refining his strategic vision before he took the reins.

Make it clear that you recognize and respect your CEO's leadership. Highlight specific methods your bosses used to lead people, products, and strategy. In town halls and meetings, actively reference how the values espoused by your CEO, along with their past key achievements, serve as guardrails for the company's future. Never present this information in a flattering or flowery way but as specific, tangible direction to employees as examples of clear principles that will not change with new leadership. If appropriate, suggest that the company publicly honor your predecessor's impact; this could be through a leadership legacy event, internal recognition, or even positioning them as an industry thought leader.

And once you're aligned with their vision, amplify it. Think about ways to find time and space for telling the previous CEO's backstory rather than just relying on the highlight reel. Seek to discover the deeper story behind major decisions and the big bets that your predecessor has taken and how that story might apply to your job as a new CEO.

Every CEO in the four hundred companies under the Virgin brand feels overwhelmed to step into Richard Branson's shoes. Everybody asks Branson for advice, and he effortlessly and enthusiastically does his best to summarize. But it was only when Mark went sailing with Branson for four hours that he was able to learn that the project they were talking about could be amplified tenfold. It gave Mark time to abandon being starstruck and instead learn what size the opportunity might be. He could feel the doubts, fears, gamesmanship, and risk-taking that were baked into Sir Richard's biggest bets.

As a CEO candidate, you're thinking there's not enough time or a real chance for a sailing trip, but there might be a long flight, car ride, golf game, or dinner. Be an opportunist to find time to brainstorm with the boss. At a minimum, add to your one-on-one business updates more than just a brief moment for conversations about the future transition. You must hear how your CEO interpreted and orchestrated their successes and how they characterize their self-described shortcomings of the past. They will feel better about ceding the role if you've engaged at this deeper level.

Don't Count On What Worked in the Past

We coached an executive whose career had soared as a trusted relationship builder and sales leader, perhaps the best in the industry, at an iconic American manufacturer. Jack knew all the right people and had a gift for getting his teams to win major commitments from the biggest national accounts. We met him when he was recruited to become North American president of the largest division of another manufacturing company.

As the business conditions tightened, Jack was feeling that his boss, George, had stopped appreciating how hard it was to carve out small wins in market share. George was part of the family that founded the business; their name was on the building. George had a few years earlier stepped into the shoes of the famous founding family's larger-than-life CEO, who had passed away. The burden of this internationally admired brand was on his shoulders, and he was turning up the pressure on every member of the team both to enhance growth and expand profitability. While George was doing what any CEO needed to do in a difficult environment, Jack worried that he could not please his boss, which hit him hard because Jack had been considered a future CEO candidate and now he felt that their relationship was drifting. He wondered if George's anxiety, combined with the weight of family legacy, might prevent Jack and his peers on the executive team from admitting difficulties or asking for help.

Whenever George and Jack met, the CEO dove into a forensic review of strategy, poring over detailed spreadsheets, adding new books for Jack to read, and floating new ideas to hack the market, attract customers, and cut costs. George was noticeably less interested in the relationship factors that Jack had mastered to win support. When George emailed Jack with a punch list of items to address in the business, Jack, exasperated at the micromanagement, reached out to Mark as George's CEO coach: "Why doesn't George trust me to do the work? Does he know I'm busting my ass to deliver, and I have legions on the team addressing all those issues?"

But Jack was missing the most conspicuous point. He was seeing George's email as a sort of a remedial threat, or that George's spreadsheet analysis and barrage of ideas were somehow a failure on Jack's part. No, it was a classic disconnect between an evidence-first leader and a relationship-first leader.

Here's a simplification of this idea from psychology. Take a moment to think about the people you know who fall into these two categories:

- *Feelers* prefer to lean in on the relationship and feelings you share first, then maybe dive into content and detail.

- *Thinkers* prefer to talk about the facts and data so they can get comfortable understanding what's going on. Then, if they feel everyone is engaged in that idea, fact, or discovery, they may become willing to share feelings about their relationship.

When either personality type is under stress, these traits become intensified. Imagine a scientist or engineer loving lab research and thinking it's seriously important—that's a thinker—but that work is also fascinating and engaging for them, as it is for George. A feeler like Jack finds it hard to believe that George is encouraging Jack to actively engage in the problem-solving with him rather than letting Jack delegate the challenge to his team.

Jack lamented, "I don't want to let him down, but I'm not an expert in finance or engineering." Mark pointed out that while George had an MBA, neither was he an expert. George didn't expect Jack to have the answers, while Jack had assumed he did. As an evidence-first leader, George needed to feel that Jack was engaging in the challenge with depth and urgency, not that he had all the answers. Jack and his peers were working really hard, but many were relationship-first leaders who viewed George's shift as a rift in the relationship. It was intimidating to Jack to iterate on evidence with the boss, while George wanted Jack to let go of worries about his appearance and other feeler superpowers for the moment and show he was wrestling with the issues. It was annoying to George that folks wanted to please him when he really wanted them to just work on the problem with him. Ironically, if Jack stuck to being the pleaser, it wouldn't please the boss, and he'd lose the chance to show the courage that George was looking for in Jack as a CEO candidate.

As you work with your CEO in the run-up to and during the succession process, you must determine if your boss is operating as an evidence-based thinker or relationship-based feeler, and whichever you tend to naturally be. Your goal is not to imitate, but to align more effectively, knowing that both exist in all of us. In times of stress, we tend to give too much prominence to our default. As a CEO candidate, strive to be both a *thinker* and a *feeler*, so that you can read the room and your boss and adapt. "It's the genius of the AND versus the tyranny of the OR," said Jerry Porras, coauthor of *Built to Last* and Mark's professor at Stanford University.[8] As a CEO candidate, you need to consider who you're dealing with when your boss reaches out to you and think about the context of the circumstances.

Make It Clear You Respect the Boss's Legacy

The succession of leadership at Ralph Lauren Corporation offers valuable insights into the complexities of CEO transitions, particularly when a founder steps down. In 2015, Ralph Lauren appointed Stefan Larsson as CEO, marking the first time an outsider led the company. Despite Larsson's successful track record at H&M and Old Navy, his tenure at Ralph Lauren was short-lived, lasting less than two years. The departure was attributed to the differing views between Larsson and Lauren on the company's creative and consumer strategies.[9]

Following Larsson's exit, Patrice Louvet, a former Procter & Gamble executive, was appointed as CEO in 2017. Louvet's collaborative approach and respect for the brand's heritage facilitated a more harmonious relationship with Lauren, who remained as executive chairman and chief creative officer. This transition underscores the importance of aligning visions and maintaining open communication between incoming leaders and founders to ensure a smooth succession.

CEOs who are founders particularly fear what they may feel is irrelevance for their brand and their career, even when they've had a successful run. Consider the following advice to avoid conflicts:

- *Seek advice from the incumbent and be explicit about what you intend to preserve* from the previous CEO's tenure, why it's important, and how you intend it to evolve, rather than framing your leadership as a rejection of their tenure.

- *Accept that the current CEO has earned the right to a tantrum.* This may become one of the harder moments of their professional lives. Hopefully it's short-lived or even unnoticed, but remember you are not CEO, so you don't know what they're feeling. Give them room.

- *Be prepared to find sincere ways to honor, celebrate, and commit* to one or two key achievements from your current CEO that you publicly cherish, even if part of your charter and mandate is to dramatically transform the company or strategy.

Find a Mentor for Your CEO

As a CEO candidate, we hope you're getting the message that the most mature and even-keeled CEOs can be understandably ravaged by moments of discomfort at the idea of leaving the job. This is a feeling you should not dismiss, because if and when you become CEO, you will also experience those moments, even if it doesn't feel that way now. One reason CEOs hold on too long is because they don't know what comes next. If they see no future for themselves beyond this role, they will resist the transition.

In moments of calm, ask them about their post-CEO plans and offer encouragement. If appropriate, connect them with executive recruiters, board advisers, or past CEOs who have made a successful transition. The goal is to help them see a future beyond the corner office, so they don't feel like they are walking into a void.

Encourage them to find a peer—a former CEO who moved to the role as chair—to serve as their coach and sounding board, like Michelle Seitz, former CEO of Russell Investments and now founder and CEO of startup MeydenVest Partners. "I want to retire the word 'retirement,'" Seitz says. "It's a really scary word when you're full of life, full of impact, when you get energized from what you love to do, but you don't know any other track other to keep doing the one you are on. Hopefully at some point along your journey, you get to stop the music for a little bit and say, 'What do I really want to experience? What do I really want to try?'" Seitz is a great mentor. Imagine tapping into her thirty-five years of experience in investing and running asset management firms.

Recently she has been pouring this knowledge into a new role in a micro-startup that's investing in women and underrepresented groups. She says, "When I thought about what gave me the most energy, I really wanted to carve out time for things that I always squeezed in during my full-time roles, trying to find ideas, find people, and find businesses

Eight Questions

During the leadership transition at Cisco, CEO candidate Chuck Robbins deliberately engaged with outgoing CEO John Chambers, seeking his insights to deepen his understanding of the company's challenges and opportunities. This collaborative approach facilitated a seamless transition and upheld continuity within the organization.[a]

As a CEO candidate, it's crucial to engage the incumbent CEO with thoughtful, strategic questions that demonstrate your respect for their leadership while also helping you prepare for the transition. Here's how you can reframe these inquiries to gain valuable insights and position yourself effectively:

1. *What aspects of your legacy would you like to see continued, and where do you believe there's room for new ideas or approaches?* As the incoming CEO, you need to understand the foundation that has made the company successful. Asking this question signals your willingness to honor the past while preparing to lead the company into its next phase. It also helps you identify which initiatives the incumbent holds dear, so you can thoughtfully balance continuity with innovation.

2. *How would you describe the leadership qualities and team dynamics that have been most critical to your success?* This question allows you to gain insights into the cultural and leadership styles that have driven the company forward. It will also help you identify gaps or opportunities for assembling a team that not only supports your vision but also challenges you constructively. By understanding the incumbent's leadership approach, you can decide which elements to retain and where to introduce new perspectives.

3. *In your view, what challenges should I expect in the first ninety days, and how would you recommend preparing as a candidate during the next year?* This question invites practical, experience-based advice from the outgoing CEO and helps you anticipate potential hurdles. It also demonstrates humility and a willingness to

learn, which can ease any tension during the transition period. Understanding their perspective on early challenges will allow you to set realistic expectations for yourself and your team.

4. *How can I support your transition out of the role in a way that honors your contributions while preparing the company for the future?* This question addresses the emotional and strategic aspects of leadership change. It shows that you respect the incumbent's legacy and are committed to a smooth, thoughtful transition. This can also open a dialogue about their future plans—whether they will remain involved as a board member or adviser—and how you can collaborate to ensure continuity during the handoff.

5. *What do you wish someone had told you when you first became CEO?* This question not only taps into the incumbent's wisdom but also fosters a more personal connection. It allows them to reflect on their own journey and share valuable lessons learned, giving you insights that might not come from formal succession planning processes.

6. *How can I best align with the board and key stakeholders during this transition?* Since the incumbent likely has deep relationships with the board and other stakeholders, their advice on managing these relationships can be invaluable. This question shows that you recognize the importance of these dynamics and are eager to build trust and alignment with critical decision-makers.

7. *What initiatives or strategies do you believe will be most important for the company's long-term success, and where do you see potential risks?* This helps you identify areas where the incumbent CEO sees both opportunity and vulnerability. It also allows you to demonstrate your strategic thinking by acknowledging their insights while considering how you'll approach these issues differently, if needed.

8. *What advice do you have for maintaining morale and continuity within the executive team?* Since the CEO is likely a stabilizing

(continued)

> leader, this transition can cause uncertainty within the organization. This question helps you understand how to stabilize and motivate the team, drawing from the incumbent's knowledge of internal dynamics. It also positions you as someone who values the well-being of the team and the continuity of leadership. We will review what most CEOs tell us about the art and science of reinforcing a strong culture as a part of their CEO transition process in chapter 9.
>
> a. Cisco Newsroom, "Cisco Board Names Chuck Robbins as Next CEO—John Chambers to Become Executive Chairman, Effective July 26," May 4, 2015, https://newsroom.cisco.com/c/r/newsroom/en/us/a/y2015/m05/cisco-board-names-chuck-robbins-as-next-ceo-john-chambers-to-become-executive-chairman-effective-july-26.html.

that I could give voice to, that I could empower with strategic advice, that I could invest in on my own."

You can offer coaching to your exiting boss. As a former CEO, board member, and chairman, Mark is frequently asked to step into that mentoring role for an outgoing CEO as they make the transition. We take them through a process of thinking about what's next for them and help them cope with the feelings of letting go.

Seitz encourages every CEO candidate to shift their role with the CEO to facilitate the transition by helping them see the opportunities beyond the corner office. When your boss looks at how much of a difference their experience, networks, and resources can make for outside organizations, it can reenergize them and, frankly, distract them from the difficulties of the transition. As a senior executive and now CEO candidate, you are already being recruited for your talents and reputation in your position. As outgoing CEO, those opportunities are significantly magnified for board positions, philanthropy, teaching positions, private equity, venture capital, consulting, or mentorship. If appropriate, as a CEO candidate, you can introduce your departing boss to executive recruiters, advisers, or leadership networks outside your company's succession process who specialize in post-CEO career paths. Your CEO deserves the opportunity to start thinking about *their* own future, not just the future of your company.

As a CEO candidate, your CEO and board are investing in you to help you grow into the role. But for the CEO, there is no clear off-ramp to guide their next stage. When it's hard to let go, you can provide empathy and support to the departing boss; you might even be able to help your boss embrace the existential crisis and enjoy the journey even more. And if all goes well, *you* will be the next to face this great, uncertain transition.

Your CEO Readiness Pulse Check

Five questions to help you partner with your predecessor—and step up with class

1. **Do you understand what your CEO is experiencing, or are you focused only on your ascent?** This isn't just a leadership change; it's an epic personal transition. Have you taken the time to understand what your predecessor may be feeling as they prepare to let go?

2. **Have you clarified how power and decision-making are evolving between you and your CEO?** Transition periods can blur roles. Are you negotiating authority with respect and transparency or letting assumptions breed tension?

3. **Do you understand how your CEO leads under pressure and how your styles may collide or complement?** Every leader has a stress fingerprint. Have you adapted your approach to consider how your CEO operates in times of change and volatility?

4. **Are you reinforcing your CEO's legacy and your vision in public?** Boards and teams want continuity with momentum. Are you signaling respect for what worked, while preparing to define what comes next?

5. **Are you building confidence with the board as your CEO exits or letting a vacuum form?** The board watches your navigation of this handoff closely. Are you showing up as a partner now, so board members can picture you leading?

7

Engage with the Owners

Your candidacy depends on what your shareholders value

Activist investors are known to disrupt CEOs in public to advocate new strategies, jettison underperforming divisions, and lobby to replace directors to give themselves influential seats in your boardroom. But with volatile markets and disruptive competitors grabbing market share, activists have embraced an additional demand, what they call *decapitation*. More than 20 percent of CEOs whose companies have been targeted by activists in the past two years have been replaced, according to Barclays.[1] And for large-cap brand-name companies, it's almost twice that: 38 percent saw their CEOs replaced in 2024 alone.

Obviously, the exit rate for chief executives has huge implications for CEO candidates. While the board of directors and the sitting chief executive typically steer succession planning, it's the company's owners—including short-term activists—who can ultimately seize control and upend the process. As the fifth of the seven key stakeholders in your CEO readiness journey, their influence can recast your candidacy in unexpected ways. For that reason, and many more we'll get to in this chapter, you will need to take your skill in investor relations to the next level beyond what you've done at board meetings, quarterly conference calls, and analyst days in your current role, even if you're a president or other C-suite executive. Your capacity to engage with myriad shareholders is key to surviving and thriving as the next chief executive, and your success or failure is widely broadcast. When a public company CEO is announced, for example, the stockholders instantly drive the price of your company's shares up or down in response, and investors openly share their hopes and fears about you with by far the loudest immediate public support or rebuke as your firm gains or loses millions or billions in market value.

If your company is public, you will prove your worth to Wall Street—usually buy-side and sell-side analysts and portfolio managers as well as the insurgent activist investors. If your organization is private, your skills in dealing with owners will be fundamentally different than with public companies. You'll build bridges with large individual shareholders, founders or family members, or the partners of a private equity or a venture capital firm.

As a senior executive who's a CEO candidate, you've undoubtedly dealt with many of these investors. But this process involves much more than just getting chummy with a few key people; it requires learning the nuances of the culture and language of each of your specific owners, understanding how they think, and accepting their expected timeline to see results. "I'm shocked how many people [CEO candidates] I advise who actually don't learn the nuances of who controls ownership of the company and where the influencers are on the cap table, like a key partner at the VC [venture capital] firm or a PE [private equity] fund," said cofounder and CEO Margo Georgiadis of Montai Therapeutics, who's also a board member for several companies, including McDonald's. She's had extraordinary experience leading almost every type of company structure, from privately held, PE-funded Ancestry.com to publicly traded Mattel. She was President of the Americas division of Google, and before that, she was chief operating officer of Groupon, executive vice president of USCard Services, and chief marketing officer at Discover Financial Services.

The capitalization table that she's referring to shows the full ownership breakdown of a company, detailing who owns what percentage of the equity (e.g., founders, investors, employees), what type of shares they hold (e.g., common stock, preferred shares, options), along with how much they've been granted, vested, and invested, and often what their stakes might be worth. Since Mark partners as a coach to CEOs of public companies, along with many PE and VC firms, he's felt privileged to be among Georgiadis's advisers as she leads a myriad of company structures. She said that ambitious executives can tend to be "so excited at the prospect of becoming a CEO that they do not ask very basic questions [like who controls ownership of the company] that can significantly affect their success."

In this chapter, we'll discuss the critical role for which you must prepare as a chief executive that investors know as a visionary leader and spokesperson for the owners so that the board can feel confident about you, particularly if you're not in finance. If you do *not* have that experience, you have a disadvantage as a CEO candidate until you prove your skill in this area to your boss and board. You will need to demonstrate that you can ignite the company's story for shareholders and understand the power politics of the ownership structure before you can be seriously considered for the big job. If you are already responsible for investor relations as CFO, you can skip forward to the next chapter.

Learn the Language of Your Owners

If you're running a division or functional area of your company and you haven't spent a lot of time with anyone from Wall Street, it's not unusual to wonder: "Buy side versus sell side; analysts versus investors. Why does that matter? What are each of these groups trying to accomplish?" In addition to trying to learn about the types of people you're talking with, it's important to map your strategy accordingly. It takes some adjustment.

As an executive who's angling to be a CEO, you need to know who you're talking with when you are addressing your owners or their representatives, just as you would any other group of crucial customers. You need to be at least conversationally fluent in their languages and cultural eccentricities. Remember, it's the owners who will determine whether someone is able to keep the job after they become CEO, and those people will use shareholder value as the long-term indicator and measurement of success or failure as CEO.

Here's the reality: in addition to honoring your company's culture, engaging your employees, calming your customers, and developing great products, if shareholder returns are poor—even for one quarter—the already high pressure on you will steadily intensify. You have likely already felt the shift in your boss's mood when investors and analysts attack the CEO and CFO on earnings calls. The owners and the analysts who write about your company on behalf of those owners are looking for anyone and anything they can blame when the quarter falls below *their* expectations. When you think about money people, they are not necessarily the most naturally sympathetic to you or your concerns. Their mindset is: "I bought the stock. I own you. Deliver on my expectations for return on my investment in the time frame that I'm demanding."

It May Not Seem Fair, But the Owners Make the Final Call

Perhaps the most fundamental truth when dealing with owners is what Peter Drucker shared with Marshall Goldsmith: "Every decision in the world is made by the person who has the power to make the decision. Make peace with that."[2] That may sound a bit obvious, but consider it for a moment in the context of the ultimate control and destiny of a company. If you become CEO, you will not always be the final decision-maker on this and many other decisions investors make as owners. The board members are going to make final calls on many big decisions, and they are going to act based on what they think is best for the owners or shareholders. In this power structure, you may be third in line in terms of pure decision-making power even when or if you become CEO.

And the decisions shareholders make are not about rightness, fairness, goodness, or logic; they are pursuing the strategy for investing that they believe is best. Now, apply that to your candidacy as a potential CEO. Decision-makers do not have to buy what you are offering; you have to *sell* your strategy by showing how it aligns with their investing strategy. You have to convince them of your worth, just as your company must to its investors.

Get More Engaged in Investor Relations

"Number one, investor relations are your responsibility as CEO. You need to have a lateral vision of how your company may be viewed by different kinds of investors," Michelle Seitz of Russell Investments told Mark at his Chief Executive Summit series.

She continued: "You are going to need to be very clear where you want to take the company, because investors in the public market can clearly buy and sell you every single day. New CEOs and CEO candidates often want to believe that investors, like them, are invested in the long-term success of the business, and those that aren't they can worry less about, since they won't be sticking around for the long term. That's a very bad way to look at it. Your job is to steward *all* your investors because they are fiduciaries for other people's money. You have to be the chief storyteller on why they should invest now in your company. You must make it clear why you believe this is the appropriate risk-return decision-making for the company and therefore the shareholders, and why we believe we'll hit these milestones along the way."

When Mark asked Seitz how a nonfinancial senior executive should prepare as a CEO candidate, she said: "Show up at as many of the investor events as possible. [And at those meetings, you will] need to prove that you are executing on the investor story that your current CEO is telling."

If you're in line for the CEO job, you have already developed some deep expertise that is of interest to investors. If your company is public, at some point you'll receive opportunities to participate in quarterly earnings investor conference calls, and many of you as senior leaders already have participated in such meetings. There may have been a merger, a big change in operations, a breakthrough in research or development, a write-off, or various other positives or negatives to report, and as an expert, you can be called on to contribute insight.

The two key players who run investor relations every day and the earnings calls each quarter are obviously the chief executive officer and the chief financial officer. The CFO is often also on the short list to be the next CEO. In 2023, 8.4 percent of CEOs at *Fortune* 500 and S&P 500 companies were promoted directly from CFO roles, compared to 5.8 percent in 2013.³ This upward trend is even more pronounced among the UK's FTSE 100 companies, where about 15 percent of current CEOs were CFOs immediately prior to their promotion, compared to a global average of 8 percent.⁴ A full 40 percent of Mark's clients are CFOs on the way up. We've seen major shifts in recent years highlighting how strategic functions like CFO and COO are being given broader organizational responsibilities like chief commercial officer, chief revenue officer, or chief strategist, beyond traditional financial management in ways that enhance their experience and viability as CEO candidates in the eyes of the board. (The point is that, if you're a CFO, you've proven substantial gravitas related to investor relations and financial management, so to be CEO ready now, you'll need to hone your expanded skills as a strategist, marketer, technologist, operator, and so on.)

Work Closely with the CFO

If you're a CEO candidate who is not a CFO, you need to demonstrate that you're a great asset to and supporter of investor relations. One way is to seek a role in investor meetings, where you can show shareholders your subject matter expertise. These meetings offer an opportunity to impress investors and the board with your special expertise, but that's only the beginning; you're broadly capable of so much more, showing sophistication across many functional areas of the organization.

Many CEO candidates have already participated in the showcase event that's called an "investor day" or "analyst day" (this is not to be confused with your company's annual general meeting for all shareholders). Investor days are often held semiannually and convene major investors and analysts interested in learning more about the company and its outlook and gauging the quality of its executive team. Just like investor calls that your CFO and CEO have throughout the year—particularly during the quarterly earnings announcement—you could be expected to add color and specificity from your area of expertise about capital expenditures, new clients, and new services.

If you haven't done this yet, get invited. Think of investors as just a different kind of powerful and nuanced customer and just as necessary to know for you to be considered for the role of chief executive.

Investor Credibility: Seven Ways to Win the CEO Audition That Never Ever Ends

1. ***Tune into the ritual quarterly reckoning—the earnings calls with investors.*** Be there even if you're not making a presentation. Too many CEO candidates see this as tedious or distracting from their day jobs, but you must understand how it feels for your CEO and CFO. It's the shareholders' quarterly airing of grievances—live and on the record. It's the owners' public, unfiltered critique of your CEO and CFO that can make or break the tenure of your executive team and company strategy, broadcast every quarter. If you're paying attention, you might notice that the earnings cycle and board meetings affect your boss's mood before and after the calls. It may not be a big deal for you yet, but it will be. It's *their* quarterly review.

   - Coca-Cola Company CEO Douglas Daft told Mark about the emotional toll of the quarterly report with a biting quip; when asked how long he'd served, he replied: "Twenty-seven quarters!" As a former COO, not a CFO, the investor relations process felt to him like an endless series of bruising ninety-day earnings cycles. This is both a huge success story and an important cautionary tale. Daft was the ideal internal CEO candidate after having become president and chief operating officer in December 1999 and CEO shortly after in February 2000 to June 2004. Before that, he had served as a long-successful division president for the Middle and Far East since 1991—tangentially steeped in the rhythm of Wall Street's quarterly scrutiny. Daft deserved the trust invested in him as an operating executive with global experience for more than thirty years rising through Coke's ranks. He was admired for strategic innovations that were initially well received. But during a turbulent period for the company, his push for decentralization and his understated communication style frustrated investors. During that period, Pepsi's stock increased more than 11 percent while Coca-Cola's fell over

       (continued)

25 percent—and so did Wall Street's patience. Daft's career was a long success story by many measures, but he knew going into the job that the ultimate tenure of the journey is judged by shareholder performance, which can turn quickly, quarter by quarter.

2. ***Understand the investor implications of your board's agenda.*** As a senior executive, you're tasked with delivering in your specific function at board meetings, but a CEO is also tasked with knowing the whole picture to deliver results for investors. The broader context and breadth of understanding, courage, and vision that your CEO must demonstrate with investors must be contextualized in the boardroom. You can help the CEO and CFO prepare, present, and cope with shareholder fallout.

3. ***Seek coaching from your company's IR team and board members who are willing to share tactics to inspire your shareholders.*** Peter Lynch, the legendary mutual fund investor with one of history's best track records of performance in the long term, cautioned against becoming too emotionally connected with the daily gyrations of your stock price. If you were lucky enough to have him invest in your company, he was the best example of a thoughtful, long-term investor who could inspire you and your management team with wise insights and a broad perspective of your competitors. He could also provide frank coaching on tough days when you as an executive felt punished by the market and investors in a personal way: "You're never as good as your stock price when it's soaring and never as bad as it seems when stocks are tanking," he told Mark. The stock market is all over the place with volatility that no one can control, and it's not fair, perhaps, but the CEO's job is ultimately judged by market performance. Think about how you can better support your investor relations in that regard, and how willing you may or may not be to carry that burden.

4. ***Volunteer to join investor visits whenever you can.*** Offer to back up your finance team and CFO whenever possible by adding an investor visit while you're traveling for other business at your company. Your investors aren't just in New York, Silicon Valley, Dubai,

Mumbai, or London, obviously; the biggest financial influencers might be where you happen to be traveling for your work.

5. *Mystery shop your competitors' investor relations presentations as often as you can.* If the competitor is a public company, anyone can sign up to listen. It's the recurring public scorecard where investors weigh in on your competitors' performance, too. We advise CEO candidates to be mystery shoppers in as many ways as they can: if your competitors have retail stores, visit them; if you can create accounts with them, do that. When Mark was producing Schwab.com, he obtained regulatory compliance approval for his team to open accounts at his competitors. This is common practice in marketing but not enough CEO candidates practice it in the context of investor relations. Surprisingly, as an investor in your competitors, you will gain insights you haven't obtained elsewhere, which make you an even more interesting and enlightened CEO candidate to your board. You should mention what you learned to your boss and your board. The breadth of your strategic understanding makes you more attractive and sets you apart from other CEO candidates. Every CEO and every company competes not only for customers but also for capital and shareholder value.

6. *Study the analyst reports that are prepared by investment research analysts commenting on your company.* They review the prospects for your industry and competitors. You can impress your CEO and board by reading and digesting those analyst reports about your firm and your adversaries.

7. *Add investor relations to the strategic plan you're incubating as a CEO candidate.* You need to think about the owner and investor story because it plays a central role in how you present the company during your CEO candidacy interview with the board. Be sure to review the discussions investors are having about your company and think about what you would do if you were running the analyst meeting. Think about the meeting holistically and how it appeals to a broad range of investors and represents the full range of services your company offers.

Know the Cast of Investor Characters and Their Ownership Dramas

Think of the stock market as a stage where key actors, each with a unique role in the financial theater, influence your company's narrative (and stock price). Again, if you're not an expert in investor relations, but you are a CEO candidate, you need to know which kinds of investors are most interested in your business and how they are evaluating your company. Let's take a brief look at the most common shareholders you must know.

Buy side versus sell side

Two influences who have the biggest impact on the market buzz about your company's stock are the buy-side and sell-side analysts and investors—both of whom you need to know as future chief executive.

Buy-side analysts research your company as an investment on behalf of mutual fund managers, hedge funds, pension funds, and insurance firms that buy and hold securities for their own accounts or for their investors, with the goal of generating a good return over time. Buy-side analysts write reports about your company and its competitors and serve as the strategists in the shadows, representing institutional investment firms that can take a significant position in your company. These are the folks who meet with your investor relations team and CFO and make a case with their institutional investment managers to assess how well your company fits within their investment strategy, based on your strategic direction, governance, and financial robustness. Those firms rely on buy-side analysts to determine if you and your company are a good bet. Their forensic analyses are detailed, focusing on the long-term potential and underlying value of your company. Their recommendations are directly tied to the specific investing direction of the portfolios they manage.

Among the most prominent buy-side players are BlackRock, the world's largest asset manager, overseeing approximately $11.6 trillion in assets; Vanguard Group, managing around $10.4 trillion; Fidelity

Investments, with $5.9 trillion; State Street Global Advisors, with $4.34 trillion under management; and J.P. Morgan Asset Management, with $4.1 trillion in assets.[5]

Sell-side analysts, unlike the buy-side analysts, are vocal in the news and generate research analysis for brokerage firms that are interested in marketing your stock or your competitors' and selling it to their investors. Think of them as narrators who interpret your company's story for a broader audience. They are a part of the sales function of their brokerage firms and investment banks, crafting those reports in which they advocate or dissuade investors with buy or sell recommendations. Their insights, whether bullish or bearish, can significantly impact your stock's trading volume and price. Popular sell-side brokerages include J.P. Morgan, Goldman Sachs, Merrill Lynch, Deutsche Bank, and Citibank, to name a few. On the sell side, top analysts in specific fields or industries earn visibility when they consistently make accurate predictions about your company and the markets. Recognition from financial media like *Institutional Investor* is like the Academy Awards for them and, in a certain way, for you in the role of investor relations. When those high-profile analysts attend your events, your stock is more likely to gain attention, attract major institutional investors, and generate greater enthusiasm for your company.

Prepare to Deal with Activist Investors

Activist investors can strike terror in the hearts of boards and CEOs. They usually seek to profit quickly by buying substantial stakes in companies to influence management and strategic decisions. Their goal is to unlock shareholder value thought to be unrealized by going public with their point of view. They often push for change: leadership, operational, financial, or strategic shifts that they argue will capture the purported value. Activists attend investor days and analyst meetings and behave like the social media influencers of Wall Street. They may start with only a few shares, or they may be major players with significant backing. Activists who seek to shake up the company's leadership often launch a proxy fight. A proxy fight at a public company is a contest

How to Prepare for Your CEO Audition with Buy-Side and Sell-Side Analysts

The CEO and CFO are in the spotlight when they're in the room, but as a rising candidate, you're not just making a cameo; you're stepping into a pivotal supporting role. Think of yourself not as a background player, but as a strategic voice auditioning in real time. Your investor narrative must be more than a polished update; it should reflect readiness to think and lead at enterprise scale.

Here's how to sharpen your delivery before the spotlight shifts:

1. *Own your scene in the strategic script.* Clarify how your part of the business advances the company's long-term plan. Whether you lead operations, technology, or innovation, analysts want to see that you grasp not just the numbers but the bigger picture. Speak fluently about performance drivers, risks, and the value you're helping to create—without veering off-message. Partner with your company's investor relations team and CFO to draft the key points and a script.

2. *Be consistently compelling.* Wall Street prizes consistency. Show a steady command of results, patterns, and priorities. Deliver your message with calm authority—clear, data informed, and forward looking. Analysts and investors want to believe that if handed the top job, you'd deliver value with discipline.

3. *Speak candidly, within the guardrails.* Trust is built on transparency, but also on judgment. Know what you can say—and what you can't. Learn from your CFO and investor relations team how to manage compliance boundaries while still offering insight. When you do speak, balance candor with control. Investors don't expect perfection, but they expect clarity and no surprises.

between competing groups of shareholders to gain control of the board of directors by persuading other shareholders to vote for their slate of board nominees, typically driven by activist investors seeking to make strategic changes or to replace the CEO. They will attack weak spots in your company's corporate governance.

As CEO coaches, we have witnessed moments when activists orchestrate the ousting of board members and the chief executive. If the idea of decapitation gains traction with other investors, a coup may ensue, which disrupts or accelerates the orderly succession process in which you thought you were a candidate like a corporate boardroom season finale of *Survivor*. The renowned auction house Sotheby's was attacked by activist Daniel Loeb's hedge fund, Third Point, which criticized Sotheby's management for weak operating margins and a declining competitive position relative to its main rival, Christie's. He called for the resignation of then-CEO William Ruprecht and sought representation on the board. Following a proxy battle, an agreement was reached, allowing Loeb and two of his nominees to join Sotheby's board, and the CEO soon announced his departure.

In June 2024, Southwest Airlines was attacked by Elliott Investment Management, as it announced a $1.9 billion stake in the company and slammed the airline's leadership for its "stubborn unwillingness to evolve the company's strategy," as Paul Elliott Singer claimed in a publicly released letter that he sent to the Southwest board.[6] He advocated for the removal of CEO Bob Jordan and Executive Chairman Gary Kelly, citing the airline's declining stock performance and operational issues. In response to mounting pressure, Southwest agreed to a board restructuring in September 2024, resulting in the early retirement of Kelly and the appointment of five Elliott-backed nominees to the board. Despite these changes, Jordan remained as CEO, tasked with implementing a turnaround strategy to restore the airline's profitability.

At the same time, a similar coup was underway at the Walt Disney Company, which was embroiled in a proxy battle with activist investor Nelson Peltz of Trian Partners. Peltz criticized Disney's strategic decisions and multiple failed attempts at CEO succession planning, seeking a seat on the board to influence the company's direction. In April 2024, Disney shareholders rejected Peltz's board nomination, effectively ending the proxy fight, and CEO Bob Iger kept his job. But the controversy did prompt an intervention by Disney's board in the lackluster CEO succession process. Iger won't return as executive chairman, nor will he remain Disney CEO after the board names his successor by 2026.

Attacking another iconic brand, Procter & Gamble, Peltz threatened its board, initiating a proxy fight to win a seat to influence the company's strategy. Initially, Peltz's bid was declared unsuccessful, but a recount revealed he had won by a narrow margin. Peltz joined P&G's board, advocating for organizational restructuring and cost-cutting measures to enhance performance. After bullying his way onto the board in 2017, he stepped down as a director in 2021, having seen several of his proposed changes implemented. This is typical of activists who, once they have achieved their initial profit goals, are happy to move on to other companies.

Activists don't need billions to increase the pressure on corporate boards; indeed, their impact far exceeds the dollars they invest in companies. Despite holding only a 0.02 percent stake in ExxonMobil, Engine No. 1, a small, activist hedge fund, launched a campaign and successfully secured three seats on the board.

To be fair, while activists' actions are painful, they're not necessarily without some merit and can be quite insightful. If a company follows their advice, it may be able to accelerate change that was needed and win investor support that increases the share price, at least temporarily. But overall, the CEOs we coach do not generally see activism as a positive trend because the activists usually cash out quickly after getting involved and are not typically committed to a company's future long-term success. As one director told Byron, it "felt like management was getting an excessively bad report card for its stewardship of the company without meaningful support" in creating a more effective organization for all shareholders.

Legendary former Medtronic CEO Bill George and Jay Lorsch, both on the faculty at Harvard Business School, argue in a *Harvard Business Review* article that the activists' "initiatives can weaken a company's competitive position (to win short-term gains) to the detriment of long-term shareholders, and the high-leverage financing structures they often propose may put companies in jeopardy in the event of an economic downturn."[7]

Nevertheless, the increasing possibility that you, as a CEO candidate, must consider is that "the boss of a public board is not the investor, it is the activist shareholders. They evaluate every company. They find the gap where they can enter. They drive it," insists Ram Charan. The world-renowned leadership adviser and author emphasized to Mark that "they almost always get collaboration with investors to unseat [and] to make the board change. People must come to terms that these activist shareholders pounce and you better pay attention to them. Listen to them. Because investors will collaborate with them."

Adds Michelle Seitz, CEO candidates must prepare to deal with activism before they take the big seat. She suggests an exercise: "If I were to write an activist letter, what would I say? And what would my response be as CEO? That's managing the risk of your business." To do as Seitz suggests, think of ways you might increase short-term shareholder value if you were an activist. Then, be ready to articulate a plan to the board, in your interview for the CEO's role, for how you would achieve similar results for shareholders as an activist might, but how you'd do it in a thoughtful manner that would benefit investors with both a short-term focus and long-term focus.

Seitz adds, "Whenever I get called to come on to even very prestigious boards . . . because they have an activist and they want someone on the board to deal with them, my answer is, 'It may already be too late.' It's no fun coming in to try to mediate at that point what should have been previously preempted." So, Seitz recommends adopting a preemptive, fluid, and well-articulated vision for where you as a potential CEO will take the company and the milestones you will keep your investors focused on.

Sort Your Opportunities by Company Ownership Type

As a CEO, you will interact with a diverse spectrum of shareholders, depending on the stage of your company's growth and its financial maturity. If your company is not yet publicly traded, then there are many stages before an initial public offering, each with different priorities for you as a potential CEO. Here's a summary of the types of firms and

Create an Investor Relations Blueprint

When engaging with owners, Wall Street, and others who own massive blocks of shares in your company, your task is to win their hearts and minds. Mastering the art of investor relations is akin to a rite of passage for a potential CEO. It's a journey that transcends mere financial stewardship; it ventures into the realm of storytelling, trust-building, and strategic foresight. So, we offer the following blueprint for navigating the multifaceted challenge of investor relations and transforming into a master of shareholder engagement.

- *Individualize your attention.* The complex landscape of each type of investor and analyst includes diverse terrains, each inhabited by distinct groups with their own priorities and expectations. Strive to deeply understand the various members of your investor base and their investing philosophies. Don't confine engagement with investors to quarterly earnings calls or annual meetings.

- *Embrace feedback.* Just as you listen deeply to the engagement of your customers and employees in surveys, lean into investor feedback to refine your approach. It provides a mirror that reflects how your leadership and the company's direction are perceived externally. Ask analysts and institutional investors for their unvarnished opinions. Embrace this feedback, both positive and critical, to improve and evolve. Use it as a learning loop to guide adjustments in communication, highlight areas for strategic emphasis, and influence corporate governance practices.

- *Weather the storms.* The way CEOs navigate challenges can define their legacy. During your journey, you will not avoid storms. There is no escape, but there are many options, so in times of crisis, be proactive, strategic, and decisive. Outline for investors the steps you're taking to address the issue, the anticipated outcomes, and how these align with long-term strategies for stability and growth. A calm, confident approach can serve as a beacon of reassurance, transforming potential vulnerabilities into demonstrations of resilience.

companies you're likely to be recruited to lead as a potential chief executive, and the types of leaders each prefers. This list will also help you to decide which type of company is the best fit for you, so that when you're tapped for an opportunity, you'll know what kind of company you'd be leading.

Public companies

In this chapter so far, we've focused largely on public company investor relations. As a CEO candidate, your current company (or every company today) is likely determined to drive massive change that requires a CEO who can navigate through transformation with skills such as:

- *Change management.* Proficiency in managing large-scale organizational change

- *Long-term strategic vision.* The ability to envision and guide the company toward long-term success

- *Stakeholder communication.* Keeping all stakeholders aligned during periods of uncertainty

- *Resilience and adaptability.* The capacity to handle setbacks and rapidly adapt to new challenges

- *Sustainable growth.* A vision to accelerate growth quarter after quarter, under the scrutiny of public markets throughout the company's transformation

Private companies on the IPO threshold

As a private company prepares to go public, the CEO role is vital to give confidence to future potential Wall Street investors. The CEO will become a visionary, helping prepare people to deal with the intense scrutiny of operating in the public sector. The leader must not only be fluent in the language of regulatory landscapes and investor expectations but also adept at establishing a governance framework robust enough to withstand public scrutiny. The narrative of the CEO and of you as a candidate must speak of the potential for consistent growth, employ transparent financial storytelling, and implement a strategy for sustainable expansion under the watchful gaze in the new public sphere.

For private companies on the cusp of going public, CEO selection focuses on:

- *Public market readiness.* Understanding regulatory requirements and the expectations of public investors

- *Corporate governance.* Establishing strong governance structures and clean audits and practices

- *Investor relations.* A background in communicating effectively with analysts, investors, and the media, as well as a track record of consistent delivery of results that investors care about, such as profit margins and quarter-over-quarter performance

- *Financial reporting.* Transparency, accuracy, and predictability in financial reporting

- *Sustainable growth.* A vision to maintain growth post-IPO, under the scrutiny of public markets

Private equity–owned firms

PE firms like to think of themselves as the architects of value—or actually the *renovators* of prior brand value. They often rescue and resculpt more mature enterprises and prioritize a different blueprint for the company. Their cornerstones are operational efficiency and financial acumen, and they seek a CEO who can navigate the complex structures of debt and capital. They value a leader who can drive growth not just organically but at breathtaking speed through the strategic amalgamation of acquisitions, all while preparing for a masterful exit that maximizes shareholder value within a precise time frame. Time is money in the extreme in this context; PE firms require spectacular returns, sometimes at any cost to the culture, customers, and community of employees. For companies in need of revival, a CEO with turnaround expertise becomes the linchpin of future prosperity. In a new CEO, they prioritize:

- *Operational efficiency.* The ability to streamline operations to improve profitability

- *Financial acumen.* A strong grasp of financial strategies to restructure debt, if necessary, and to manage capital

- *Sales leadership.* Ability to build a sales pipeline, hire and manage sales talent, and drive toward sales goals and high-level customer service needs

- *Growth through acquisition.* Skills in identifying and integrating acquisitions to drive growth

- *Turnaround expertise.* For underperforming companies, a proven ability to lead a successful turnaround

- *Strategic exit planning.* Maximizing shareholder value through strategic exits, often within a four-to-five-year time frame

A classic case of a PE-owned company is Ancestry.com. The company had swelled beyond $1.5 billion in market capitalization when it was a public company, but business conditions and strategic missteps put the company's valuation into a freefall. This is the perfect scenario for a PE firm, in which its knowledge of an industry or product gives it confidence to swoop in and capitalize on the opportunity to turn it around. In this case, Ancestry was acquired for a fraction of its former value and taken off the public market so the new owners could reinvent the company in private. PE firms routinely map a fresh strategy that will reclaim the company's market opportunity; that is where you may have an opportunity as a CEO candidate. They're looking for senior executives with experience running the operations of a bigger company or as chief financial officer or strategist to lead the transformation. A key part of that ambition involves hiring a new CEO to orchestrate a turnaround. In this case, that leader was Margo Georgiadis, whom you met earlier. The owners thought that, with her extensive experience, she was the perfect choice. They were right. She engaged the company's resurgent mission-based culture and shaped its renewed value by more than tenfold during her tenure. BlackRock bought the company for $4.6 billion.

Georgiadis insists that you must learn how the ownership structure of a company informs addressing the specific needs of your unique owners, who have different priorities. "If you're in a two-tiered structure where a founder has control, that's very different than a traditionally publicly traded company, where generally you have large institutional investors and the board is a well-qualified group that understands the different areas of the company," Georgiadis says. She explains that in a public company, CEOs often feel intense pressure from institutional investors that are comparing you with a peer group of companies. "They're thinking about your ability to provide them visibility and relative returns on investment, and if the type of company you are building aligns with their investment profile. If the company is dependable, with big dividends, it's going to have one type of shareholder. If the company is high growth, it's going to attract a different kind of shareholder. You have to make sure that you tell your story in a way that aligns your shareholder base. Those people do not want to be surprised by a shift in business performance against that."

In a private company, perhaps one owned by a private equity firm, Georgiadis says a potential CEO needs to think about the concentration of the capital table. "Typically, what you have is a small group of investors that come in, and they have a hypothesis on the return on capital expected. Private equity tends to have a minimum of a 3X return threshold within three to four years. There are PE people who look for profitability, some who tend to be more growth oriented, and others who are more after cash flow. If you are going to be CEO, you have to be clear on their expected return profile. It's your job to deliver on the agreed strategy."

Private equity investors tend to invest in more established companies that have the potential to increase profitability, as Georgiadis was tasked to do with Ancestry.com.

Venture capital–funded companies

Think of VC firms as the pioneers of potential. They stand on the frontier of innovation, their sights set on startups brimming with explosive growth to optimize a possible, but not entirely certain, total available market. For these firms, selecting a CEO means finding a captain who can steer the ship through tumultuous waters with an eye firmly on the horizon. VC firms are oriented toward lightning-fast growth to prove the concept or shut it down quickly. They seek to capture market share and new clients rapidly to confirm whether the idea is viable, while choosing to offer a limited number of products to test in the marketplace and to initially prioritize share growth over immediate profitability. They seek a senior leader who can rapidly adapt to ever-shifting market winds while also charting a course for future fundraising. The ultimate treasure map? An exit strategy that aligns with the VC's timeline. When selecting a CEO, their priorities revolve around:

- *Growth orientation.* A clear track record of identifying product-market fit and then scaling those experiments rapidly

- *Proof-of-concept leadership.* The ability to foster swift iteration of the product (until it works) and to adapt to market changes

- *Fundraising skills.* Proficiency in securing additional funding

- *Exit strategy.* Understanding the road map for eventual exit, be it through acquisition, IPO, or sale to a private equity firm that aligns with the VC's investment horizon

- *Risk management.* Balancing aggressive growth with sound risk management strategies

Georgiadis is now CEO of a venture-funded company in the biotech industry. She says, "The mindset is completely different in venture versus a public company. People are looking at portfolio risk across a range of companies that they own. They want to underwrite something that has between 5X and 10X growth potential because they're going in earlier. So, you need a big idea, and you need a way to demonstrate milestone improvement to that 10X return. You really need to be good at laying out the mileposts for how you demonstrate that you're making meaningful progress with the capital that you have as well as setting yourself up to be able to raise the next group of capital. That could be a big shock for people who have not worked in those environments. They are intensely driven by how well their original plan and investment thesis for the growth of the company is working out, and they're very steadfast about the timeline for returning capital."

Do your homework before you join any company, or even if you're asked to take over at your current firm. "Ask to review the last four years of financials and the current year financial plan, because you're going to own that," says Georgiadis. "When I was hired in my first CEO role, I asked nine questions about the numbers because I didn't think the numbers added up. You need to ask them about their investment thesis and how far they are from it. It's such a basic thing, but unless you're experienced in the industry, people don't ask that."

Honor the Founder

A final caution about navigating the ownership structure of a company as you consider your candidacy for CEO: if the company is controlled by private equity or a venture capital firm, there is often a founder of the company who could be a large or significantly influential shareholder. They have a passionate point of view about how the company should be run. That founder is or has been CEO and currently sits on the board as chair or in some other crucial role, like chief technology officer. As a candidate to become the new CEO, your story of how you will run the company must consider thoughtfully how it may or may not align with the founder's and the controlling shareholders' story.

Before you take the CEO role, you need to unpack many uncertain, slippery issues, like time horizons for investment and return. If you don't, conflict will ensue. This timing mismatch comes up as an issue in almost every private equity or venture capital–funded company because of the limited visibility on how long things take to be invented, built, rebuilt, tested, and retested. Innovation is messy, and experiments are necessary but unpredictable. It's a bit of a paradox, because investors want predictability. For instance, if you are being considered as the new CEO at the start of year three of a four-year horizon in private equity or your five-year plan, your horizon is tight, and it could be very hard to ramp up the company for the results the investment partners are looking for. The runway could be just too short for takeoff. If you cannot live with the time horizons for goal setting, we advise you not to take the job.

Sometimes a CEO candidate will tell us, "I'm just interested in what's in the long-term best interest of the company, not in some two-year exit strategy." While it's OK for you to feel noble that way, and you may be right, remember that as an incoming CEO, it's not your money. As the hired gun, it's never your money. If the shareholders have a plan, and you have a different one, you need to sell it to the partners or not take the job.

Some candidates still think about the CEO role as the ultimate goal regardless of the company type. We encourage you to think deeply about ownership structure and even rule out some opportunities based on whether you can live with the requirements of the shareholders. Understand what types of companies and owners you're the best fit to lead. There's nothing wrong with saying that you don't do PE or VC or IPOs or whichever ownership model doesn't match you.

The landscapes of CEO leadership vary wildly, from the wild frontiers of venture capital to the Machiavellian realities of private equity, the existential leap to IPOs or the quarterly scrutiny of public company leadership. Those who traverse these terrains typically share a common quest: shareholder value, in its many guises. How leaders champion growth to get there, partner with stakeholders, and manage risks provides a unique portrait of the legacy you will build as the next CEO.

Applying this logic, you'll see that you need to actively listen and speak in languages that a broad network of people who are invested in or reporting on the financials and fundamentals of your company will understand. To say you'll need to be financially multilingual is an understatement. Herein lies the essence of mastering the CEO's role in the dynamic world of owner's expectations. Prospective CEOs become investor relations experts adept at identifying and aligning with the nuanced priorities of their company's owners. By doing so, they can ensure not only their own success but also the long-term prosperity of the organization they lead.

Your CEO Readiness Pulse Check

Five questions you must answer to become CEO ready

1. **Who really owns your future, and have you earned their trust to lead it?** Every CEO selection is shaped by those who influence capital application. Do you know the top decision-makers in your shareholder base? Have you built the credibility, visibility, and investor fluency to make them bet on you when the moment comes?

2. **If you were to write a letter as an activist investor to your board, what would it say?** Think through how to defend the business while accelerating transformation. Can you preempt activist pressure by articulating a strategy that delivers both short-term wins and long-term value?

3. **Are you fluent in the language of shareholders, or are you still monolingual?** Being financially multilingual is not a bonus skill; it's a requirement. CEOs are judged by how well they align their company's vision with investor priorities.

4. **How are you prioritizing investor relations to become CEO ready?** If you're not the CFO, are you showing up on earnings calls, investor days, or roadshows to prove you're aligned with the financial story and worthy of carrying it forward?

5. **Have you ruled out the types of ownership structures that are the wrong fit for you?** Just because a company is offering the CEO role doesn't mean it's the right opportunity. Are you clear on whether you're suited for the expectations of public markets, PE pressure, or the volatility of venture-backed growth?

8

Embrace the Scrutiny

Learn to live under the microscope of assessors and consultants who've never had the job

Your selection as CEO can be life or death for a great company. Some 53 percent of the time, the "obvious heir apparent"—the anointed successor in a CEO search—proves to be the wrong choice, according to data from ghSMART, one of the leading firms conducting senior executive assessments.[1] These mistakes cost shareholders billions. *Forbes* notes: "Companies that have to fire their CEO forgo an average of $1.8 billion in shareholder value."[2] Throughout this book, we have emphasized how difficult it is for a board to select any chief executive with so much at stake, particularly a first-time CEO compared with executives who have been CEOs at other companies who may seem more accomplished and less risky. That's why it's crucial to understand why you as either an internal or external CEO candidate—whether a first-timer or serial CEO—will continue to run through a tornado of psychological, behavioral, and business scenario tests.

"It's a huge leap of faith for the decision-makers to choose you as a CEO candidate, because it's an absolute certainty that, if we get it wrong, it will be not only be highly visible public failure, but could be existential for the company," Shahzada Dawood said at a late dinner at a World Economic Forum that Mark hosted. All six CEOs at the table nodded. The table topic that night was "Risk Management for Board

Members," and the group agreed that CEO selection was the biggest risk for any company and every director. As chair of a family-owned international conglomerate, Dawood was frustrated with the CEO candidate recommendations he'd received for their most prominent portfolio company. (He died in the tragic Titan submersible accident before a final choice was made.) During the dinner, he asked rhetorically: "Who are these people—I mean how well do we really know them—and how can we possibly de-risk the process based just on how much we like their interviews and their references?"

Dawood advocated going well beyond interviews and references to use "every assessment tool from which we can ferret out as much forensic evidence about the executive as possible," he said as he pushed his plate away, wringing his hands. "We're not getting this wrong on my watch."

At this point in your career, as a senior executive and now CEO candidate, you have likely been subjected to a blizzard of reviews, simulations, and evaluations. In the competition to become CEO, you should expect that to intensify and prepare for multiple types of assessment tools from recruiting firms and independent assessors that the boards decide to hire; this group represents so much power that they are the sixth stakeholder among the seven you must address in your bid to become CEO.

We'll share with you many of the specific and complex tools that the board and your boss are using to filter your candidacy. The tools screen for myriad skills, behaviors, and derailers that the board and your boss believe they cannot fully detect through personal interviews. They also use the tools as a filter to get a pure view of what they learned while reviewing back channels about your reputation and references. Your board, CEO, and chief human resources officer (CHRO) expect your standard references to be biased.

Only the Paranoid Survive

What keeps boards, CEOs, CHROs, and succession committees awake at night—and fuels the rising rigor of CEO assessments—is the nightmare scenario: even the most seasoned, seemingly perfect candidate can fail to deliver the transformation they were hired to lead. The risk? Betting on a CEO candidate whose *past* achievements—no matter how impressive, whether as an internal executive, an outside leader, or even a sitting CEO—may not translate into future success. The worry is that none of that might guarantee success or readiness for the *future* inflection points your organization is facing.

Intel, once a trailblazer in Silicon Valley, had been losing technological dominance over the course of a decade. During that period, the board identified many CEO candidates and tapped three CEOs in succession with very different personalities and very different professional profiles. Brian Krzanich was a widely respected semiconductor industry veteran operator who the board appointed CEO after his more than thirty-five years at the company. Then Bob Swan, a globally admired CFO who had joined Intel in 2016 as CFO from EDS and eBay, was promoted to Intel's CEO from 2019 to 2021. Then came Pat Gelsinger, a technologist who started at Intel at eighteen, rose to chief technology officer, and, after leading successful runs as president of EMC and CEO of VMware, was brought back as Intel CEO to restore the company's glory.

Gelsinger's tenure included twenty years working many layers below the legendary Intel CEO Andy Grove, whose book *Only the Paranoid Survive* warned against the "inevitable complacency and arrogance bred from too much success." Grove's message came at a time when he led industry-shaking changes that resulted in epic growth at Intel, never allowing leaders to rest on their laurels. "Disrupt yourself or be disrupted by others during moments of strategic inflection," he insisted.[3] Grove's disciplined paranoia fueled Intel's dominance and helped put the "silicon" in Silicon Valley. His legacy shaped generations of tech leaders—launching Mark's coaching career while working with Grove—and his books are required reading for CEO candidates.

But Gelsinger's return in 2021 may have been too late to reignite that playbook. Intel's market cap fell another 50 percent to $92 billion by the end of 2024. The company was removed from the Dow Jones Industrial Average, replaced by its neighbor and rival Nvidia—the first public company to surpass a $3 trillion valuation.

Now contrast that with another tech titan, Microsoft, whose board was also concerned about the company's slowing growth and its strategic senior leadership pipeline, including future CEO succession candidates. Under CEO Steve Ballmer, investors increasingly weighed in about how the company had missed several strategic inflection points, especially in mobile and internet services. As with Intel, stock performance stagnated, and Microsoft's relevance was seen to be fading, as faster, more agile competitors surged ahead. Though technically an insider, Ballmer's bombastic leadership style and focus on an aggressive sales culture also were seen as a departure from the company's original ethos of innovation and engineering excellence.

When looking at many outside and inside CEO candidates to succeed Ballmer, the chairman of the board—founder Bill Gates—was initially hesitant to endorse Satya Nadella as Ballmer's successor. Nadella, a twenty-two-year insider, was respected for his steady temperament and operational depth but considered by some as too understated to command the top job and was almost passed over. Yet it was precisely Nadella's embrace of innovation principles like Grove's—that "only the paranoid survive"—that made the difference. He refocused Microsoft's vision around cloud computing and AI, revitalized the company's culture, and restored its long-term orientation. The result? Microsoft's market capitalization skyrocketed from $300 billion in 2014 to over $3.4 trillion by 2025, making it the most valuable company in the world.

These two stories show why succession decisions are so fraught. Both insiders and outsiders can either succeed—or fail—spectacularly. Boards have seen enough to know that leadership pedigree alone isn't predictive. That's why they are leaning more heavily on assessments, simulations, and deep diagnostics. They're not just looking for someone who fits today. They're searching for a CEO candidate like you who will not only survive but thrive and drive the next strategic inflection point in your industry.

That's why your CEO readiness will be tested using every technique possible to lower the apparent risk of the board's decision. During this process, you will inevitably meet a small army of assessors and recruiters looking to further pinpoint your strengths and weaknesses and predict your prospects for that bigger role in ways that traditional methods of interviewing might not completely reveal.

Korn Ferry research found that leaders who scored higher on an assessment "more than doubled the annualized market capitalization growth over four years, generating 109 percent more than those who scored low. They also achieved a 20 percent higher annual revenue growth, and a 26 percent higher EBITDA margin than their low-scoring counterparts."[4] Beyond financial metrics, Spencer Stuart and Korn Ferry research also found that candidates who scored higher on the overall assessment enjoyed significantly longer tenures. Longer tenures lead to more organizational stability and continuity, attributes that are invaluable for long-term strategic success.

Search firm Egon Zehnder, in collaboration with McKinsey & Company, revealed similar correlations between executive leadership as defined by their assessments and organizational performance. Their study identified key leadership competencies that are reviewed in tests and evaluations, such as strategic vision, collaboration, and resilience, which were strongly tied to improved financial outcomes. Companies led by executives with these competencies experienced revenue growth rates that exceeded industry averages by up to 25 percent.[5]

The New Power of Recruiting Firms over Your Candidacy and Promotability

What this means for you as a candidate is that leading CEO recruiting firms like Korn Ferry, Egon Zehnder, Russell Reynolds, Spencer Stuart, Heidrick & Struggles, and others are a new set of stakeholders to consider as curators of your succession process. Their reports give search firms a new level of strategic impact on your candidacy for CEO and—in a surprising trend—huge sway over your future career opportunities, as those tests elevate your visibility or vulnerability for any other promotion at your company.

Executive search firms have far evolved beyond the headhunters who once just sourced outside candidates for the human resources department; they have moved upstream to assess you in your current role as they conduct CEO readiness evaluations for the CHRO, CEO, and the board. They wield enormous, expanded access and power as a driver with vested interest in knowing you and your company's other internal candidates who might be considered for CEO or other roles in the C-suite.

The CEO readiness assessments developed by leading recruiting firms help keep those retained search firms not only relevant but seated front and center in the boardroom, with game-changing influence over your company's long-term succession planning. This influence holds even when an internal candidate is ultimately selected, which remains true in roughly three out of four cases. Given the political sensitivity and high stakes of replacing a CEO, many boards and CHROs prefer to delegate the second opinion to trusted advisers—often engaging consultants like Byron or Mark to provide an outside perspective. These assessments are designed not just to evaluate candidates but to give the board, CEO, and CHRO a broader view of the leadership pipeline, identifying high-potential executives who could benefit from development and coaching. You as a candidate need to be strategic about whose guidance you seek. The consultants interpreting your assessment may also influence your readiness trajectory or shape how the board perceives your future. Choose carefully. Look for advisers who not only understand the process, but who can offer truly independent insight.

The fact that the recruiting firm has assessed you can elevate or diminish your potential as a future candidate, so think of the firm as a customer and stakeholder in the succession process. Hopefully, it is not a political kingmaker but stays in its lane to help provide insight about your leadership journey, listening for content and demeanor that's helpful for you and your board. Depending on their evaluation of you, these firms can hold sway over your prospects of getting promoted internally. The good news is the firms can enhance your visibility for consideration and recruitment to a better job at another company—or they could worsen your prospects, depending how they assess you.

In contrast to recruiting firms that specialize in executive search, independent assessment firms—focused solely on evaluation and coaching—often argue that search firms face an inherent conflict of interest. Because recruiting firms are retained to fill roles across many organizations, they may be incentivized to promote candidates from their broader talent pipeline rather than objectively vet the best fit for your company's specific CEO role. Independent assessors contend that their exclusive focus on evaluation ensures an impartial, rigorous review of leadership potential. Search firms, for their part, reject this criticism and assert that their assessments remain unbiased because their compensation does not depend on whether an external candidate is ultimately selected. Still, independent assessment firms distinguish themselves by not offering recruitment services at all, reinforcing their position as neutral evaluators in the succession process.

Independent firms like Assess International, Hogan Assessments, Development Dimensions International (DDI), ghSMART, RHR International, MDA Leadership, YSC Consulting (now part of Accenture), and Mercer—known also for advising boards on executive compensation and organizational design—do not offer recruitment services. Instead, they focus on assessing and developing leadership capabilities with what they describe as "greater objectivity." Among the most frequently used are Assess International, which specializes in data-driven evaluations; Hogan Assessments, which provides insights into workplace behavior and leadership effectiveness; DDI, which offers tools to align executive capabilities with organizational goals; and ghSMART, recognized for its forensic-level C-suite assessments.

Recruiting firms such as Korn Ferry, Spencer Stuart, Egon Zehnder, and Heidrick & Struggles have developed their own internal assessment capabilities and leadership institutes. Korn Ferry operates the Korn Ferry Institute, which conducts extensive research on leadership competencies and offers proprietary assessment tools. Spencer Stuart offers services through its Leadership Advisory Services division. Egon Zehnder integrates assessment through its Leadership Advisory practice, anchored in its proprietary Potential Model. Heidrick & Struggles runs Heidrick Consulting and the Heidrick Leadership Assessment framework, which evaluates executives based on agility, performance, and culture fit.

We've listed and described many additional resources, evaluative methods, diagnostic tools, and firm profiles—both from assessment specialists and search firms—in the appendices, along with guidance on how to interpret their role in your candidacy. These approaches to the evaluation processes could give you added opportunity for reflection and insight for your boss, along with exposure to recruiting firms that might help give your candidacy for the CEO's role a bit more visibility within and outside your company.

Make Your Assessment a Strategy Off-Site for Yourself

For any busy executive, the assessment tools and processes can seem tedious and time-consuming, stealing you away from your job. To overcome this feeling, we advise candidates to think of the various tests and interviews as an individualized professional strategy offsite for yourself. You're prepping a go-to-market plan for your career moves. Shift your mindset from necessary imposition to CEO-ready opportunity. Glean insights from the assessments and scour the process for helpful feedback. Consider it another refresher course in management and leadership 101, as the tests attempt to review the primary drivers of success.

For example, Geoff Smart founded ghSMART to conduct in-depth assessments of CEO candidates. Smart eschews many of the off-the-shelf psychological and behavioral tests that you may have taken already, because most are not validated—in a scientific sense—so they cannot predict CEO success. In Smart's view, self-reporting in such assessments can cause results to shift considerably depending on an individual's mood and career status at the time the assessment is made.[6] He prefers instead to have experts on his team perform unique, forensic, in-depth interviews, which can lead to what he considers extraordinary discoveries.

Jim Citrin, who leads the CEO practice at Spencer Stuart, has extensively studied the relationship between CEO tenure, leadership practices, and financial performance. In his book *The CEO Life Cycle* and in his boardroom counsel, Citrin consistently reminds CEO candidates that boards, shareholders, and employees often rely too heavily on anecdotal impressions formed under pressure, especially in high-visibility moments when communication skills and executive presence dominate. These traits may earn you a seat at the table, but they're just table stakes, not differentiators.

There are two key lessons here. First, you must relentlessly grow as a communicator—under pressure, across settings, and with every stakeholder group. Moving from good to great in this area is not optional. Second, Citrin warns boards about what he calls the "trap of the great interviewer." While charisma and composure are necessary, they can mask gaps in critical areas. That's why boards are increasingly urged to go deeper, evaluating not just communication but a candidate's analytical skills, problem-framing capabilities, cultural alignment, and their capacity to inspire followership and trust across stakeholder groups.

The rise of rigorous CEO assessments is, in part, a response to this trap. These tools aim to depersonalize the process, not to strip away personality but to surface deeper insight beyond what an exceptional interview might reveal.

Get Ready for the Assessments

Just as legendary shareholders like Michelle Seitz recommend that you as a candidate draft a letter from an activist investor, Citrin urges boards to consider "that among the best assessments is to ask candidates to write a five-page vision memo about being the next CEO, outlining strategy, operating opportunities, and financial performance. Then the board can look at each candidate as a representation of alternative futures." As a candidate, challenge yourself with that five-page goal. Curate and test it on others as you continue to draft and redraft that vision memo so that when you're asked, you're ready.

Your memo should be a living document that evolves every time you meet board members and interact with colleagues. Review it with your boss. Rehearse and revise it with your executive coach. Think of it as a discipline to get more insight each time you meet with them to build your visionary story. That's not remotely how most candidates think during their busy day, but the candidates who become CEOs find it very useful.

As a CEO candidate, don't be lulled into comfort that you're the candidate that everyone is thinking about and hoping for, even though they've given you that impression. Remember that they have a vested interest in making you continue to feel motivated in your current job, but they're likely finding other authentic things to flatter your competitors so they stay in their jobs happily, too. Force time on your schedule to prepare for the assessment process, and if you're an inside CEO candidate looking for the promotion, think about it as you would an outside job interview, because that is what this is for your outside competitors. And it's likely to be useful to you the next time you get an outside interview.

You, the CEO-ready candidate, should prepare for the assessor to ask you about *all* of your prior jobs, bosses, strengths, weaknesses, accomplishments, who you've worked with and how you got along, why you left each role, and so on. They'll ask about mistakes you've made—and don't pretend that they didn't happen. And, yes, sometimes they go all the way back to your teens. As a CEO coach, Mark often also checks in with a family member during the 360-degree feedback process, not to measure your competencies but to glean surprisingly useful insights about how you show up at the office that inform your leadership effectiveness.

"There was a lot of rigor to the reference checks and assessment tests," Steve Hasker of Thomson Reuters recalls. "Jason [Daumeyer, a partner at ghSMART] sat me down for a half day and went through my experiences, all the way back to my childhood. He'd ask, 'Why did you do this, and why did you do that?' After sitting in the seat for five hours, I finally said to him, 'I can't talk about myself anymore. I'm going to have to start making stuff up soon.'"

It may sound cliché, but "the school of hard knocks makes for better chief executives," says Hasker. Thus, he adds, when you are asked about your failures, be ready to be vulnerable and to share how you took action. "People need to be prepared to have the confidence to say, 'Let me tell you about something I really screwed up, and how long it took me to recover.' That's impressive. Most candidates when asked about weaknesses or missteps will say, 'I worked too hard, or I tend to be too intense.'" That, of course, will be dismissed by the assessors as a humblebrag.

Hasker continued: "I'm talking about being honest about something where you had a target and an objective, and you just didn't get it. Those are the kinds of experiences from which you learn. The first time you publicly screw something up is a very difficult thing. I wouldn't want to endure that as a chief executive. Assessors want to see how you reacted to a failure. How did you fix it and what did you learn?"

As a CEO candidate, consider the experience of Michelle Riley-Brown, who won the top job as president and CEO of Children's National Hospital after such an assessment process. "The process was a journey marked by transparency, rigorous evaluation, and a profound understanding of organizational fit," she said. "I think the board's understanding and clarity in terms of qualifications, leadership style, and who they were looking for in the next CEO role really helped make the process run a lot smoother."

Riley-Brown told us about her interview that lasted most of a day: "It starts from the moment you're born, through your schooling, what you were involved in at school that helped shape you to be the person you are. It covers your education, your community involvement, your upbringing with your family, to the leadership roles that you've held over the years. They want to know how you make decisions, your challenges, your strengths, and weaknesses. They're assessing you, understanding who you are as a person."

Identify Your Most Compelling References

Think for a moment about how *referenceable* you truly are—would other professionals actively and credibly vouch for your leadership, your integrity, and your impact? Sure, you have plenty of friends and colleagues, but as a CEO candidate, you likely have not been job hunting; you've been busy doing your job, delivering on your promises. Given your demanding day job, it is likely that you have not thought enough as an internal candidate about developing a deep and diverse group of people ready to speak up on your behalf inside and outside your organization, as you would if you were job hunting outside the company. This should not be a marginal matter of scratching your head to come up with a few pals and former bosses.

Assessment analysts routinely find that "the simple act of telling someone that we're going to do reference checks on them and then asking for their insights into what their bosses will say gets us amazing data that is specific," Geoff Smart says. "We'll also find out why they left each job. We listen for themes. Our statistics indicate that if people are getting pushed out of more than about 20 percent of their jobs, the chance that they're going to delight you suddenly in this next job goes down by a lot. We aren't looking for someone who's perfect. Sometimes you work for bad bosses. Your mistakes are interesting; they are not deal killers. What we want to know is that people generally think you're a pretty awesome leader for reasons that are relevant to the job for which you're applying."

Smart told us about a financial services firm that asked him to interview a finalist for a senior executive role with a $10 million base salary. As with most jobs like this, his upside salary based on performance was multiples of that, and the client thought he was more than worth it for the value he created. Smart said, "It was more of a formality, they said, as the guy was extraordinary in their view. But we found that he had been convicted of selling drugs in his college years, and then discovered that he had left his last job for a 'difference of opinion.' As we dug further, he said it was technical. Finally, it came out that he had falsified financial information to inflate his annual bonus. The SEC got involved and the guy was fired. Somehow the search firm missed it, and the psych test didn't ask the question, 'Were you fired for SEC securities fraud in your last job?'"

That's exactly what boards are hoping—or, rather, are hoping not to ferret out of these assessments and references of every CEO candidate like you. Assuming your conscience and background are clear, we recommend you take your preparation to the next level to think through how to approach your assessments. Thoughtfully go over your personal and professional background; recall the names of bosses and coworkers and how they are spelled. Think about the highlights, lowlights, and learnings from each role and leader. Especially, think through some honest answers to questions about interpersonal challenges you've faced along the way. While fraud is obviously a nonstarter, interviewers and assessors love hearing about hard-won learning experiences and an honest assessment of your weaknesses and growth.

Don't Expect Unity

Your board has been diligently working to build—and continues to revise and revisit—a very specific set of criteria to help choose the next CEO. Factoring the CEO candidacy into the changing market conditions is a moving target for every company in this volatile environment. "It is basically translating the business into a set of outcomes and competencies that the new CEO must be able to execute on. But as a candidate, no one's going to show that to you. You don't get to see that because we don't want you gaming your answers," Smart says. And in fact, your assessors have been privy to all the relevant boardroom conversations. As coaches, we make it our business to meet as many of the board members individually as possible to learn about their divergent professional interests in the company's strategy and future leadership, just as you should.

"We were brought into a global fashion brand," Smart says. "One board member told me, 'We already know what we're looking for. Let's skip that part of our conversation.' I said, 'That's great news. What are you looking for?' She was looking to go upmarket. The next board member looked on with befuddlement and said, 'I thought we were going to go more mass market, more down-market.' And someone else said, 'Hold on, weren't we going to lean into technology?'" Considering the varying levels of the board's alignment and the shifting market needs—and in light of the assessment that they'll review about you as a CEO candidate—you will have to demonstrate enormous patience as you map thoughtful CEO ready strategy.

Be Patient with Your Assessors

While your board includes experienced CEOs, the same cannot be said for most of the recruiters, assessors, psychologists, or analysts evaluating you. Few—if any—of them have ever held the job you're seeking, let alone in a company comparable to yours. Yet they are tasked with reviewing your operating plans, judging the soundness of your business scenarios, and assessing your leadership potential. They haven't done what you're doing. What they have done is conduct hundreds of interviews, studied best practices, and applied frameworks grounded in social science. Their methodologies are built on data, but also shaped by academics and professors in a well-intentioned way. As with any human judgment, an ultimately subjective echo chamber of predictive assumptions can ensue. For seasoned CEO candidates, the experience can feel frustratingly fictional, like being coached for hours on how to hit a major league fastball by someone who's never stood at the plate. Fortunately, the assessment tools can offer great insight—but they can't predict your success as a CEO.

Resistance is futile, of course, as you have no choice but to participate in this process. So we advise you to lean into what may feel like fantasy based on your vast résumé. Imagine the training of your assessors. Remember they have good intentions. Don't condescend, fret, fuss, or complain. You're not wrong to feel those things, but like every other circumstance in which you have succeeded despite the seemingly opaque parts of the process, you will find that patience and good humor (not sarcasm) will serve you best.

This will be important to getting the job and good practice for when you have it. After all, it won't be the only time you must think and speak with an open heart with very influential and important people who have never done your job. As a CEO, every time you talk to the press, or Wall Street analysts, or government leaders, or even most employees and customers, you must have great appreciation for folks who do not have a technical foundation in your role and who have rarely ever run a business or large organization. They never have the whole picture. But they will be certain they have great ideas and often outsized confidence they can make valid recommendations about how you should run your business. They can't, of course, but your job is to listen for useful insights, applaud their willingness to engage and contribute, and respect their intentions.

You don't have to take the advice, but you do have to hear it and thank them for it. Treat it like a generous gift, and you may even regift it to others. Likewise with your assessors and the coaches who may be assigned to you. Think of them the way Olympian athletes think of their coaches: Learn from them and thank them, whatever the result. Let them know how much you have discovered from their efforts. Again, this is great practice as a senior leader and future CEO: always know the people you touch have *their story*—and their expertise—and you have yours. It is an honor and privilege of your candidacy to engage with them as a candidate and as the CEO.

Be Aware That Some Assessors May Lead the Witness

We've seen assessors unintentionally bias their advice based on insights into the candidate preferences that the CEO, the CHRO, or board members explicitly stated. They may have their early favorites, and both assessors and analysts can unintentionally bias the inquiry and their reports with those inferences, highlighting strengths for some candidates and weaknesses for others. We know this happens because, as CEO coaches, we've been directly involved in the process—reading the reports and participating in dozens of candidate interviews conducted by analysts over the past thirty years.

In some cases, the arduous process of assessment could be used purposely or unintentionally to increase or reduce your chances for the CEO role. As a candidate, you don't have power over that, but awareness of this possibility can help with unexpected results either way. Don't be heartbroken if the assessments don't swing your way or feel ebullient with overconfidence if they do. Do not confuse rigor in the tests with the results. Great assessors know that this evaluation is not a search for the *truth*, but rather useful perceptions that matter.

Today's assessment processes are far better than many ad hoc methods we've seen over thirty years. Smart of ghSMART is right to say that assessments elevate the succession process above what was historically susceptible to a superficial sniff test. Smart said, "I had one board member tell me that he likes to take CEO succession candidates out for a drive. He drives fast and aggressively, and he's seeing if they politely say something. That's a good answer."

Yikes! Smart continued: "Another board member of a large company asks candidates what kind of animal they would be; another chooses by the sports teams they like. There are a lot of bad methods out there that are unfair, biased, data-light, gut-feel type of methods that [as a candidate] you might have to just accept." Whether the results are relevant to the job you're seeking or whether the process is entirely impartial is not in your control, but how you show up is worth considering in advance of each interaction.

Accept That You Might Be the Third Horse

During the assessment stage, sometimes coaches will hear a board member describe a CEO candidate as "rounding out the three-horse list." We mentioned this in an earlier chapter in reference to Enrique Lores, the highly regarded CEO of Hewlett-Packard. Mark shared that comment with Lores the day after he heard it. The CEO smiled and nodded, unfazed, a response that represents one of the many reasons he was the perfect candidate and won the role, according to the board. Here's how he dealt with being "the guy who rounded out the list": He described himself to them as already having been a very fortunate and a very successful executive committed to a great company he loved in every post around the world. He described his highlights and lowlights with authenticity. He shared how his self-worth and net worth were wrapped up in the success of HP, not in his job title. Of course, he said he'd be honored to be selected, and then he presented a powerful vision and plan for the future. He could have pouted or gotten angry at being labeled the third horse. Instead, he continued to lead authentically and did not let such an assessment affect how he went about the process. That won over all seven stakeholders we've described in this book.

That's not to say he didn't prepare for this process. He certainly did. As a CEO candidate, you may encounter people who say you can't really prepare for the assessments. "Try not to overthink or stress about it," you might hear, or "Just be yourself." We disagree. Throughout this chapter, we insist that you prepare as if you're going on a job interview, because you are. The rigor and time you set aside to prepare should be similar to what you'd invest to take the GMAT, LSAT, MCAT, and GRE. It may take a few tries, and you will get better with practice.[7]

Master the CEO Assessment Process

Our CEO candidates have experienced twenty-three different types of assessments. For those of you wishing to prepare in greater depth, beyond what you've read in this chapter, we've crafted a three-dimensional review of them in the appendices. First, you'll find a summary of each with a description of how they came to be used in leadership assessments, so that you might gain greater context. Second, we break down those tests into nine categories of assessment—like personality tests versus competency tests—again with some hacks to address them. And third, we review what the search firms and notable independent assessment firms have created to take you through their succession process so you can understand the nuanced and philosophical differences among them.

Those resources will be invaluable as you go through the process, but they are quite extensive; in the sidebar "Seven Fundamentals to Mastering the Assessment Phase" we offer you a condensed list of seven fundamentals to master your preparation for the assessment phase of your CEO candidacy.

"CEO succession remains one of the mysteries of the business world," Smart contends. Short tenures and tragedies plague the headlines. Botched successions weaken corporate cultures, are a huge pain for boards, and hurt real people—employees, customers, and suppliers. Smart continues, "Yet this problem is self-inflicted. The low rate of success in CEO succession is not due to bad luck. It's not because it's impossible to accurately assess what's likely to be repeated human behavior. It's due to a failure to follow every method that works."

As the sixth stakeholder among our seven crucial customers that you must engage as a CEO candidate, the independent assessors and major recruiting search firms who evaluate you might be unexpected decision-makers. They provide an increasingly important milestone you must pass for the board, CHRO, and CEO as a candidate. The increasing impact of these stakeholders in many ways mirrors the rise in analytics driving the assessment of pro athletes. The insights and advice in this chapter increase your chances of being selected, because you will become better prepared for the ever more rigorous CEO succession ritual.

Seven Fundamentals to Mastering the Assessment Phase

1. Shift Your Mindset Regarding Psychoanalysis and Fictional Scenarios

Candidates who are exposed to the search firms might be shocked at just how much power recruiters now have in running succession programs. Some CEO candidates rail against it or think it's unfair. We implore you to keep an open mind about it and have faith that assessment, no matter how maddening a process, is helpful in building your capacity to strategize for your CEO candidacy.

Also, harvest the insights gained from any of the assessments, no matter the outcome of your candidacy. They are not just evaluating your prospects as a CEO but looking at any future role you might seek at the company.

There's an easier path—to grin and bear the process or marginalize it in your mind and in your actions. We don't recommend this. Assessment is almost always a real eye-opener about how others perceive you and how you perceive yourself. It's a process that can deepen self-awareness.

2. Create a Clear Story about Your Journey

For the sake of your candidacy and as preparation for the assessments, reflect on your own career; imagine describing yourself to an outsider. Think about each role you have held and how it offered lessons and, in particular, tough setbacks that contributed to your growth. This is a surprisingly difficult and time-consuming project that you need to take seriously because your interviewers and assessors have nothing else to base their judgments on besides this process and the story you tell. The board will use many criteria, but your assessors don't have that perspective. Identify patterns of success, challenges overcome, and key moments of professional and personal transformation. While doing so, demonstrate authenticity and humility, balancing confidence in your abilities with openness to learning and growth. As an internal candidate, this reflection should directly align with showcasing how your journey prepares you specifically for the CEO role within your organization in ways that an outsider would find difficult.

3. Build Internal References across Every Division and Function

Internal references can be more important than external ones. While your peers don't select you, they can kill your prospects quickly and decisively. The assessors assume that your peers in the C-suite have agendas to boost or reduce your candidacy, depending on whether they're willing to work with you as their boss. Build strong bonds throughout your company to gain insights into organizational culture and politics, strategic priorities, and governance dynamics.

4. Create and Articulate a Bigger Strategic Vision

Develop a transformative vision for the organization that addresses critical pain points and aligns with long-term goals. Revise it and research it, then revise it again. Be prepared to present this as a comprehensive five-page strategy, whether you are an internal candidate or an external prospect. Account for the expectations of the board and leadership team that you're learning about so your vision bridges their current view to your future one. Ensure this vision is more than empty ideals. It should also demonstrate your ability to execute and adapt to evolving priorities.

5. Hone Decision-Making under Pressure

Put yourself in a position to demonstrate your decision-making skills under pressure. You've made many tough calls in your career; you have already had enormous responsibilities and accomplishments. Now take it to the next level by looking at what your predecessors have done and putting yourself into similar situations. Read case histories of other new CEOs and engage in real-time simulations to refine your approach and build confidence in high-stakes environments.

(continued)

6. Seek Bold, Standout Experiences

A search firm will present any outside candidate as the hero whose story has been unintentionally embellished to sweep the directors off their feet. This is a hard narrative to compete with. The assessment process is an attempt to even the playing field and help make a more objective comparison between you, someone they know well, warts and all, and this mythical knight from outside. Boards still prefer the insider 77 percent of the time, according to a 2024 study of S&P 500 CEO successions.[a] But for you to stand out, you still must seek diverse experiences that give you a bit of a knight-in-shining-armor image. Pursue cross-functional projects, global assignments, or high-stakes initiatives that broaden your perspective and demonstrate your readiness to lead at the highest levels. These key factors make the outsider appealing.

7. Expand External Networks

Leverage targeted development resources such as executive coaching and feedback loops to strengthen key leadership capabilities. Beyond internal preparation, take a more intentional approach to building an external network of peers, experienced CEOs, and coaches. Participate in professional associations, attend conferences, and engage with leaders outside your industry to gain broader perspectives and insights that will enhance your strategic thinking and leadership readiness.

a. Matteo Tonello et al., "CEO Succession Practices in the Russell 3000 and S&P 500," Harvard Law School Forum on Corporate Governance, November 19, 2024, https://corpgov.law.harvard.edu/2024/11/19/ceo-succession-practices-in-the-russell-3000-and-sp-500-3/.

Your CEO Readiness Pulse Check

Five questions to navigate the assessment gauntlet

1. **Have you crafted a strategic vision memo—one that could win over your board and clarify your unique leadership edge?** This document serves as a test of your thinking and differentiates you from competitors who rely solely on formal or standardized tests.

2. **Do you know how the independent assessors and the recruiting firms evaluating you could shape—or shadow—your entire succession path?** Top consulting firms run readiness reviews long before formal searches begin. Their reports influence not only your current candidacy but your future promotability within and beyond your company.

3. **Can you lead—without flinching—when you're being judged by people who've never done your job?** Most assessors and recruiters who evaluate CEO candidates have never led a company, built a team from scratch, or delivered results at your level. Yet they'll dissect your strategy, critique your decisions, and measure your readiness using academic frameworks built on data and theory, not experience. Can you resist the urge to push back and instead model composure and gratitude, even under pressure and when the process feels surreal?

4. **Can you narrate your leadership journey—including missteps—with clarity, humility, and strategic insight?** Assessment interviews will go deep, sometimes to childhood and personal values. Are you ready to frame mistakes as growth moments and connect your past roles to the company's future needs?

5. **Are you prepared to be the "third horse" and win anyway?** Boards often bring in candidates to round out the list, even skipping levels of seniority, not realizing they may end up hiring them. Your ability to stay grounded, positive, and persuasive despite being underestimated could be your greatest advantage.

9

Honor Culture, Comfort Customers, and Manage Celebrity

Employees and customers must believe you're ready

Sarah Hirshland was asked to consider becoming CEO of the United States Olympic & Paralympic Committee (USOPC), an organization she described as "a burning house" in 2018. Mark coached her minutes before her congressional testimony on behalf of the Olympic team, as it reeled from its worst scandal in its history. The most harrowing systemic ethical failure in modern sports history occurred when physician Larry Nassar, unchecked by the team for years, abused three hundred athletes. High-profile athletes including Rachael Denhollander, McKayla Maroney, Aly Raisman, and later, gymnastics legend Simone Biles courageously stepped forward to admit they were among Nassar's victims.

These are hardly the circumstances most candidates imagine for their first chief executive role. Yet in today's relentlessly disruptive environment, nearly every company is facing existential threats to its relevance, customer trust, and long-term growth. That's why you, as an internal or external CEO candidate, are being sought not just for experience, but for your readiness, willingness, and courage to lead and even accelerate growth through uncertainty.

The only way to do that is to be anchored in your values and passionately driven to demonstrate a deep, visible commitment to all seven stakeholders we've outlined in this book, especially in ways that reconnect the organization's identity with a future worth believing in. The seventh stakeholder—and perhaps most defining—is your customers, and the employees willing to engage them, through triumph and turbulence alike.

In the case of the Olympic team, the crisis was so severe that several seasoned candidates turned the job down, wary of inheriting a deeply damaged institution. But that's the question every CEO candidate must confront: Are you ready—and is it worth it? Sarah Hirshland was.

But for her, the real challenge wasn't just stepping into the role; it was stitching back together the torn cultural and organizational fabric of a team, a brand, and an iconic institution under attack. For Hirshland, this was *personal*. As an athlete, she had grown up admiring the Olympic team as emblematic of integrity and excellence. As news broke about the horrifying abuse, the USOPC board responded to the shock by seeking credible advisers to represent it. It appointed Susanne Lyons as interim chairman and CEO. Lyons is a veteran financial services executive known for helping lead the investment industry through the financial crisis of 2008; Mark worked with her at Charles Schwab. She recruited Hirshland, whose remit was to steady the organization, repair the damage, and assure the world it would not happen again. Hirshland saw this as a mission compelling enough to risk her own career. She was willing to take the role because she believed the organization could—and must—be saved.

Ask yourself a simple question, for your sake and for the sake of your company, that will define this moment in your career: Is this the challenge that justifies the sacrifices you've made to get here? Lacking the same level of drama in your CEO candidacy that Hirshland's had, what makes becoming a CEO candidate personal for you? How much do you care about the people who support, serve, and are inspired by your organization? Is this truly worth it?

The Olympic team meant so much to the country and had elevated the hopes and dreams of young athletes in the past, and it could again.

As her coach, Mark asked Hirshland whether this was a battle worth fighting. "There is so much good in what sport brings to society," she said. Her passion was unequivocal.

Is Your CEO Candidacy Worth the Risk?

For any leader, the CEO's job can be overwhelming intellectually and emotionally. "It's really difficult to manage a team of people who are dealing with those very real emotions at the same time you are," she told Mark. "But the benefit of running an organization like that is that you don't need to secure permission to change; [in this case] I had the mandate to make changes. I just had to figure out which ones, and then how much to put my foot on the gas or the brake to determine both the organization's and community's readiness to change and navigate through all of that."

Congressional hearings soon followed, with scathing reports highlighting "how systemic failures allowed Nassar's abuse to persist."[1] The US Senate investigation concluded that a "culture prioritizing medals over the welfare of athletes created an environment ripe for exploitation. The USOC and USA Gymnastics fundamentally failed to uphold their responsibility to protect athletes."

Imagine yourself as a CEO candidate inheriting this debacle. Are you sure you want to be the CEO to do this? Are you sure that you have not been recruited to be a first-time CEO as the expendable executive facing a difficult or impossible turnaround? "Will I be the sacrificial lamb?" one CEO candidate asked us metaphorically as he watched his company file for bankruptcy and then was invited to become CEO while a competitor was acquiring it. On the other hand, the greater risk represents the greater reward as you reinvent a great legacy to make history—hopefully in a good way.

Hirshland was courageously willing to be a candidate in the midst of the perfect storm. To be able to perform extraordinarily well as a CEO candidate under pressure, you must wear seven hats, building your credibility in the seven roles you may need to play with each stakeholder.

1. Chief engagement officer

Hirshland clarified how the team could reignite what had been a great culture through long-term transformational change, not just manage the fallout. This is somewhat different from the cheerleading role that former Best Buy CEO Hubert Joly called *chief energizing officer*. That's a critical and continuous effort that every CEO must make to feed light and energy into the room. As *chief engagement officer*, Hirshland was additionally providing the context needed for all employees and athletes to understand how to play the long game, not just put out a fire. As you craft your strategic narrative—or your activist investor letter—as a CEO candidate, remember that you are articulating the foundational story of how every employee can *engage* in the organizational change you intend to lead. That's what Hirshland did. In her interview to become CEO and from the day she started as chief executive, and every single day after, she emphasized specific, enduring ways everyone could invest in, reinforce, and therefore reclaim the organization's pride and value in the culture. While acknowledging that she would be steadfast in aggressively removing vestiges of the cancer that had lurked inside the organization, Hirshland reminded people that she was equally committed to creating policies, procedures, and transparency to ensure safety and growth long term. As CEO, she would not be there just to perform a quick operation, but to reclaim the organization's legacy that deserved to flourish.

2. Chief customer officer

Hirshland comforted customers in the crisis without overpromising. If, as a CEO candidate, you already have a track record and deep relationships with your company's customers, you know how important this is. If you're a CFO now, you'll have to demonstrate that you can embrace the company's customers with the same elegance that you brilliantly engage Wall Street. The board wanted to know if Hirshland would be OK with immediately reaching out to resuscitate all of the Olympic team's historically close customer relationships and sponsors, even when the scandal was radioactive and everyone awaited congressional actions. Procedures and policies would need to change, but it wasn't entirely obvious what systems would have to be rethought to create greater safety for athletes. The situation was still embarrassingly unclear and threatening. Nevertheless, her mission was to reassure US athletes, sponsors, sports fans, and America that the USOPC would present plans that showed a clear path to healing the damage.

As a candidate expected to drive wave after wave of uncomfortable change, Hirshland said, "Be comfortable with the fact that you're not going to have it all figured out, and nobody expects you to, but you do have a compelling belief and point of view about what target you're going after. Part of this is the journey of figuring things out, finding people you can trust, trusting your judgment, and trusting yourself. Those are hard things to do in an environment where the pressure seems intense."

3. Chief gratitude officer

Hirshland showered gratitude on all stakeholders and showed confidence to lead change despite the fog. The key principle for a CEO candidate is that you must have a vision for reform without complete visibility into what may happen. You need to be prepared for many scenarios that won't match the ideal one. You need to demonstrate that you're willing to take a leap of faith under difficult circumstances to recruit hearts and minds to the mission. "I wasn't accepting a job; I was embracing a mission to create generational change," Hirshland said. She was taking the biggest bet of her life for the sake of the Olympics.

She expressed how honored she felt to lead the campaign, embracing the weight of responsibility with humility. "Pressure is privilege," as Hubert Joly puts it, "because your role as CEO has given you the opportunity to make a real difference when it's needed most." You've worked your whole life for the biggest job of your life as CEO, so it's a privilege to be in a position to actually make a difference no matter how difficult. Hirshland's tone wasn't just appreciative; it reflected a deep sense of purpose and pride in being entrusted with the challenge.

When the board interviewed Hirshland about her past accomplishments, she was a gratitude machine. She gave credit to those around her. She never stopped learning. She set the expectation for the board that all her prior roles involved gathering input and evidence, spending "time listening to our coaches talk to their teams," she said, "and listening to groups of our high-performance athletes talk about the nuances of what they were going to tweak. Not because I'm a sports expert or had any value to add to the conversation, but I always got a nugget that made me think about how I was going to run our team."

4. Chief architect

Hirshland ascended from CEO candidate to chief firefighter, then to chief foreperson of the renovation. As a CEO candidate, you're preparing for the most demanding and high-stakes role of your career—one that comes with massive risks and visibility. The lesson here is about the extraordinary potential to lead a meaningful transformation. Hirshland proved how powerful this approach can be, even in dire, high-pressure, and deeply scrutinized circumstances. If she could drive that level of success under fire, imagine what *you* may discover about the impact you can have as chief executive.

Hirshland started the journey in the darkest days leading up to the 2020 Tokyo Olympics, when the US team delivered its worst performance amid scandal and controversy. At the 2024 summer games in Paris, the USOPC and Olympic team demonstrated a spectacular return of ethical and athletic credibility. The well-deserved congressional reprimand accusing the USPOC of swapping ethics for medals before the Tokyo games was appropriate at the time. Four years later, the criticism melted as Hirshland galvanized the confidence and commitment of these athletes to achieve their most historic performance: 132 total medals, including 47 gold, unprecedented in modern history. This surge not only reclaimed global athletic status for the team but also underscored the empowering moral lift of this organization's mission as envisioned when Hirshland was interviewing as a CEO candidate.

Hirshland adds that mentoring from a peer and a coach "was lifesaving for me at a time when I was in the trenches of a difficult environment. There is nothing more powerful than hearing someone who understands where you are and says, 'I get it. I've been there.'

Honor Culture, Comfort Customers, and Manage Celebrity

Sometimes it's just 'Atta girl, keep going. It may feel like the sky is falling today, but it's not. You're doing a good job.' A little bit of encouragement can go a long way."

From Sarah Hirshland's example, we can learn a great deal about how to prepare for the seventh and final stakeholder group: employees, customers, and the broader organizational culture. What Hirshland got right in her candidacy—and later in her tenure—was her ability to confront a culture that had skewed toxic, shine a spotlight on what needed repair, and offer a path forward that promoted healing and clarity. Much like Satya Nadella at Microsoft, she provided not just comfort to employees and customers concerned about past inconsistencies in leadership, but a compelling blueprint for a brighter future. It's a reminder that effective CEO candidates don't just step into a role—they step into a narrative, one that must be reshaped with empathy, vision, and credibility. Unfortunately, the employees of every organization wonder why leaders let toxicity simmer and take too long to protect and promote the best parts of the culture—to coach and to fire executives who do not follow the stated culture, regardless of their business performance.

As the incoming CEO, that responsibility now rests with you. All seven stakeholder groups are watching to see whether you have the courage to lead with conviction—or whether you'll look the other way. They're watching to see if you can resist the intoxicating flattery that often accompanies the selection process, when people suddenly tell you you're funnier, smarter, or more charismatic than ever before. Don't drink the Kool-Aid. Stay grounded. Real leadership requires clarity, humility, and the strength to challenge the narrative being served to you.

5. *Chief culture curator*

Hirshland made it a priority to celebrate the most venerable parts of the Olympic culture—a move every CEO candidate must emulate in interactions with their team, peers, and board. Let's define culture as the collective behaviors, values, and beliefs that shape how people operate within an organization. A strong culture connects people to a shared sense of meaning and purpose, but sometimes it doesn't. Your job is to help your team discern what should be cherished as sacred and what must evolve. The more clearly you guide that process, the more agile and effective your organization becomes. A well-aligned, energized culture is a force multiplier. As Nadella did for Microsoft and Hirshland for the Olympic team, the best culture leaders understand how to honor what's working while boldly improving what's not, earning the trust of both employees and customers in the process.

Hirshland won hearts by reminding the team, peers, and the board about the special role and unique position the organization held in the world—not in a Pollyanna way, but with substantive evidence. She said, "We are a nonprofit, the only Olympic committee in the world that does not receive government funding. We generate our own resources. And this is fact—not me bragging—that we have been the best team in the world on the Olympic stage, especially in the summer games, for a very long time. We are the winningest team in history. It's fun to be part of that." By setting her sights on reclaiming the culture—in addition to just managing the crisis—she established herself in the board's eyes as the best candidate to become CEO.

In times of deep organizational crisis—like the one Hirshland stepped into—culture may become your most important strategic compass for employees and customers. It's not enough to inherit or admire a culture; you must live it visibly and consistently, especially under pressure. As a CEO candidate, you must be able to articulate exactly what elements of the culture you will preserve and which ones you intend to elevate. Your team, board, and customers are looking at this transition under a microscope, not just to hear your values but to see if you embody them. When your actions align with the culture you espouse—especially in moments of uncertainty—others will follow, often before you even hold the title.

6. *Chief transformation officer*

Only 22 percent of CEO-led transformations succeed, according to *Harvard Business Review* research, a very sobering one in five.[2] So, if you know and understand that every board *craves* a transformation, but most fail, it's a call to action for you as a CEO candidate. The most common missteps? Failing to think bigger, start smaller, and move faster, according to Sandy Ogg of CEO.works. Hirshland flipped that script by not creating a vision that had to be "spread like peanut butter" slowly oozing into every corner with great effort, but starting smaller instead. She advocated a razor-sharp approach that started not with a shotgun but a rifle, not a blinding floodlight but a pinpoint set of crucial tasks that were laser focused, moving with urgency and prioritizing only areas that moved the needle, producing outcomes with precision.

Hirshland was surgical, enforcing clear, actionable, consistent systems that made the Olympic team safe again for athletes. She didn't change everything; she did a few things brilliantly well at the speed of light. She narrowed the goals to the shortest list of powerful changes to guarantee success. It's common in times of stress or uncertainty, and particularly during a crisis, to start by launching a thousand ships that confuse the culture. Instead, Hirshland defined the most limited, tight set of achievable objectives that could measurably deliver a clear win. Legendary author Jim Collins calls it "bullets before cannonballs." For you as a CEO candidate, that kind of disciplined thinking shows boards you're not just a visionary, but a leader with situational fluency who can actually get things done. You recognize that transformation isn't about launching dozens of initiatives; it's about identifying the *fewest* high-impact moves, sequencing them intelligently, and holding people accountable to the outcomes.

At CEO.works, Ogg highlights three essential tools that can help you do exactly that: the *value creation agenda*, the *operating model architecture*, and the *talent capital balance sheet*. As a candidate, you will benefit from becoming fluent in each tool. The value agenda helps you define *what* needs to be done and *where* the value lies—pinpointing six to eight hot spots and sequencing them into a practical road map of "now, next, and later." You're not trying to boil the ocean. You're showing the board you know how to prioritize and move fast on what matters first.

Just as important is showing *how* that value will be delivered. The operating model architecture clarifies how the business must evolve, starting with today's operating reality and mapping toward the capabilities needed to win tomorrow. As a candidate, your ability to diagnose that gap and propose actionable shifts will be scrutinized when you make your pitch to the board. It doesn't expect you to have all the answers, but it does expect you to know where and how to look for them—and how to lead the organization through the pivot.

Finally, the question that haunts every transition when a new CEO is appointed, as you consider your first one hundred days: Do you have the right people in the right roles to deliver value in time? This is where Ogg's concept of the talent capital balance sheet is helpful, but it might be scary for the culture and your peers. As a candidate, you'll need to assess whether your leadership team—and the individuals in mission-critical roles—are up to the challenge. This means going beyond résumés and org charts. It means identifying capability gaps and offering a clear plan to close them. In a room full of CEO hopefuls, the candidate who can talk specifically about fit, speed, and execution is the one who earns the board's trust.

You would do well to emulate Mike Clem as a strategic and culture champion leading his company's transformation. Clem invited Mark to partner with him when he was named a candidate a year before his eventual appointment as chief executive for Sweetwater Sound, a $1.7 billion music instrument retailer and one of the fastest-growing companies in an otherwise stagnant industry. As a long-term Sweetwater executive, Clem had an advantage over outside candidates because he knew that its culture has differentiated the company from its competitors in a tough business. Clem says, "The first principles of this company, indeed, the entire business model is based on one-to-one relationships and taking the long view with a customer, saying we're not in it for any one transaction but for a lifelong journey through music with lifelong purchases."

Here are a few key principles from Sweetwater and others for you to consider as a CEO candidate when you present your case for to the board in the interview.

DEMONSTRATE A STRATEGIC UNDERSTANDING OF YOUR CUSTOMERS' EVOLVING NEEDS. Build durable brand loyalty and long-term competitive advantage by learning from the frontline employees who shape their experience. Like any long-tenured leader at a great company, Clem, as a CEO candidate, had an advantage few outsiders could match: deep familiarity with Sweetwater's people and culture.

But that alone wasn't nearly enough. With employees feeling uncertain what it meant to be operating under expanded private equity ownership, and with Clem's background rooted in technology rather than enterprise-wide leadership, he still had to prove he could honor the legacy of beloved founder Chuck Surack. To win the board's confidence—and the trust of a fiercely loyal customer base—he needed to show he could not only preserve Sweetwater's deeply held values but amplify and evolve them in a rapidly transforming industry.

The board was looking for a candidate who could step into the founder's shoes without missing a beat. As we explored in chapter 4, boards rarely seek a carbon copy of the outgoing CEO, but in some cases, sentimentality can cloud judgment. It's natural for board members to hold deep affection for the founder and deserve continuity. In others, the board is eager for change or divided over which direction to take next. Regardless of where the board stands emotionally, one truth remains: as a CEO candidate, you must convince the board you can preserve, embody, and amplify the cultural ethos that made the brand beloved in the first place.

At the same time, outsiders have some advantages by not being steeped in the culture. Frankly, Sweetwater's competitors might not be good role models, and perhaps the board members would have been better off looking outside their industry for greater inspiration. As a CEO candidate, you can count on that. Your board has a fiduciary duty to consider folks outside your industry when conducting the CEO search at your company. As discussed in earlier chapters, outsiders can be much more attractive choices because they might look with fresh eyes at growing the business. An insider like Clem had the potential to be too self-absorbed or overconfident about Sweetwater's amazing history, missing key signals from the industry about its future.

As a CEO candidate, Clem doubled down on what captured employees' loyalty in the culture but at the same time got excited about how to redefine the future for customer service. He held a great ambition to drive changes and lead customers there. He dug deeper into the data and evidence, differentiating service that would win customer confidence. Clem is an incessant learner, reading about and studying other service companies that Sweetwater aspires to match or exceed in service. Clem said, "The Sweetwater culture is very similar to a Chewy or a Zappos"—that's the standard to which he insisted he would hold the company if he were to become CEO. Success "is based on over-the-top customer service and truly caring for customers as human beings and doing the right thing. That's our North Star. That really depends on hiring the right people to come in and really want to pour into the lives of others." That attitude won over Sweetwater's board and the founder.

The decision-makers are looking to you to become the company's reinvigorated culture champion when you become CEO, just as Clem has, so think about how you can demonstrate how that role excites you in a practical way. Clem's approval rating and engagement scores have been impressive.

As Peter Drucker is often (if somewhat inaccurately) quoted: "Culture eats strategy for breakfast." While the Drucker Institute clarifies that he never said those exact words—his actual phrasing was that culture is "singularly persistent"—the sentiment has endured for good reason. It's taken decades for some leaders, particularly new CEO candidates eager to make their mark, to fully grasp just how foundational culture is to successful transformation. Some still haven't. Your board is now looking for CEO candidates who not only understand the existing culture but who can use it as a springboard for institutional alignment and large-scale change. And they know one thing for sure: no one else can truly own the unofficial title of culture champion; your HR leader can and should be your greatest partner. Although you need everyone to own the campaign and play a key role in the outcome, as a CEO candidate you must realize you cannot delegate culture—not to a direct report, not even to a "chief culture officer." As CEO, that's your job.

If, as a CEO candidate, you cannot demonstrate a track record of building culture at your company or elsewhere, "it won't be good. I sometimes hear people say, 'We don't *have* a culture at our company.' They have one. But if it hasn't been nurtured, if no one has spent on any time on it, you can assume it's the wrong culture," said Bill Emerson, vice chairman of Rock Holdings, the parent company of Quicken Loans.[3]

LEARN TO STEP BACK. In early 2024, Eric Kessenich was identified as a leading CEO candidate at U.S. Venture, a $14 billion diversified

Honor Culture, Comfort Customers, and Manage Celebrity 171

firm spanning energy, tire distribution, and software. His predecessor, John Schmidt, a charismatic entrepreneur who had grown the company's value sixfold, planned an eighteen-month transition to chairman. During the 360-degree feedback process, both Schmidt and Kessenich voiced a shared reflection about the challenge of this transition that Mark hears in *every* succession transition. Schmidt talked about the need and challenge to downshift from his role meeting the day-to-day requirements—stepping away from operations and management—while at the same time Kessenich would also have to step back in important ways from his tactical leadership as a division leader. "The higher you go," Kessenich mused, "the less you get to *do things* and the more you oversee the doing of things by other people."

That shift—from decisive operator to enabling architect—is one of the hardest transitions for rising CEOs and their bosses. The very instinct that propelled your rise—making the call, driving execution—must now evolve into something broader: scaling your leadership through others. It requires building trust, stepping back, and empowering a culture of accountability where evidence-based decision-making doesn't flow from you, but is an accountability of your team. This isn't theoretical for a CEO candidate. Your board, peers, and employees are wondering how you will make that transition with elegance and class. If you hope to win their confidence, you must demonstrate that you're not just leading projects, you're building a leadership pipeline for others to do that.

To manage this shift during the year *before* the transition to CEO, Kessenich spent "a lot more time thinking about organizational design and culture and how we would operate as opposed to what I was operating on." It's been a permanent evolution for his mindset, as it must be for every CEO candidate. "I think about how we go about problem-solving versus being the one who's doing the problem-solving. You have to focus on culture."

BECOME CHIEF COACHING OFFICER. CEOs who now coach other CEOs, like Garry Ridge, legendary former chairman and CEO of WD-40, invite you to think of the following as your mantra during your interviews with stakeholders: "Building great cultures in an organization is not a microwavable event—it takes a crockpot approach." Under his transformative leadership, WD-40's market capitalization grew from approximately $300 million to $2.5 billion. He envisioned a workplace culture where the leaders looked to hire and train "people who love their work every day, arrive to make a contribution to something bigger than themselves, learn something new, and go home happy." That's the kind of leader he was looking for when recruiting his replacement.

"You might think all we [WD-40] do is make oil in a can, but of course, that's not what drives the organization—the leader who would become our next CEO knows that it's culture," said Ridge. During his tenure as CEO, Ridge coauthored four books about culture including his latest, *Any Dumb-Ass Can Do It: Learning Moments from an Everyday CEO of a Multi-Billion-Dollar Company*. For Ridge, the leader's role is not to manage but to coach. "You *manage* your bank account; you *coach* human beings," he declared, emphasizing the importance of nurturing talent and fostering personal growth within the organization. This vision exemplifies Ridge's dedication to creating an environment of purpose, learning, and fulfillment. As a leader, he believed in balancing compassion with courage, encouraging leaders to embody "a heart of gold but a backbone of steel"—a mindset that allowed them to connect with people while making tough, necessary decisions.

KNOW YOUR SCORE WITH YOUR EMPLOYEES. As you build a reputation worthy of becoming CEO, understand this fundamental truth: if the culture in your current area is working, everything else will work better for you. Most companies now run regular engagement surveys with employees, and they will closely scrutinize the scores from the business or function you lead as part of your CEO candidacy. As you know, boards and executive committees no longer focus solely on companywide averages. They examine engagement results by division, department, region, and leader. Why? Because it's a proxy for leadership effectiveness and organizational health. Your track record on employee experience is now part of your CEO readiness scorecard.

Are you and your company considered an employer worth recommending? That's no longer just a philosophical question; it's a measurable data point that could define your trajectory as a CEO candidate. Many companies now rely on employee Net Promoter Scores (eNPS), a concept that originated with the customer-facing Net Promoter Score (NPS) developed by Fred Reichheld of Bain & Company in collaboration with Satmetrix, and introduced in his landmark 2003 *Harvard Business Review* article, "The One Number You Need to Grow." His breakthrough was simple and powerful: by asking customers, "Would you recommend this company to a friend?" you could predict future business growth. The idea transformed how companies measure loyalty and customer satisfaction.

Soon after, HR leaders applied the same principle inward, asking the same question of employees. If customer referrals could predict performance, could employee advocacy predict cultural health and retention? That point of view has been widely adopted as part of a larger set of assessments across many platforms, including Gallup's Q12, which measures twelve core drivers of engagement linked to retention and high performance; Glint, now part of LinkedIn, which specializes in real-time Pulse surveys and AI-powered feedback loops; and Culture Amp, known for its customizable surveys and analytics aligned to company values. Qualtrics integrates employee engagement data with customer and operational metrics to offer a comprehensive view of organizational health, while Peakon, now under Workday, delivers dynamic dashboards and sentiment analysis across teams. WorkBoard is increasingly popular for aligning engagement data with objectives and key results, tying culture directly to business performance. Other fast-rising platforms like TinyPulse and Lattice focus on frequent check-ins, recognition, and agile feedback cycles—tools especially favored by fast-moving, high-growth organizations seeking real-time insight into employee morale and manager effectiveness.

For CEO candidates, the employee survey is no longer a score that is reviewed exclusively by your partners in human resources; now boards and search firms and assessment analysts increasingly track these engagement metrics by business unit, geography, and leader, sometimes well before formal succession discussions begin. In this way, engagement surveys have become a quiet but decisive signal of whether you're ready to lead at scale and whether others will follow.

As a CEO candidate, your leadership is also judged by the brand reputation you inherit as an employer—and what you do with it. Public platforms like Glassdoor reflect anonymous employee reviews that influence your company's standing with job seekers and investors alike. Other key evaluators include Comparably, which benchmarks pay equity, leadership, and culture in real time; Great Places to Work, which certifies companies and feeds rankings like *Fortune*'s "100 Best Companies to Work For"; and Indeed's Company Reviews, which aggregate sentiment around work-life balance, management, and career growth. These external perceptions—fair or not—become part of your brand equity. As a CEO candidate, your leadership must engage both internal teams and the public narrative. As Kessenich notes, "You have to be intentional around finding the right measures and creating the culture you want."

COMFORT YOUR CUSTOMERS. Ask yourself an equally critical question: "How well do I know my customers?" This goes beyond knowing who buys your products or services to *why*. Do you understand their evolving needs, values, and frustrations? Can you anticipate how they might respond to your leadership—and how any shift in strategy or tone will affect their loyalty? The best CEO candidates don't just study the customer base; they re-earn its trust through insight, empathy, and vision. Making customers feel confident in the transition isn't enough—you must demonstrate that you *see* them, that you're ready to serve them even better.

Head to the front lines. How, other than through research or customer surveys, does a potential CEO learn about what customers want and need and what might potentially come down the pike that might derail their trust? If you are not already serving your company in a role that does this every day, one of the best ways to build your understanding is to talk with the people who deal with customers—all types, not just the buying type—every day. We're talking about frontline employees. Maggie Wilderotter, chairman of DocuSign and former CEO of Frontier Communications, has interviewed many CEO candidates. She's impressed when the prospective leader shares stories of face-to-face interactions with those who serve the paying type of customers: "I believe the front line is the bottom line. I used to put two-hour blocks on my calendar, so that any place I went to visit, any of my markets, I had 'lion hunts' on my calendar. I'd take two hours, just prowl around the offices, bump into people, go to their cubes and offices, and ask: 'How's it going?' and 'What are you working on?' and 'Tell me what we should be doing different.' I'd also ask them, 'Tell me what you like that we're doing' and 'Tell me what's not working.'" Most CEO candidates are already so far up the ladder in the corporate hierarchy that they've long since abandoned that kind of employee engagement on behalf of seeing firsthand how customers feel. Wilderotter says, "People love to tell you. You just have to ask and then listen."

When she was CEO, Wilderotter would then take this information back to the area's leaders and ask what their plan was to rectify the situations. "They'd go, 'How did you know about that?' And I'd say, 'I talk to your employees.' And then they'd start prowling around the office too; they'd start those conversations because they didn't want to get surprised."

As Wilderotter interviews CEO candidates, she says you will separate yourself from the pack of others in her mind by showing your resourcefulness about customers, "going to the truth tellers, because they're going to tell you what's really happening, especially those in customer service roles." Ask those folks who are answering the phones, making deliveries, or working the front desk every day what customers are saying, and they'll tell you.

Are customers and employees unable to tell you the truth? Eric Kessenich of U.S. Venture said that as a CEO candidate, no matter how much you think you have your finger on the pulse of the organization, "in a lot of ways you [the CEO] are the most ill-equipped person to make a specific decision because people aren't telling you the truth. Not that they're lying; it's just information comes with bias and filter. They think, 'I don't want to waste the CEO's time,' or 'This issue isn't important enough for them,' or 'I don't want to throw my boss under the bus.'"

Measure engagement by how often people tell you what you don't want to hear. As a candidate, Kessenich worried because he had another thing working against getting good customer feedback: he is an imposing mountain of a man. "I'm a lot more intimidating than John [our founder]. So, if people were afraid to talk to him, I have to work even harder to combat that." Kessenich put extra effort into reassuring the board and boss that he would not fall victim to employees or customers who just patronized him as heir apparent. For that reason, he stepped up attendance at "next-level leadership meetings of my direct reports. I started doing skip-level meetings. I overshared and am intentionally more vulnerable, sharing things that are more personal than people might expect. I incorporate humor. I try to be genuine and authentic so people can come and tell me the bad and not just the good." You've got to behave and act the part of the CEO in "professionally vulnerable and authentic ways" that make people feel safe to follow you and be more transparent.

Klaus Kleinfeld, the former CEO of Siemens AG and Alcoa, echoed this challenge: "The higher you rise, the more filtered the information you receive," he warned. Crises don't usually erupt because the data is wrong—they escalate because essential nuance gets lost in translation. That's why Kleinfeld developed a habit every CEO candidate should adopt: go directly to the source. When something serious arose—whether a safety incident, a customer meltdown, or a culture breakdown—Kleinfeld showed appreciation for the sanitized summary, but he didn't rely on it; he didn't bet his career or the customer on it. He picked up the phone and, when possible, went straight to the site. "Your team may resist," he admitted, "worried it implies a lack of trust." But in moments that truly matter, it's not micromanagement; it's your obligation to double-check. "They may momentarily hate you for it," he added with a wry smile. Still, when the stakes are high and time is short, your direct involvement can clarify what others can't and ultimately support the very leaders you might be second-guessing.

As Kessenich and Kleinfeld discovered, people may admire or fear you too much to be fully honest. You just have to be careful that you never shoot the messenger. Great CEOs overcome this by creating environments where candor isn't punished and dissent is welcomed. They are not just informed; they are trusted enough to hear what's wrong while there's still time to fix it. Your ability to draw out those hard truths and demonstrate them as a CEO candidate may determine whether you're selected and how effectively you lead once you're there.

Get to know the customers you don't know now. Most businesses have key customers that provide a significant share of their company's total revenue. As president or a leader of a division, you might already know these customers. But if you're a CEO candidate who's currently CFO or in some other C-suite role where you have less customer contact, then you'll want to reach out to those executives to participate in sales calls and presentations. The board and your boss need to see you get out of your staff role and onto the factory floor with employees and meet customers.

If your company's customers are primarily transactional, buying products and services with little concern for ongoing relationships, they're unlikely to have much influence on your run for the CEO office. However, if your company has key relationship customers who generate a substantial amount of revenue, customer feedback may be a critical factor in whether you get the job. Many financial services firms, for instance, have clients who want to deal directly with the CEO. Given the social and business circles they move in, these clients often have relationships with the company's board members. Building ties with them before becoming a CEO candidate will improve an executive's chances of getting the job and succeeding in it.

7. *Chief communication officer*

Many of the CEO candidates who became chief executives admit to us that they were not prepared for the glare of the spotlight that hit when they first took the big job. To rise to a position where stakeholders feel comfortable with you, your natural self-confidence must be blended with genuine humility, which acknowledges that we each have been given certain gifts or talents, and we are obligated to use them in the best way we can to benefit those around us.

"Confidence is the sweet spot between arrogance and despair—consisting of positive expectations for favorable outcomes," says Rosabeth Moss Kanter of Harvard Business School and author of

Earning Customer Trust before Day One

As a CEO candidate, here are some more ways to help ensure that you have the support of key customers when you're up for the top job:

- **Prioritize working with your current CEO and senior leadership team to identify the company's most important customer relationships.** Make it a point to connect personally with the key decision-makers behind those accounts, especially those you haven't yet met. Don't limit your conversations to immediate business needs; take the time to build long-term rapport. Trust-based relationships with your most critical customers aren't just a commercial asset; they're a strategic differentiator that strengthens your credibility as an incoming CEO.

- **Determine which customers have close personal relationships with board members**. Work with your CEO to understand those relationships and the CEO's role in them.

- **Discuss with your CEO the balance between customer satisfaction and your company's business needs**. In some cases (such as pricing), you may have to make hard decisions that anger customers. If this happens, quickly go to the customer and explain what is happening and why. They may not be thrilled with your rationale, but they will at least know that you value them as a client and that you want to maintain the relationship.

- **Get involved in those company programs that recognize key employees who serve clients well**. Legendary founder Herb Kelleher of Southwest Airlines and Sir Richard Branson, founder of Virgin, both emphasized the same core truth to Mark: While clients are vital, employees must come first. Take care of your employees, they believed, and your employees will take care of the customers. Frank Blake, former CEO of Home Depot, would spend each Sunday writing some two hundred messages to store leaders who had high customer-service scores for the previous week. "I'd see these notes framed at the stores, so I knew it mattered," he said.[a]

a. Elisa Boxer, "Home Depot's CEO Did This 25,000 Times. Science Says You Should Do It Too," Inc.com, November 10, 2017, https://www.inc.com/elisa-boxer/home-depots-ceo-did-this-25000-times-science-says-you-should-do-it-too.html.

Confidence.[4] True confidence is believing in yourself and believing in others to reach those favorable outcomes.

PREPARE FOR PUBLIC VISIBILITY. With so many celebrities featured in the media who may strike you as less than ideal role models—and so many reporters heralding stardom—the transition to become CEO creates visibility that is harder than you imagine until you actually are the next chief executive. For some, it's tempting for many employees and onlookers to view the CEO as a celebrity, not just the face of the company—the famous executive, the person with an answer for everything, someone who is full of grace and charm—or for others the CEO is a melodramatic and intimidating public figure. While that persona might work for central casting in Hollywood and geopolitics, it's not comforting and usually not highly motivating in organizations. Employees, customers, and shareholders, while prone to the exciting entertainment value of occasional showmanship, privately far more appreciate and are loyal to CEOs who inspire steady, stable, predictable vision and confident decision-making. But any point of view that you present as CEO can be expected to be constantly reviewed, *twisted*, and reinvented, all with the hope of finding any blemish that will call attention to the conspirator. Even understandable behavior, such as looking at your smartwatch too often or yawning in a meeting, can become fodder for your team's watercooler resentment or even content for late-night comedians if it's caught on video.

Many years of a positive reputation can be lost in a day. Potential successors need to clearly understand, before being considered for the job, how much CEO behavior matters to the people they will be leading and how closely that is watched by the media. Our friend John Dickerson has a front row seat on the drama that consumes leaders. He is coanchor of *CBS Evening News*, and also an anchor on CBS News 24/7, the network's streaming news platform. Dickerson told us that, while anchoring *Face the Nation*, he learned "you may be sending signals you don't know you're sending, or the message you're sending isn't being received in the way you hoped it would be. Even the great communicators can't change public opinion. They can shape the flow. They can guide the flow. But they cannot redirect the flow. In business you have more power than that, but you still have to answer to boards of directors and shareholders, so you can't rule by fiat."

Yes, as CEO, you're suddenly larger than life, at least to those around you. Most candidates for chief executive never fully internalize how dramatically the power dynamic shifts until they are in the job. Most want to believe the admiration and attention are sincere, not inflated or performative. But behind the scenes, people—internally and externally—are scrutinizing your every move, second-guessing your decisions, and reinterpreting your tone, words, and even body language. When Mark ran investor relations for Charles Schwab, he witnessed investors and analysts speculating on whether Schwab or any of the senior leaders "looked tired," "seemed rattled," or "were overly upbeat," searching for any signal to predict what the next quarter might bring, up or down, good or bad. As Marshall Goldsmith wisely puts it: "As CEO, you no longer own your face."

What Does *Authenticity* Mean When You No Longer Own Your Face?

Are you prepared to redefine what *authenticity* means in the spotlight of modern leadership and social media? Can you stay centered when your facial expressions, tone, and every word are dissected in real time and sometimes distorted by those with their own agenda? What once felt like honest communication may now require a more intentional and strategic approach. Today, CEO candidates—and especially sitting CEOs—must accept that every mobile phone is a camera and they are walking lightning rods for attention, admiration, and attack. The pressure has never been higher. Well-meaning leaders are now pressured to speak out on myriad issues. But what begins as principled leadership often becomes weaponized in the public sphere. Many media influencers aren't always interested in nuance or debate. Some are looking to hijack your platform, amplify outrage, or create controversy where none exists. A single offhand comment, a facial expression caught on a phone, or an awkward pause can go viral in minutes. In some cases, the media won't wait for a mistake;

they'll invent a scandal and pressure your company into silence or submission just to gain clicks or notoriety.

Escalating Risks for Senior Executives

This is the new normal. As a CEO candidate, you must decide for yourself and discuss with your family the risk of greater public visibility for you and for them. To the world's horror, Brian Thompson, the CEO of UnitedHealthcare, was tragically shot on his way to the annual investor day. This shocking event underscored the increasing risks that corporate leaders face. Protests and defacement of homes have intensified with personal attacks. These incidents highlight the mounting dangers and public scrutiny that leaders endure.

You will have to make peace with all this and plan for it or pass on your candidacy for the CEO role. The demands of modern CEO visibility—relentless scrutiny, sudden backlash, and high emotional stakes—will test your clarity and composure at every turn. That's why your preparation as a CEO candidate must go beyond strategy and messaging. You need media training, of course, and trusted advisers, coaching, and a grounded sense of purpose that can anchor you when perception shifts against you. Boards want to know that you've built that inner stability, anchored to values long before you take the chair, because once you're in it, the pressure only grows.

We're not saying you *should* feel good about stepping into this intense spotlight. In fact, it's OK if part of you doesn't. Our goal isn't to glamorize the chaos or pressure, but to give you the truth. This is the terrain of leadership today: unpredictable, amplified, and often unfair. What matters is that you prepare for it with clarity, courage, and support. See how it feels in your body and heart. Ask yourself whether the responsibility overwhelms or ignites your purpose, as it did for Hirshland. That's not a decision to rush. But it *is* one on which you as a CEO candidate should reflect, refine, rehearse and own, so that when the lights turn on, you're not just ready. You're steady.

Becoming the Boss and a Beacon

So your rise to CEO comes with unprecedented exposure. But think of that spotlight as a beacon. You can illuminate a path forward for a company ready to change the world, to grow, to transform. You are not expected to be flawless. You are expected to be realistic, prepared, coachable, resilient, and purpose driven. The board is not just seeking your strategy; it is sensing your character. Can you do the evidence-based homework to assess what motivates your customers and employees and hone your skills and emotional intelligence to honor what works in the culture? Can you find the strategic clarity to evolve it, the courage to speak with conviction, and the humility to listen deeply to those who serve your customers and define your brand? That is what will earn you not just the job, but followership.

If you're truly CEO ready, you already know that this role is not about being celebrated; it's about being trusted. And you're ready to earn that trust every day, with every one of the seven stakeholders, in every room you walk into.

CEO Ready Pulse Check

The seven officer roles of the chief executive

As you've seen throughout this book, a successful CEO candidate must engage seven core stakeholder groups—each with its own culture, expectations, and language. But understanding them isn't enough. To earn their trust and lead effectively, you'll need to play multiple roles. In fact, for each stakeholder, you may find yourself wearing more than one hat. That's why the most credible and trusted CEO candidates master not just stakeholder alignment—but also role fluency. Here are seven essential leadership roles—your "officer hats"—that every CEO must be prepared to wear:

1. **CHIEF ENGAGEMENT OFFICER**
   Are you reading the signals in your employee data to energize your team and build your reputation as a credible, inspiring leader? As former WD-40 CEO Garry Ridge says, "You manage your bank account; you *coach* human beings. You're chief coaching officer."

2. **CHIEF CUSTOMER OFFICER**
   How well do you understand your customers as they face times of uncertainty? Every dimension of your leadership is now measured. Are you seeking unfiltered feedback directly from frontline employees and the customers they serve?

3. **CHIEF GRATITUDE OFFICER**
   Are you anchored enough to honor the people and culture that got you here? Do your team and customers see you as grounded and anchored by your values, as someone who listens deeply, who leads with loving admiration of the people serving your mission, bringing the team with you, especially at high-stakes moments?

4. **CHIEF ARCHITECT**
   Can you reinvent what must change while preserving what works? Your objective is not just sweeping transformation but thoughtful reinvention and renovation. Can you identify the load-bearing walls of your business and culture? Have you sequenced your change agenda to maximize alignment?

5. CHIEF CULTURE CURATOR

Do you know which cultural elements to protect and which ones must evolve? Can you name the behaviors and values that make your organization proud? Can you challenge what's toxic or outdated? Boards are looking for leaders who can honor the soul of the company while driving lasting renewal and greater accountability.

6. CHIEF TRANSFORMATION OFFICER

Do you know the fewest, most powerful things that will drive value? You'll be judged on your ability to execute. Can you articulate your value creation agenda, operating model shifts and a talent alignment plan in a way that feels focused, realistic, and fast? Boards want someone who gets things done without boiling the ocean, and employees need to feel they're making tangible progress.

7. CHIEF COMMUNICATION OFFICER

Are you ready for the spotlight and prepared to lead when every word, gesture, and pause is amplified? You no longer own your face. Can you project calm, conviction, and clarity in the public arena, even under attack? Can you lead with authenticity when your privacy, reputation, and tone are under 24/7 surveillance?

Conclusion

Permission to Be Happy

What anchors you, what fuels you, what lights your sky

When you spend so much time with CEO candidates, as we do, you come to appreciate just how harrowing the process is for people who've spent their lives aspiring to this achievement. We romanticize actors striving to make it in Hollywood, athletes battling to get to the pros, inventors devoting their lives to that one breakthrough, but no less a human drama is playing out in companies worldwide when the CEO role opens. Many will get only one shot at it.

This crash course on how to manage the process—and win over the seven key stakeholders—will improve your odds when your moment comes. It's difficult to summarize all of what you've read to this point, so let's highlight several of the most critical lessons with clarity and precision. We'll use the example of Blackstone, which has over $1 trillion in assets invested in more than 250 companies and enforces one of the world's most rigorous CEO candidacy processes, offering critical insights for any executive aspiring to lead as chief executive, especially in high-stakes environments.

1. Partner with Your CPO to Scope Nuanced Details of Your Next Role

A promising executive up for a CEO position at Blackstone, though highly accomplished at another Blackstone-owned real estate firm, lacked expertise in local market dynamics, regulatory affairs, and relationships with regional policy makers—skills essential for the new position. Within six months, the company's performance lagged, as reported by Ruth Umoh in a *Fortune* article about Blackstone's CEO search process. Reflecting on this, Courtney della Cava, Blackstone's senior managing director and global head of portfolio talent, acknowledged, "If we had simply stepped back and asked ourselves, 'What do we uniquely need this CEO to do to get us where we need to be?' we would have realized he wasn't the right fit."[1]

LESSON FOR CANDIDATES: Partner early and earnestly with your chief human resources officer (CHRO) or chief people officer (CPO) as a strategic ally. Many CEO candidates initially underestimate HR's influence because, in your previous jobs as CFO, president, or other C-suite executive, the HR team may not have played a central role in your daily leadership. But during CEO succession, when rumors run high and uncertainty deepens, embracing HR as a key partner becomes a critical competitive advantage, as it can help you define and articulate the plan the board expects you to deliver. As an internal CEO candidate, you're navigating the critical transition from peer to chief, where you're deepening your relationships with your peers in the C-suite. Your HR business partner can help.

Boards—especially nominating committee chairs—now view HR leaders as the "quality-control agents" of CEO succession.[2] As della Cava at Blackstone sees it, top HR executives operate as confidantes, peers, and objective advisers, holding panoramic influence over talent decisions.[3] Our advice is for you to take your relationship with the CHRO to the next level by seeking deeper insights about the next role and encouraging frank feedback about yourself; you will inspire them with your maturity and humility. CHROs often quietly nurture multiple potential

CEO candidates behind the scenes, like Ronald Schellekens, executive vice president and chief human resources officer at PepsiCo, who stresses that boards rely on CHROs to deliver candid, sometimes uncomfortable truths during succession deliberations.[4] Often acting as informal coaches, CHROs invest in preparing internal candidates, regardless of who is ultimately selected.[5] If your CHRO advises you to deepen your financial skills, expand customer insights, or enhance executive presence, you should listen. Acting on their guidance strengthens their confidence in your readiness and encourages their advocacy on your behalf.

Before pursuing even the most obvious CEO role, your HR partners can help you assess whether your skills align with the needs of the company and the next phase of the transformation and change, beyond your general executive experience. Tailor your candidacy to the company's context, market, and strategic priorities, and be honest with yourself about your ability and desire to lead in different contexts. How you engage with HR during this succession journey may define your future candidacy.

2. Prepare for an Exhaustive Evaluation Process

Blackstone's CEO selection is not for the faint of heart. Under della Cava's leadership, candidates undergo a three-to-four-month recruitment process involving nearly a dozen interviews, third-party assessments, board presentations, and a five-hour psychometric evaluation. Dan Kaplan, a senior client partner at Korn Ferry, emphasizes the competitiveness of these roles: "Everyone wants to be there. It has become a brand synonymous with being best in class."[6]

LESSON FOR CANDIDATES: The big awakening for most CEO candidates is that you must earn readiness twice—first, demonstrate that you're steadily expanding your skills, and second, invest in the relationships necessary to be selected, as described in chapter 2. Be ready to demonstrate your technical competence, emotional intelligence, resilience, and cultural fit. Plan for deep scrutiny of your leadership style, decision-making under pressure, and long-term vision. Do not be surprised if the process is sometimes combative.

3. Recognize That Leadership Is the Engine of Value Creation

Blackstone's success in growing its business hinges on selecting leaders who can drive both operational efficiency and cultural transformation. Della Cava stresses that "an underperforming leader results in an underperforming company" and emphasizes that "leadership is the number one driver of value creation."[7] Since CFOs work at the center of financial performance, increasing numbers are appointed CEO. Yet even for those executives, the CEO role demands a shift from guardian of financial outcomes to visionary leader of the whole enterprise.[8] Boards are increasingly promoting CFOs, but candidates must demonstrate readiness far beyond finance, inspiring teams, and adapting enterprise-wide strategy under pressure.

LESSON FOR CANDIDATES: Boards aren't just looking for financial engineering; they are seeking leaders who can translate cultural strength of the company into long-term value creation. Be prepared to show how you will lead through crisis, manage conflict, and sustain performance against headwinds. Show them your plan to not just protect the balance sheet, but build a resilient culture that accelerates growth. In every job, you have independent variables, like people, and dependent variables. The dependent variable for the CEO is shareholder value. If you can't generate it, you're not going to be in the job for very long.

We encourage you to ask every CEO you meet about your aspirations to become chief executive. If you're shooting to become a first-time CEO, every one of them will say that you are never fully prepared for it. They are not intentionally trying to discourage your ambition; after all, every CEO must start their first rodeo with a leap of faith as a rookie. Veteran CEOs just want you to know how to avoid the most common trap: the candidate's assumption that the next level of leadership is simply a broader version of their last very senior role and that their relationship with each of the decision-makers is secure. You already had a big job, right? Not like this one; it's a role like no other that fundamentally shifts the point of view and your power dynamic with every one of the seven stakeholders whom you thought you knew during your prior role.

"Becoming CEO is a jump-shift. There's no real preparation for the job," A.G. Lafley, former chair and CEO, Procter & Gamble, remarked at the CEO Academy, where Mark is former chief executive officer. The academy hosts two dozen CEOs twice annually in partnership with Wharton and McKinsey and is owned by the Society for Human Resource Management. "If you're hungry to take the leap to CEO, the biggest job of a lifetime, you're about to discover that you're not as ready as you think," said Aicha Evans, CEO of the Amazon company Zoox. Evans reflected on how she felt when she got the call from Jeff Bezos to become chief executive: "I thought I'd summited Everest, but found another higher peak just behind it!" Born in Senegal in West Africa, Evans's leadership journey required constant reinvention—adapting, building new skills, and cultivating relationships without ever feeling she had arrived at a destination. She credits much of her growth to being "vulnerable enough to be coachable." She instills that discipline in everyone who works for her, and it's helped her navigate from senior leadership roles at Intel to becoming CEO of Zoox, where Bezos, the iconic Amazon founder, recruited her, and Mark became her coach.

"What the world's most influential leaders know is that the secret to achieving effectiveness is becoming coachable," said Scott Osman. He and Jacquelyn Lane run the world's leading executive coaching placement agency, 100Coaches, and together wrote the *Wall Street Journal* bestselling book, *Becoming Coachable*. As a part of the 100Coaches Readiness Practice, they have developed a programmatic strategy to solve the talent management transition challenge by curating matches for top CEO candidates with elite experienced executive coaches.

Most leaders rising through the ranks underestimate the leap, says Klaus Kleinfeld, former Alcoa and Siemens AG CEO. "And we need coaching to better understand what is involved in this next vulnerable step," he told Mark during his CEO Summit interview. Kleinfeld, like many executives, struggled with the transition at first. The reason is that "even though your jobs over time get massively bigger, we still ultimately report to one boss," Kleinfeld observed. And while you must deal with many influencers, there's still just one person who matters most in each of your jobs for your entire career. Over time, you have learned how to read that boss—what earns trust, what sets off alarms, and where the invisible boundaries lie, he explained. Then one day, you become CEO, and your "boss" is no longer a single person—it's a board that suddenly shifts from a group you thought you knew well to a powerful tribe with sharply differing individual expectations and power dynamics. There's a fundamental change by definition when you become chief executive, evoking drifting alliances, divergent expectations, and political undercurrents. That, Kleinfeld says, is where many executives are caught off-guard before becoming first-time CEO candidates. They continue to behave as if performance alone will carry the day, not realizing they now need to manage alignment and perception at the group level.

"Boards only have two stable states," he quipped. "They either love the CEO and brag about you to everyone—or they suddenly decide you need to be gone yesterday." And that shift can happen in seconds.

4. Embrace the High-Stakes Nature of the Role

Being a CEO is a "high-intensity sport," della Cava emphasized, requiring a leader who can thrive under pressure, navigate volatility, and handle the oscillation between being celebrated as a hero and criticized as a villain. Blackstone's disciplined approach to CEO candidacy is increasingly typical.[9]

LESSON FOR CANDIDATES: Prepare yourself mentally and emotionally for the intense reality of the role. Find ways to practice resilience, adaptability, and the ability to manage criticism while staying focused on long-term goals. As former United Technologies Corporation CEO George David advised us at the CEO Academy, "Maintain laser-like focus on your top three to five priorities—avoid the trap of trying to do everything at once." During that same session, Alan Mulally, former

CEO credited with transforming Ford Motor Company, agreed, cautioning that success demands "relentless implementation." Mulally added, "Without clarity of focus and love for the mission, the role's complexity will overwhelm even the most talented leaders."

As a CEO candidate, think of yourself as an elite athlete. Gold medalists recognize that they play their best when challenged by the hardest competition, energized to elevate their game by the demands of performing at a world-class level. Serena Williams shared at Wimbledon in 2018, "I always play everyone at their greatest, so I have to be greater."[10] Over her career, Williams captured twenty-three Grand Slam singles titles—the most for a woman in the Open Era—while Novak Djokovic now holds the record for men with twenty-four Grand Slam titles.

Notably, Williams claimed her final major victory at the Australian Open, where she defeated her sister while eight weeks pregnant, a fact she revealed publicly several months later. Both Serena and Venus Williams have since become prolific entrepreneurial CEOs, building on decades of business preparation that began when they were children in the backseat of their father's car, driven to tennis practice with dreams bigger than the court. Mark coached Venus and her executive team as they reinvented two of her companies during the pandemic, V Starr Interiors and EleVen by Venus Williams. The Williams sisters applied their decades-long discipline for preparation as athletes to structure their journey as CEOs, and so must you. Their extraordinary clarity of purpose and passion under pressure can summon a superhuman level of performance—something we wish for each of you as you prepare for your own leadership moment.

5. Understand That Nobody Does It Alone

Identify your trusted truth tellers and get help. "With the volume of problems you face, and the higher you rise," Kleinfeld says, "the more crap lands on your desk." You must embrace all the issues—"most of which you had nothing to do with"—because once you're the CEO, everything is on *your* watch. This point underscores a deeper insight at the heart of your preparation for this next step in your career: there is a difference between being accountable for everything and having to come up with every solution. As a candidate—and later as a chief executive—it's never about having all the answers. It's about having the judgment and humility to know that nobody does it alone and surrounding yourself with great leaders with whom you can be a partner and empower.

LESSON FOR CANDIDATES: You'll need to expand your circle of trusted advisers because you'll often receive incomplete information. You'll need the courage to challenge assumptions—including your own—cut through the noise, gather data, and engage the group with clarity and confidence when the stakes are highest.

6. Get Ready, Even When Your Company Might Not Be

If you, as a CEO candidate, sense that your organization does not have a clear succession plan with disciplined milestones, there may be a deeper reason behind the gaps. This is exactly what Byron Loflin found when he first created Nasdaq's Global Governance Pulse survey of senior executives. Its 2024 survey revealed that "alarmingly, 26% of respondents report their board has no CEO succession plan, which presents risk to organizational stability and continuity. Additionally, 21% report the board only has an emergency CEO succession plan and 46% indicate there is a formalized, detailed CEO succession plan that includes an emergency provision and long-term plan."[11] That means less than half have an official ongoing plan for succession.

At the same time, Nasdaq observed that turnover at the top is increasing rapidly, opening more opportunities for which CEO candidates need to ready themselves. "The number of CEOs who announced departures in early 2024 increased 49% over the first quarter of 2023 (the highest ever recorded)."[12] The shortening of CEO tenure reinforces this urgency. In the S&P 500, median CEO tenure dropped from approximately six years in 2013 to 4.8 years in 2022—a decline of about 20 percent—while average tenure edged downward from 7.6 years to 7.2 years.[13]

The Nasdaq survey also provided a shortlist of what boards look for in a candidate: "The CEO succession planning process must account for experience, industry knowledge, leadership skills, and the evolving needs of the organization to ensure a smooth transition that sustains the organization's culture, short- and long-term strategic direction, and performance," it said, urging board members to invigorate their succession planning process or face "serious setbacks and potential failures."[14]

Further underscoring the opportunities for CEO candidates at the largest companies, fifty-eight incumbent chief executives departed from S&P 500 companies in 2024, marking a 21 percent increase from 2023 and representing the second-highest annual departure total on record.[15]

LESSON FOR CANDIDATES: Don't wait to be asked. Paraphrasing Gandhi, "Be the change you wish to see in the world." The call to action is clear: take the initiative; treat your CEO candidacy more seriously than anyone else might. Launch your own strategic plan. Your preparation and process may even influence how succession is defined by your company. Position yourself to be CEO ready.

7. Champion a Worthy Mission—and Lead at the Crossroads

Every organization stands at a crossroads, and every board is seeking someone like you—if you're prepared. They need a leader who will honor their proud history while recognizing that succession isn't a continuation—it's an urgent reinvention. For all the cautionary tales—and encouragement—we've offered throughout this book, we hope that the cause or company you are called to lead feels worthy of your preparation, resilience, imagination, and sacrifices. We hope that it feels worthy of shaping a future that impacts not just quarterly earnings, but the lives and livelihoods of everyone your organization may touch. And if it is worthy to you, know this: organizations and their boards *need you* more now than at any other time in history.

As a CEO candidate, you may already be feeling the pressures mount. NBA Hall of Famer Pau Gasol reminded Mark, during one of their coaching sessions, "Highs and lows will cycle through your demanding days, but lasting fulfillment comes only when you anchor yourself in a mission worthy of the burdens you will bear." As you prepare to lead at the crossroads, Gasol asks you not just whether you can handle the role, but whether you are *called* to it—with the depth of commitment and conviction that true leadership demands.

That's the opportunity ahead of you. The bridge you must convince the board you can build depends on earning the confidence of seven distinct stakeholder groups. Now that you've read about what that takes, it's time to assess your own readiness honestly and surround yourself with people committed to your collective success. Understand what the board fears. Anticipate what investors demand. Honor what employees value. Energize your customers. Align with your assessors. And manage your growing visibility with a level of self-awareness and narrative control you've likely never needed before.

. . .

As we come to the end of your crash course on what it takes to get the job, we have one more task for you: *reflect*. Take some time away from imagining the issues surrounding your potential ascent. Stop for a moment going over again your understanding of the company culture and your connection with customers. Detach and reflect on three key questions.:

Where do you come from?

Who do you serve?

What lights your sky?

Where Do You Come From?

What anchors you? What foundational story grounds you in your values, from which you can connect to the mission you hope to lead? The board is not just hiring a strategist; it's hiring a steward of trust, a symbol, a very human story. As Sarah Hirshland witnessed the collapse of the US Olympic team during its hardest moment in its history, it shook her soul. It erased all doubt for her as a CEO candidate and elevated her commitment to change what happened to an institution she admired, anchoring her candidacy firmly to her roots.

Anyone interviewing Hirshland could see why she won that role. Early in her life, she saw the good that sports can do for individuals and communities. With that background, she dug deep to represent a humiliated institution with the cameras broadcasting her every move. Forgive the melodrama, but that is the kind of executive that the board wants to lead the next chapter of your organization.

Adversity is not your enemy—it is your architect

As a CEO candidate striving to convince your boss and the board that you feel the conviction to lead, one of the best ways to sharpen your story is by studying leaders who built enduring organizations through wave after wave of setbacks and the hazing of critics. That's what Mark did in his research and book, *Success Built to Last: Creating a Life That Matters*. Seeking to identify the traits that supported careers lasting two decades or more, Mark conducted face-to-face interviews with two hundred world leaders, from self-made billionaires to long-serving CEOs, sovereign leaders to Nobel laureates, Oscar and Emmy winners, and gold medalists who returned to more than one Olympic Games. No one-hit wonders, only those whose impact was repeated time and again.

In addition to live conversations, Mark and his research partners—Jerry Wind at Wharton, Howard Moskowitz of Harvard, *New York Times* bestselling author Bonita Thompson of the University of Pennsylvania, and *Built to Last* coauthor Jerry Porras at the Stanford Graduate School of Business—conducted a unique global conjoint analysis with Wharton to understand what separates leaders who win the ultramarathons of their field or industry from those who do not.

What they discovered is that enduring success is anchored by convictions forged through adversity as much—or even more—than through achievement. Enduring leaders "turn their wounds into wisdom," as we wrote in *Success Built to Last*. The greatest, most lasting rewards for leaders occur when they align three distinct dimensions of their talent. In the original study, these dimensions were described as meaning, thought, action. But after twenty years of applied leadership science and coaching real-world transitions, we have reframed them—more precisely and usefully—as purpose, passion, performance. The three Ps are often mistaken in the leadership literature as interchangeable—widely misunderstood as synonymous—when, in fact, each conceals a missing link for aspiring leaders: a *signature force* as unique as your fingerprint:

> *Purpose.* A cause or mission to which you are publicly committed that energizes you
>
> *Passion.* A personal private pursuit for which you're incessantly curious that excites you
>
> *Performance.* An obsession with excellence and a drive to prove yourself competitively

Put all three together into one objective and you can run through walls. These signature forces drive the leadership behaviors that successful leaders ultimately master to create success that's built to last. The problem is that talented high achievers rarely suffer from a scarcity of opportunities; instead, they face an overabundance. The true challenge for elite executives is finding the signal through all the noise; it's not about finding meaning but rather choosing the most meaningful next pursuit that will sustain you.

As a CEO candidate, to go from good to great in your next role demands the discipline to sift through myriad worthy options—those that ignite your deepest curiosity or heal prior wounds—so you can surface the insights needed to identify the path that maximizes both external impact and internal fulfillment for you. To support this discernment process, we created a tool designed over the past twenty years to help high achievers better curate and align purpose, passion, and performance into one unified objective to better define what's next for you. It's called STAR: the Strategic Transition Alignment and Readiness test for chief executives. Leaders who unlock their intrinsic and extrinsic motivations find the strength and the endurance to create impact that lasts.

A great example is first-time chief executive Srikanth Velamakanni, cofounder of Fractal Analytics. Raised by a father who believed "all businessmen are corrupt," Velamakanni had long been discouraged from entering the business world, until an encounter with Infosys cofounder N. R. Narayana Murthy in 1997 convinced him that entrepreneurship could be a "force for integrity."[16] That conversation crystallized his purpose: to become an advocate for positive impact through business, rooted in his passion for math, having earned distinction as a National Talent Search Examination scholar and representing India at the International Mathematics Olympiad. Passion, we learned, is what you would secretly do for free—that signature force where you're absorbed, losing all track of time—something that captivates you completely. Velamakanni is also a voracious reader who devours four books a week across a wide range of disciplines, and is particularly passionate about political science, channeling his lifelong curiosity about how leadership and power shape the world.

The third pillar in this triad of signature forces is performance—the competitive spirit that draws you toward your next achievement. Every leader is drawn by a special pull—a purpose that calls you, a passion that captivates you, and a push—an athletic drive that demands your best. Velamakanni combined all three when, inspired by this vision, he left a secure banking job at age twenty-five to cofound Fractal with his classmate Pranay Agrawal at the Indian Institute of Management Ahmedabad.

When Fractal launched in 2000, it became a pioneer in a world that was just beginning to buzz about how data analytics could create greater efficiency, delivering service smarter, better, faster. The name *Fractal* itself is drawn from a scientific principle describing complex patterns that recur at every scale, reflecting Velamakanni's enduring love for math and his belief that elegant structures—whether in nature, business, or technology—could create outsized impact. But then the dot-com crash hit, funding dried up, and the fledgling startup teetered on collapse. "I used to sleep in the office," Velamakanni recalled, grinding through nineteen-hour days in a cramped one-room space to keep the dream alive. The two entrepreneurs doubled down, convinced that their sense of purpose, passion, and performance in building its capacity to deliver great data science, robust analytics, machine learning, and large language models would make a difference in the world and would be worth the investment—all of which have been contributing precursors to the AI revolution.

Over the next twenty-five years, as complexity intensified, Velamakanni, Agrawal, and their growing band of Fractalites transformed that vision into large-scale AI, engineering, and design solutions that forged partnerships with industry leaders like Microsoft, Google, C3.ai, and Amazon. Mark has served as executive coach, investor, and mentor to Fractal for many years. Across every season of growth and challenge, he observed how Velamakanni and Agrawal embraced their fears and failures, harvesting their lessons and anchoring themselves in humility, resilience, and a simple personal credo: "Never let ego drive decisions."

Fractal's journey is a reminder for you as a CEO candidate: the crucibles that test and reaffirm your loyalty to the mission are exactly what will convince a board you are ready to lead the future. Today's boards are looking for CEO candidates whose hard-won accomplishments—and the setbacks that tempered them—prove they have the stamina, wisdom, and emotional clarity to lead at the next level. They know that great future CEOs are not forged in ease but defined by challenge. Indeed, board members are looking for a striking rise in energy and presence in CEO candidates—even those who are otherwise measured or introverted—when they speak about the heart of the mission they're pursuing. That surge of conviction is one dimension of what management thinker Jim Collins calls *level 5 leadership*: quiet resolve fused with an unshakable sense of purpose and a commitment to empower others to serve.

Mark and Jim witnessed this vividly in CEO David Kohler during a leadership meeting at the headquarters in Kohler, Wisconsin. Known for his rigorous, evidence-based approach and operational discipline, Kohler visibly lights up when engaging employees around their shared mission—not only to create and manufacture stunningly beautiful, even fashion-forward products, but more importantly, to promote new levels of health and well-being for millions. When Mark interviewed his board and team, it was obvious how much they value and feel at a visceral level how this deeper purpose draws out his passion and fuels a sense of loyalty across an organization led by the Kohler family for generations.

Jesper Nordengaard, CEO of Dechra Pharmaceuticals, embodies the same principle. After a successful career culminating in his role as president of Colgate-Palmolive, Jesper now speaks with not only disciplined focus—for which he is legendary—but infectious joy and excitement about developing medical solutions for the animals that millions of people depend on. This is what boards are seeking in CEO candidates, regardless of your background or personality. When asked about your expertise and the mission that drives you, they're looking for you to come alive—for even the most reserved technical leaders to become unexpectedly magnetic.

As we described in *Success Built to Last*, the cause itself carries charisma. Purpose ignites a quiet leader in a way that is deeply compelling. In a volatile and fast-changing market, companies must constantly evolve—but boards are no longer satisfied with managers of transformation. They want leaders of causes. Of movements. Of missions that inspire teams, attract talent, and remind everyone why the work matters.

Who Do You Serve?

You must show the board and your team that you want this role because you want to serve—and you know how. "Your insights, wisdom, and strength are going to come from people at all levels," Hirshland added. You will inspire board members when you make it obvious that "you want to build relationships at all levels, keeping yourself grounded in the reality of having a network of peers, customers, and friends—and sometimes those who challenge you the most are the most valuable to have in your circle. If you think about those relationships and how you can help them, it will help you tenfold." You can't view the role of the CEO as something you want only for yourself. Those making the choice will have little patience for a candidate who clearly only wants the job for its power and perks, for themselves.

"Whatever success you may have is just the residue of you making others successful—your team, your employees, your customers, your business partners, or your investors," said former chair and CEO Mark Turner, WSFS Financial, during our CEO Academy in New York.

Former CEO Maggie Wilderotter recalls receiving a stern reminder years ago from her boss that she needed to demonstrate extra clarity about who "I was hired to serve and develop the skills to do that better." She said he was pushing her far beyond her comfort zone to expand the company's operations centers. Wilderotter told Mark in his CEO Summit interview that she initially resisted, explaining that she had no experience doing that kind of work. Her boss responded, "You don't know anything about marketing either!" She accepted the criticism as a challenge—realizing that her boss was calling her to serve in a bigger way. In fact, it was an invitation to leap toward the breadth of experience she would need to serve as the future CEO.

Wilderotter rose to the occasion, serving as chief executive of Frontier Communications, where she transformed a $1 billion regional telephone company into a national provider with revenues of $10 billion. Today, she's chair of DocuSign and has served on more *Fortune* 500 boards than any other chief executive in history. When her boss and the board were looking for her to stretch herself to become chief executive, they did not expect perfection; they were looking for someone who had embraced discomfort, learned to lead in unfamiliar terrain, and built the emotional and strategic courage required to guide the organization at its most pivotal moment.

Curtis Martin, the Hall of Fame running back who overcame poverty, injury, and personal loss to become one of the NFL's greatest players, said, "You will never achieve your ultimate purpose inside your comfort zone." He's now building one of America's most influential sports entertainment and development investment firms, where Mark is a coach and adviser. In high-stakes moments—when the future of an organization or a movement hangs in the balance—Martin says your ability to prioritize becomes your true capacity to lead: "Your priority determines your capacity."

As a CEO candidate, Eric Kessenich realized his capacity to have impact would be calibrated by the level of engagement of his team when he became chief executive. He deeply valued U.S. Venture's culture and was intentional in every signal he sent, careful not to inadvertently shift the swiftly growing company toward a hierarchical structure that, in his words, would be "going counter to what we want to do." Instead, he guided the organization toward a flatter, more cohesive design—energizing his team, boss, and board with that vision. "Where we sit is important," he reflected. "As a CEO, I would be moving into an office for the first time. As the president of our energy business for ten years, I didn't have walls. I wanted to sit with my people." This wasn't symbolic—it was deliberate. His purpose was to reinforce a high-performance culture grounded in transparency and fast, free-flowing information sharing. He understood that accountability and empowerment go hand in hand, and that even subtle decisions—like office layout—must align with and promote the desired culture. "I think that leadership style resonated. The feedback I got during my assessment was that people found me easy to talk with. That kind of communication style resonated with a lot of people and let them know the kind of culture we were creating."

Hubert Joly, former Best Buy chief executive, reminds CEO candidates that your emotional state defines how your people will respond. Whether you're happy or sad, how you show up and manage your mood will be felt by all. He urges: "Be the thermostat, not the thermometer."[17] In turbulent environments, boards want to see you as a chief executive who is neither impulsive nor temperamental, who has the discipline to set the temperature rather than react. As a CEO candidate, it's your responsibility to demonstrate emotional stability, calibrating urgency and optimism regardless of external mayhem.

What Lights Your Sky?

The reality is that if the job of chief executive doesn't bring you joy, it will crush you. The weight is too much to carry without a North Star. As a CEO candidate, think about what gives you oxygen as you make the climb. What ignites your energy or meaning-driven purpose empowers you to thrive despite criticism, pressure, and setbacks in this new role. At the Olympics, Hirshland didn't inherit a job; she had no entitlement. She ran into a burning building because it mattered deeply to her. She didn't just survive the firestorm; she charged into it, carried by conviction that was stronger than the chaos around her, determined not merely to endure but to rebuild, fueled by a joyful cause that called her forward. It made her happy.

The question is, what makes *you* happy?

As the next CEO, you will set the tone. Hopefully, that includes a sense of humor. Legendary investor Warren Buffett frequently shares unforgettable advice about following your passion in your work, because your career is a marathon that must be energized and lifted by the joy of savoring the journey—with delight and wit. At one session that Mark attended at the University of Florida business school, Buffett recalled a conversation he had with a twenty-eight-year-old Harvard MBA who planned to accept a consulting job solely to enhance his résumé, despite lacking true interest in the role. Buffett advised against this shortsighted approach, as he cautions anyone who refuses to commit to doing what they love. He scolded the student with a smile: "Isn't that a little like saving up sex for your old age? There comes a time when you ought to start doing what you want." Buffett's point is cute, but powerful: abandoning passion in pursuit of status undermines your long-term strategy.

"How do I go back to a place where I'm finding incredible joy in the work, but I'm also inspiring that joy in others, and making sure that everybody feels *permission to be happy* and joyful?" Hirshland asked herself this question as she considered moves in her career, and so should you. If you don't find light and joy in the business, in the role, it will be incredibly difficult to succeed. It's just too hard a job to do in darkness.

That mindset—leading with conviction and joy, even in the hardest moments—didn't go unnoticed. Not only did the US Olympic team achieve its greatest performance in history on her watch, Hirshland was named 2025 Sports Executive of the Year by *Sports Business Journal*, only the second time in Olympic history. For her, the award wasn't about individual accolades; it was a signal that a once-broken institution was again leading the world. "It feels like we're back at the big kids' table," she said, acknowledging both how far the movement had come—and how far it still had to go. Her recognition affirmed that joy and mission are essential to high performance.

Ask yourself, why are you doing this? Do you *love* this business? Can you take some delight in the adventure? "Sometimes it's difficult to do that for ourselves, let alone lead an organization or a team of people to a place that says, '*This is fun!* It's OK for us to have fun at work. We're here to enjoy ourselves.'" Hirshland insists. "But we've got to find that space." Happiness is a discipline, an intention you set for everyone as a leader.

Reflect on these three questions, and when, as a candidate to become chief executive, you finally believe your answers tell you it's time, then you just might be CEO ready.

Appendix A

CEO Candidate Assessments That You Can Anticipate

What follows is a list of nine commonly used diagnostic tools and approaches designed to gauge a wide range of candidate competencies, personality traits, leadership styles, and strategic thinking capabilities that are used at every level, and a few ideas to prepare yourself for each.

- *Cultural fit analysis.* These assessments measure how well a candidate's values, behaviors, and leadership style align with the company's culture. Evaluators may explore the candidate's adaptability, communication style, and relationship building with stakeholders. Prepare by actively seeking feedback from trusted colleagues or mentors on how they perceive your leadership style. Make sure your feedback assessments are up to date and you've honestly evaluated how you are seen by others. Also look at factors that impact culture in your organization's engagement survey data regarding your department, function, or division of your company. Consider participating in a more visible way in cross-functional projects to broaden your cultural adaptability, strengthen your relationships, and expand perceptions about your level of engagement with the entire enterprise as you would if you were to become CEO.

- *Competency assessments.* These assessments are designed to evaluate specific skills and behaviors critical for success in a CEO role. They often cover areas such as strategic thinking, financial acumen, leadership, and decision-making. Prepare by conducting a self-assessment to identify gaps in your skill set and seek targeted development opportunities, such as executive education programs or mentorship in areas like strategic planning or financial management. Engage in decision-making scenarios that stretch your abilities to think critically and lead effectively under pressure. Whatever roles that you have not had—that your CEO has had—should be key areas where you seek opportunities. You can also ask your board about these dimensions as you interact with them.

- *360-degree feedback assessments.* This process gathers feedback from a wide range of stakeholders, including peers, subordinates, and board members—likely you've had many over the years. The feedback is confidential at some companies and for your use only, but not at others where it might be shared with HR, your boss, and the board. It is intended to provide deeper insights into your leadership effectiveness, teamwork, management skills, and how any executive is perceived by others within the organization. Prepare by proactively seeking informal feedback from colleagues at various levels to identify blind spots and areas for improvement. Regularly request feedback after key projects or interactions and demonstrate your willingness to act on it, showcasing your commitment to growth and collaboration.

- *In-depth behavioral interviews.* Experts from executive search firms and independent assessment firms conduct thorough interviews to explore a candidate's past experiences, leadership challenges they've faced, their problem-solving approach, and how they have driven growth or transformation in previous roles. These interviews are often structured to elicit examples of strategic thinking, resilience, and adaptability. Prepare by reviewing your professional milestones and creating a portfolio of STAR (situation, task, action, result) examples that highlight your leadership successes. Practice articulating these stories clearly and succinctly, focusing on outcomes and the skills demonstrated. Mock interviews with a trusted adviser or coach can also help refine your delivery and boost confidence.

- *Case studies and simulations.* Candidates may be asked by the assessors and board to work through business case studies or participate in simulation exercises designed to replicate real-world business challenges. These exercises assess how a candidate thinks through difficult challenges, their problem-solving skills, and their ability to navigate complex issues. Prepare by studying real-world business case studies from reputable sources, such as *Harvard Business Review* or McKinsey reports. Practice analyzing scenarios under time constraints, focusing on identifying key issues, weighing options, and proposing actionable solutions. Consider participating in workshops or business strategy games to sharpen your decision-making and strategic thinking in dynamic environments.

- *Leadership assessment centers.* Some firms send candidates to assessment centers where they participate in a series of exercises simulating the conditions of a CEO's role. Activities can include strategic planning exercises, group discussions, role-play scenarios, and presentations. These centers are designed to observe candidates in situations that mimic the complexities and pressures of leadership at the highest level. Prepare by practicing high-pressure scenarios, such as presenting to senior stakeholders or leading discussions with cross-functional teams. Seek opportunities to role-play with mentors or peers to refine your strategic planning and decision-making skills. Additionally, stay informed on industry trends and develop a clear, articulate leadership philosophy that you can confidently communicate in various settings.

- *Reference and background checks.* Comprehensive reference checks with former colleagues, subordinates, and other industry contacts provide additional insights into a candidate's leadership style, achievements, and areas for development. Can you obtain meaningful references? Often internal candidates fail to realize that being considered for a promotion into an internal role is like searching for a job outside the company when it comes to having good references from your stakeholders. Prepare by reactivating and maintaining strong, positive relationships with former colleagues and supervisors. Reach out to potential references ahead of time to ensure they feel informed about your recent accomplishments and career trajectory. Providing them with context about the role you're pursuing can help them highlight the most relevant aspects of your experience.

- *Specific diagnostic tools.* Each assessment firm may have proprietary tools developed based on its research and experience in executive searches. For instance, Korn Ferry uses the Leadership Architect and the Four Dimensions of Leadership and Talent framework to assess candidates, while Egon Zehnder employs its Competency and Potential Assessment framework. In appendix B we have outlined some specific methodologies and tools used by the leading firms like Spencer Stuart, Korn Ferry, and Egon Zehnder. Review any publicly available materials or case studies related to these frameworks and align your self-reflection or preparation exercises with the core principles of the company doing your assessment. Consulting with professionals who have experienced similar assessments can also provide valuable insights.

- *Psychometric testing.* These tests measure a candidate's personality traits, cognitive abilities, and emotional intelligence. Tools like the Hogan Assessment, Myers-Briggs Type Indicator (MBTI), and the Occupational Personality Questionnaire (OPQ) are popular in executive searches to understand how a candidate's personality might influence their leadership style and effectiveness. Prepare by familiarizing yourself with these tools and reflecting on past experiences where your personality traits influenced your leadership outcomes. We discuss a few of them specifically in appendix B. Consider engaging with a coach or psychologist to better understand your strengths and areas for growth, and practice mindfulness techniques to enhance your emotional intelligence.

Appendix B

Assessment Frameworks

Our clients have experienced twenty-three different psychometric, behavioral, and business tests that cover all of the frameworks discussed in appendix A. They fall across four categories of executive leadership assessment:

1. Leadership style and effectiveness
2. Personality and behavioral insights
3. Conflict and change management
4. Team dynamics and collaboration

Let's take a quick look at how each one serves a different purpose and is based on a unique set of psychological theories. At the end of appendix C, we will give you a punch list of practices that you can use to optimize your prospects as a candidate.

1. Leadership Style and Effectiveness

HOGAN DEVELOPMENT SURVEY (HDS). This tool is the gold standard that has stood the test of time in large cohorts of executives globally. Among other insights, it identifies "dark-side" personality traits that emerge under stress and can derail careers, such as being excitable, skeptical, cautious, reserved, mischievous, bold, and leisurely. By understanding these risks, leaders can proactively mitigate behaviors that impact their effectiveness. Created by Dr. Robert Hogan in 1997, the tool is based on decades of pioneering research into personality and workplace behaviors.

EMOTIONAL INTELLIGENCE (EQ-I 2.0). This tool measures emotional intelligence across domains like self-awareness, interpersonal skills, and decision-making. It evaluates competencies such as emotional self-regulation, empathy, adaptability, and stress management to enhance leadership effectiveness and resilience. Developed by Reuven Bar-On in 1997, the EQ-i was one of the first scientifically validated, emotional intelligence assessments.

LEADERSHIP PRACTICES INVENTORY (LPI). The LPI evaluates leadership behaviors based on James Kouzes and Barry Posner's "Five Practices of Exemplary Leadership." These practices include modeling the way, inspiring a shared vision, challenging the process, enabling others to act, and encouraging the heart, offering clear strategies for leadership growth. Created by Kouzes and Posner in 1987, it is widely used for leadership development.

LEADERSHIP ASSESSMENT SUITE (CCL). The Leadership Assessment Suite includes tools like Benchmarks 360 and Skillscope, which assess leadership traits such as strategic vision, communication, self-awareness, resilience, leading change, influence, teamwork, results orientation, and emotional intelligence. It provides a comprehensive view of leadership effectiveness. Developed by the Center for Creative Leadership (CCL) in the late 1980s, these tools have been refined over decades of leadership research.

GLOBAL LEADERSHIP ASSESSMENT (GLA). The GLA evaluates competencies essential for a global context, including cultural agility, strategic thinking, stakeholder management, decision-making, and adaptability. It helps leaders navigate the complexities of diverse and international teams. Developed by the Center for Creative Leadership in the early 2000s, it focuses on preparing leaders for global challenges.

MERCER LEADERSHIP ASSESSMENT. The Mercer Leadership Assessment evaluates leadership potential across dimensions like strategic vision, operational focus, change management, collaboration, innovation, and decision-making. It helps organizations identify high-potential leaders and align them with critical roles. Developed by Mercer, a global consulting firm, in the early 2000s, it is grounded in extensive talent research.

CALIPER PROFILE. The Caliper Profile assesses traits such as assertiveness, empathy, resilience, decision-making, problem-solving, and time management. It links these traits to leadership potential and provides actionable insights for development, succession planning, and role alignment. Created by Herb Greenberg in 1961, the Caliper Profile is one of the longest-standing assessments used in business.

2. Personality and Behavioral Insights

MYERS-BRIGGS TYPE INDICATOR (MBTI). The MBTI categorizes individuals into sixteen personality types based on preferences like extraversion/introversion, sensing/intuition, thinking/feeling, and judging/perceiving. It helps individuals understand communication styles, decision-making tendencies, and areas for personal growth. Developed by Isabel Briggs Myers and Katharine Cook Briggs in 1943, it is based on Carl Jung's psychological type theories. While widely used, the MBTI is debated among experts. The American Psychological Association notes it lacks predictive validity and test-retest reliability—people often get different results, and it doesn't reliably predict job performance or leadership success.

FIVE-FACTOR MODEL-BASED PERSONALITY TEST (FFM). The FFM assesses personality dimensions (OCEAN: openness, conscientiousness, extraversion, agreeableness, neuroticism), providing a detailed understanding of traits such as curiosity, self-discipline, sociability, cooperation, and emotional stability. This model was first conceptualized by Lewis Goldberg in 1981 and has been widely adopted for personality research.

16 PERSONALITY FACTORS (16PF). This test evaluates sixteen traits, including warmth, reasoning, emotional stability, dominance, liveliness, and openness to change. It provides a nuanced view of personality to guide recruitment, leadership development, and team alignment. Created by Dr. Raymond Cattell in 1949, the 16PF is a cornerstone of modern personality assessments.

SHL OCCUPATIONAL PERSONALITY QUESTIONNAIRE (OPQ). The OPQ assesses thirty-two work-related traits across categories like relationships, thinking style, and emotions. Traits such as adaptability, creativity, sociability, and attention to detail are linked to job performance and organizational fit. Developed by SHL in 1984, it is widely used for recruitment and talent management.

BIG FIVE INVENTORY (BFI). The BFI measures the Big Five personality traits (OCEAN) and their sub-dimensions, such as assertiveness under extraversion and anxiety under neuroticism. It provides a quick snapshot of personality influences on teamwork and leadership. Introduced by Oliver P. John and Sanjay Srivastava in 1991, it is a widely used version of the five-factor model.

THE ENNEAGRAM. The Enneagram categorizes individuals into nine types, focusing on motivations, fears, and behaviors. Types include the reformer (principled), helper (caring), achiever (goal-oriented), and others, fostering self-awareness and team harmony. While the symbol and system have ancient roots—possibly linked to early mysticism, sacred geometry, and even astrology—the Enneagram's contemporary psychological model was developed in the 1970s by Oscar Ichazo and further refined by psychiatrist Claudio Naranjo. Despite its widespread use in coaching and personal development, the Enneagram—like the MBTI and many other popular tools—faces skepticism from the American Psychological Association and academic psychologists due to its lack of empirical validation and standardized measurement. In their opinion, it's more of a self-reflective framework than a scientifically grounded leadership assessment.

THE BIRKMAN METHOD. This tool evaluates interests, usual behaviors, needs, and stress responses, identifying traits like problem-solving, adaptability, communication style, and stress tolerance. It aligns strengths with organizational needs while improving team dynamics and collaboration. Developed by Dr. Roger Birkman in 1951, it has been refined to address modern organizational challenges.

FIRSTMIND BEHAVIORAL ASSESSMENT. FirstMind categorizes individuals using a framework of thirty-four talents and ten core dimensions based on cognitive, emotional, and behavioral patterns. It draws from over twenty-five years of neuroscience and positive psychology research to identify how people think, feel, and act across various contexts. It is designed to support talent alignment, increase job satisfaction, and enhance team performance.

3. Conflict and Change Management

THOMAS-KILMANN CONFLICT MODE INSTRUMENT (TKI). The TKI identifies five conflict-handling modes: competing, collaborating, compromising, avoiding, and accommodating. Each mode is suited to specific situations, encouraging flexibility and productive conflict resolution. Developed by Kenneth Thomas and Ralph Kilmann in 1974, it is rooted in conflict management research.

CHANGE STYLE INDICATOR (CSI). The CSI categorizes individuals as conservers (preferring stability), pragmatists (balancing change and tradition), or originators (embracing innovation). It highlights adaptability and helps teams manage diverse reactions to transformation. Created by Discovery Learning, Inc., in the 2000s, it focuses on effective change management.

SITUATIONAL JUDGMENT TESTS (SJTS). SJTs assess decision-making, teamwork, and adaptability through realistic scenarios. They measure traits like judgment, prioritization, problem-solving, and collaboration under pressure. Originating in the early 2000s from psychological research, SJTs are widely used for practical skills evaluation.

CULTURAL INTELLIGENCE (CQ) ASSESSMENT. The CQ Assessment evaluates cultural adaptability, cross-cultural communication, and strategic thinking. It includes cognitive, motivational, and behavioral aspects to prepare leaders for global and diverse work environments. Developed by Soon Ang and Linn Van Dyne in 2003, it is a key tool for global leadership.

4. Team Dynamics and Collaboration

FIVE DYSFUNCTIONS OF A TEAM ASSESSMENT (LENCIONI'S TABLE GROUP). This assessment identifies dysfunctions like lack of trust, fear of conflict, and inattention to results. By addressing traits like openness, accountability, and results orientation, it fosters team alignment and high performance. Developed by Patrick Lencioni in 2002, it is based on his bestselling book.

WORKING GENIUS (LENCIONI'S TABLE GROUP). The Working Genius evaluates six natural talents: wonder, invention, discernment, galvanizing, enablement, and tenacity. It helps teams optimize collaboration by aligning roles with individual strengths. Created by Patrick Lencioni in 2020, it builds on his team development expertise.

GALLUP CLIFTONSTRENGTHS (STRENGTHSFINDER). This tool identifies top strengths across domains like strategic thinking, execution, relationship building, and influencing. It helps individuals focus on their natural talents to improve engagement and team effectiveness. Developed by Donald Clifton in 1999, it is rooted in positive psychology, which emphasizes human potential, strengths, and well-being rather than deficits.

DISC PERSONALITY ASSESSMENT. The DISC evaluates behavioral tendencies in dominance, influence, steadiness, and conscientiousness. It enhances team collaboration by understanding communication preferences and conflict management styles. Based on Carl Jung's theories—a Swiss psychiatrist and pioneer of analytical psychology—it was developed by William Moulton Marston, an American psychologist and creator of the first lie detector test, in 1928.

MOTIVATIONAL APPRAISAL OF PERSONAL POTENTIAL (MAPP). The MAPP assesses intrinsic motivators, such as achievement, independence, and service orientation. It helps align roles with personal drivers, improving job satisfaction and career planning. Created by Assessment.com in 1995, it is focused on career alignment.

VALUES IN ACTION (VIA) SURVEY OF CHARACTER STRENGTHS. This tool identifies core virtues like wisdom, courage, humanity, and justice. By leveraging strengths such as creativity or perseverance, it promotes well-being and leadership growth. Developed in 2004 by Martin Seligman, the founder of positive psychology, and Christopher Peterson, a renowned character strengths researcher, it is a cornerstone of positive psychology.

Appendix C

Recruiting Firm Assessments

Let's review four assessment processes developed by search firms that recruit world-class CEOs, with readiness succession plans at Egon Zehnder, Spencer Stuart, and Korn Ferry, along with the framework from independent assessor ghSMART. We've presented these in broad terms to get a general sense of their approach as you think about your preparation as a CEO candidate. These are our high-level summaries, not theirs, as they do not publish all the details of their proprietary data and the breadth and depth of their research would fill volumes and are changing continuously. We are making very broad generalizations without any preferences or representations about the merits of any of them, based on our experiences with more than a hundred clients who have experienced their processes and more than three hundred various reports that have resulted from those processes, so that you can consider the subtle differences. Our goal here is to help you as a CEO candidate get a sense of the breadth of possibilities in your assessment. Whatever search firm or assessment company your company selects, all of them add incredible value for your leadership development as a senior executive, regardless of your progress and candidacy as CEO.

Egon Zehnder's Executive Assessment Framework

Egon Zehnder's executive assessment framework is renowned for its comprehensive and multidimensional approach to evaluating *leadership potential*. The framework largely focuses on three distinct aspects: *performance*, *readiness*, and *potential*. These pillars guide the assessment process and provide a robust understanding of an executive candidate's suitability for high-level roles.

- *Performance: analyzing past achievements.* Performance, the first pillar, delves into a candidate's past achievements, exploring their career trajectory, their leadership experiences, and the value they have delivered in previous roles. By analyzing functional leadership and accomplishments, the assessment aims to build a clear picture of the candidate's historical impact.

- *Readiness: alignment with organizational needs.* This retrospective analysis is complemented by an evaluation of readiness—the second pillar—which focuses on the present alignment between the candidate and the organization. Readiness examines how well the candidate's leadership style, strategic orientation, and ability to collaborate fit with the company's culture and goals.

- *Potential: assessing future growth.* Finally, potential forms the third pillar, looking forward to assessing key traits such as curiosity, determination, insight, and engagement. These qualities serve as predictors of the candidate's ability to grow and adapt to future challenges.

CORE DIMENSIONS EVALUATED. Central to Egon Zehnder's framework is the evaluation of core dimensions. These include *cultural fit*, which assesses the congruence between the candidate's values and the organization's culture; *identity*, which examines how the candidate's self-perception aligns with the responsibilities of a CEO; and *market benchmark*, which evaluates the candidate's standing relative to industry standards and expectations. By integrating these dimensions, the framework ensures a holistic assessment of leadership potential.

Recruiting Firm Assessments

ASSESSMENT TOOLS AND METHODOLOGIES. Egon Zehnder employs a variety of tools and methodologies to carry out these assessments.

- *Competency evaluation* measures eight critical leadership competencies. These range from strategic orientation and results orientation to change leadership and inclusiveness. Candidates are evaluated on a developmental scale that spans from basic management capabilities to transformational leadership.

- *Psychometric assessments*, such as the 16PF (16 Personality Factors) and the HDS (Hogan Development Survey), are employed to gain deeper insights into personality traits and potential derailers under stress.

- *360-degree referencing* complements these tools by gathering feedback from peers, subordinates, and senior leaders, providing a rounded perspective on the candidate's leadership capabilities.

- *Benchmarking* against both internal standards and external industry leaders ensures that the assessment is rigorous and contextually relevant.

THE TAILORED ASSESSMENT PROCESS. The tailored assessment process unfolds in several stages.

- *Pre-assessment* is when the candidate's career trajectory and alignment with the company's strategy are reviewed.

- *Interviews and psychometric evaluations* form the next stage, providing an in-depth look at the candidate's competencies and personality traits.

- *Reference checks* involve consultations with at least six cross-functional stakeholders, adding a layer of validation to the findings.

- *Feedback and development planning* concludes the process, synthesizing insights into actionable recommendations that align with the candidate's growth and the organization's needs.

DEVELOPMENT INSIGHTS. Development insights are a key outcome of Egon Zehnder's assessments. These insights focus on enhancing strategic foresight, fostering cultural alignment, and improving adaptability.

HOLISTIC GROWTH METHODOLOGY. The methodology for development combines experience, exposure, and education, creating a holistic growth approach. For organizations, the assessments provide a window into the candidate's vision for addressing challenges, their ability to lead transformational change, and their alignment with leadership goals.

BENEFITS FOR CANDIDATES. For the candidates, the process reinforces their visibility and credibility as senior leaders, enhances self-awareness, and prepares them for the transition to high-stakes roles.

PREPARING FOR AN EGON ZEHNDER ASSESSMENT. In our opinion, preparation for an Egon Zehnder assessment, particularly for internal CEO candidates, requires a proactive and strategic approach.

- *Reflect on leadership contributions.* Candidates should begin by reflecting on their leadership contributions. This involves conducting a thorough self-assessment of achievements and challenges, focusing on experience in team-building, decision-making, and adaptability. Seeking feedback from peers and mentors can validate these reflections and help identify areas for improvement.

- *Engage with key stakeholders.* Engaging with key stakeholders is another crucial step. Building strong relationships with leadership and board members provides insights into governance dynamics and strategic priorities. These interactions allow candidates to demonstrate their ability to collaborate and align with the company's vision.

- *Analyze organizational challenges.* In addition, candidates should analyze organizational pain points and opportunities, using this understanding to craft a transformative vision that addresses critical needs and aligns with strategic objectives.

- *Communicate a strategic vision.* Communication plays a vital role in showcasing readiness for the CEO position. Candidates should practice articulating a clear and compelling strategic vision that reflects their leadership style and understanding of the organization's trajectory.
- *Exhibit CEO-ready behaviors.* Exhibiting CEO-ready behaviors in their current roles—such as composure, collaboration, and strategic foresight—further signals their preparedness for top leadership responsibilities.
- *Leverage development resources.* Leveraging development resources is also essential. Internal programs, mentors, and executive coaching can help candidates address skill gaps and prepare for the expanded scope of CEO responsibilities.
- *Align aspirations with company goals.* Finally, candidates should align their aspirations with the company's goals, clearly connecting their leadership vision with the organization's mission and long-term strategy. By demonstrating a shared commitment to success, candidates can position themselves as natural successors for the role.

Korn Ferry's Executive Assessment Framework

Korn Ferry's executive assessment framework is a structured and comprehensive approach to evaluating leadership potential. By integrating four key dimensions—competencies, traits, drivers, and experiences—the framework offers a holistic evaluation of candidates. This method is enhanced by its focus on learning agility and the identification of risk factors, ensuring a thorough understanding of a candidate's strengths and developmental areas.

COMPETENCIES: THE SKILLS FOR SUCCESS. At the heart of Korn Ferry's framework lies the evaluation of competencies, which are tailored to the specific needs of the role and organization. These competencies encompass a variety of critical leadership skills. A strategic mindset enables candidates to envision future possibilities and transform them into actionable strategies. The ability to cultivate innovation is essential for developing new solutions that drive organizational success. Ensuring accountability highlights a leader's capacity to hold themselves and others responsible for commitments. Collaboration is key to building partnerships that achieve shared objectives, while driving engagement motivates teams to perform at their best.

TRAITS: CORE CHARACTERISTICS OF LEADERSHIP. Traits are the core personality characteristics that shape behaviors and influence leadership effectiveness. Composure is a crucial trait, reflecting a leader's ability to maintain calm under stress. Optimism ensures a positive outlook, even in challenging circumstances. Curiosity drives the desire to explore new challenges and identify patterns in complex issues, while adaptability reflects a leader's flexibility in dynamic environments. Together, these traits provide insight into how candidates respond to the demands of leadership roles.

DRIVERS: MOTIVATION AND CAREER ASPIRATION. Drivers reveal the motivational factors that influence a candidate's engagement and career aspirations. Achievement orientation reflects a candidate's drive to thrive on challenging goals. Collaboration indicates a preference for success achieved through group efforts, while independence emphasizes the desire for autonomy in decision-making and execution. Understanding these drivers helps organizations align candidates with roles that match their intrinsic motivations.

EXPERIENCES: THE FOUNDATION OF LEADERSHIP. A candidate's *experiences* form a critical part of Korn Ferry's assessment. Career milestones and developmental opportunities are examined for both breadth and depth. Breadth encompasses diverse roles and global exposure, while depth focuses on specialization within key areas. High-stakes roles involving ambiguity, failure risks, or significant visibility are also considered, as they demonstrate a candidate's ability to navigate complex challenges.

LEARNING AGILITY: ADAPTING TO NEW CHALLENGES. Learning agility is a cornerstone of Korn Ferry's framework, measuring a candidate's capacity to adapt to new challenges and perform effectively in dynamic environments. Five key dimensions define learning agility:

- *Mental agility.* Tackling complex problems with curiosity and creative thinking

- *People agility.* Building effective relationships, understanding diverse perspectives, and influencing others

- *Change agility.* Embracing and leading through change while taking calculated risks

- *Results agility.* Overcoming obstacles to achieve ambitious goals in unfamiliar situations

- *Situational self-awareness.* Remaining present and adaptable to evolving circumstances

RISK FACTORS: IDENTIFYING POTENTIAL PITFALLS. Korn Ferry's assessment also identifies risk factors that could derail otherwise successful leaders. These include tendencies such as avoidant behavior, inflexibility, emotional volatility, excessive ego, micromanaging, resistance to change, excessive skepticism, and opportunistic behavior. By addressing these potential pitfalls, organizations can better support leaders in mitigating risks and optimizing performance.

ASSESSMENT METHODOLOGY: A HOLISTIC APPROACH. Korn Ferry's assessment methodology integrates multiple tools to provide a comprehensive evaluation.

- *360-degree feedback.* Perspectives from peers, subordinates, and managers offer a holistic view of leadership behaviors.

- *Behavioral interviews.* These evaluate decision-making, resilience, and adaptability under stress.

- *Benchmarking.* Candidates' skills are compared against industry standards and role-specific expectations.

- *Feedback synthesis.* Insights are combined into actionable development plans tailored to the individual's growth needs.

DEVELOPMENT INSIGHTS: ENHANCING LEADERSHIP POTENTIAL. Development insights are a crucial outcome of Korn Ferry's assessments. Tailored development plans focus on three key areas:

- *Exposure.* Providing opportunities for global roles, cross-functional projects, and high-stakes leadership assignments
- *Education.* Offering focused training in strategy, governance, and leadership
- *Feedback loops.* Regular engagements with mentors or coaches to track progress and refine skills

PREPARING FOR KORN FERRY'S CEO ASSESSMENTS. In our opinion, candidates aiming to excel in Korn Ferry's CEO assessments must adopt a proactive and strategic approach.

- *Reflect on leadership contributions.* Conduct a self-assessment of achievements, team-building efforts, and adaptability
- *Engage with stakeholders.* Build relationships with leadership to align with organizational goals
- *Analyze organizational challenges.* Identify pain points and opportunities to develop a strategic vision
- *Demonstrate learning agility.* Showcase adaptability, curiosity, and innovative problem-solving in current roles
- *Mitigate risk factors.* Address tendencies such as micromanaging or avoiding accountability to ensure readiness for leadership
- *Communicate vision.* Articulate a clear, transformative strategy aligned with company objectives

CAREER BENEFITS: ADVANCING LEADERSHIP TRAJECTORIES. Korn Ferry's framework not only benefits organizations but also enhances candidates' leadership trajectories. By participating in these assessments, executives strengthen their credibility and visibility, build adaptability to complex challenges, and prepare for broader leadership roles. Exposure to tailored feedback and continuous learning opportunities ensures that candidates are well equipped to excel in high-stakes environments.

Spencer Stuart's Executive Assessment Framework

Spencer Stuart's approach to executive assessment represents a strong methodology for identifying and nurturing leadership talent. By integrating Executive Intelligence (ExI), leadership capabilities, and the Individual Style Profile, the framework offers a multidimensional evaluation of a candidate's ability to solve problems, lead effectively, and align with organizational culture. This appendix has delved into many of the core components of this framework already, showcasing how the assessment process equips organizations to identify and develop leaders who can thrive in complexity and ambiguity.

FRAMEWORK COMPONENTS. At the heart of Spencer Stuart's executive assessment are three interconnected components: Executive Intelligence (ExI), leadership capabilities, and the Individual Style Profile. Each element contributes uniquely to the creation of a comprehensive leadership profile.

Executive Intelligence (ExI). The cornerstone of Spencer Stuart's framework is its focus on ExI, an innovative real-time case study method designed to evaluate how candidates approach complex business challenges. This methodology examines not only what decisions leaders make but also how they arrive at those decisions.
The evaluation emphasizes three key dimensions:

- *Critical and conceptual thinking.* Candidates are assessed on their ability to analyze information comprehensively, apply creative problem-solving techniques, and anticipate future challenges.

- *Interpersonal and social awareness.* This dimension highlights the candidate's skill in recognizing diverse perspectives, responding adeptly to social dynamics, and achieving outcomes through empathy and influence.

- *Self-evaluation and adjustment.* Leaders are measured on their capacity to incorporate feedback, evolve their perspectives, and confidently defend well-reasoned positions when necessary.

This nuanced approach ensures that organizations gain insight into a leader's thought processes and ability to adapt to dynamic scenarios.

Leadership capabilities. Spencer Stuart identifies six core leadership capabilities that serve as benchmarks for evaluating effectiveness in executive roles. These capabilities, refined through years of research, reflect the qualities most critical to organizational success:

1. *Strategic thinking.* Leaders must envision long-term strategies that address both market opportunities and organizational challenges.
2. *Driving results.* Achieving ambitious goals and consistently improving performance are hallmarks of impactful leadership.
3. *Leading change.* Executives must align and empower teams to embrace transformation and guide them through uncertainty.
4. *Collaborating and influencing.* Building enduring partnerships across organizational boundaries is essential for fostering alignment and achieving shared goals.
5. *Building capability.* Effective leaders prioritize talent development and foster systematic growth within their teams.
6. *Personal integrity.* Modeling fairness, authenticity, and trustworthiness anchors the credibility of leadership decisions.

By focusing on these areas, Spencer Stuart's framework ensures that leadership assessments are deeply aligned with an organization's strategic and cultural needs.

Individual Style Profile. Understanding a leader's personal style is crucial for determining their alignment with organizational culture.

The Individual Style Profile measures personality traits, values, and interpersonal tendencies, offering a lens into how candidates naturally operate and engage with others.

This profile categorizes individuals into eight distinct sociocultural styles:

1. *Caring.* Collaborative and relationship-focused

2. *Purpose.* Visionary and driven by altruistic goals

3. *Enjoyment.* Positive, spontaneous, and enthusiastic

4. *Results.* Goal-oriented and ambitious

5. *Learning.* Curious and adaptable, embracing challenges

6. *Order.* Structured, organized, and detail-oriented

7. *Authority.* Decisive and assertive

8. *Safety.* Risk-averse and cautious

These styles provide a nuanced understanding of how leaders navigate interpersonal dynamics and align their personal values with the organization's mission.

ASSESSMENT METHODOLOGY. Spencer Stuart's assessment process combines multiple methodologies to deliver a holistic evaluation. The process includes:

- *Multipart interviews.* These in-depth interviews explore candidates' career reflections, motivations, and key leadership moments. Real-time case studies test executive decision-making skills under pressure.

- *360-degree feedback.* Gathering insights from peers, subordinates, and senior leaders provides a comprehensive view of leadership behaviors and their impact.

- *Individual style assessment.* Online surveys capture personal drives, strengths, and self-perceptions, offering valuable context for development.

DEVELOPMENT INSIGHTS. A hallmark of Spencer Stuart's framework is its emphasis on actionable development insights. Assessments not only identify strengths but also uncover areas for growth. Key takeaways include:

- *Strengths.* Highlighting core capabilities, interpersonal dynamics, and problem-solving tendencies provides a foundation for leveraging existing leadership skills.
- *Opportunities.* Pinpointing growth areas, such as balancing sociocultural styles or enhancing strategic communication, ensures that leaders continue to evolve.
- *Personalized development plans.* These plans translate assessment findings into measurable, actionable goals that guide leadership growth and success.

HOW TO PREPARE FOR SPENCER STUART'S ASSESSMENT. In our opinion, preparation is critical for candidates aiming to excel in Spencer Stuart's rigorous evaluation process. Prospective leaders can take several steps to ensure they present their best selves:

1. *Reflect on leadership stories.* Reviewing critical career events that demonstrate leadership, problem-solving, and decision-making abilities is essential for articulating experiences effectively.
2. *Refine decision-making skills.* Practicing the analysis of complex case studies prepares candidates to showcase critical thinking and Executive Intelligence (ExI).
3. *Understand personal styles.* Exploring one's sociocultural style profile can help candidates align their natural tendencies with organizational expectations.
4. *Emphasize collaboration and influence.* Highlighting examples of building relationships and leading through influence reinforces a candidate's interpersonal strengths.
5. *Prepare for feedback.* Openness to 360-degree evaluations and a willingness to integrate feedback into development plans demonstrate a growth mindset.

6. *Balance strengths and styles.* Avoiding overemphasis on dominant traits ensures a well-rounded leadership profile.

ghSMART's Executive Assessment Process

ghSMART is a renowned leadership advisory firm that specializes in executive assessment and development. Its approach provides a thorough evaluation of a candidate's leadership capabilities, potential, and alignment with organizational goals. By employing innovative methodologies and evidence-based insights, ghSMART helps organizations identify and develop exceptional leaders. The assessment methodology in the ghSMART process covers five key areas:

IN-DEPTH CAREER INTERVIEW. Central to ghSMART's process is the SmartAssessment, an extensive career interview that explores the candidate's entire professional journey. This conversation encompasses early life and education, diving deeply into each professional role. For every position held, the assessment examines responsibilities, key accomplishments, challenges faced, and reasons for transitions. This meticulous approach uncovers the experiences that have shaped the candidate's leadership style and effectiveness.

SCORECARD DEVELOPMENT. A pivotal element of ghSMART's methodology is the creation of a customized scorecard. This tool defines success for the specific role by outlining two key components:

- *Business outcomes.* What needs to be achieved in the role
- *Leadership competencies.* How these outcomes should be accomplished

The scorecard serves as an objective benchmark, ensuring candidates are evaluated consistently against the role's unique demands.

PATTERN RECOGNITION. ghSMART leverages an evidence-based approach to identify patterns in a candidate's past behaviors and achievements. By analyzing these patterns, it predicts future performance with a high degree of accuracy. This insight-driven process ensures that assessments are rooted in measurable evidence rather than subjective impressions.

POTENTIAL MODEL. At the core of ghSMART's evaluation is its potential model, which breaks down leadership potential into three observable and measurable dimensions:

- *Cognitive quotient (CQ)*. Analytical and strategic thinking abilities

- *Drive quotient (DQ)*. Motivation, resilience, and results orientation

- *Emotional quotient (EQ)*. Interpersonal skills, self-awareness, and adaptability

This model provides a structured framework for assessing the behaviors and traits that contribute to long-term leadership success.

FEEDBACK AND DEVELOPMENT PLANNING. Following the assessment, ghSMART provides detailed, actionable feedback. Strengths are highlighted alongside areas for improvement, and candidates receive tactical advice for skill-building. Through tailored coaching and leadership advisory services, ghSMART ensures that candidates align with both their current roles and future organizational objectives.

PREPARATION TIPS FOR CANDIDATES. In our opinion, preparation is helpful for candidates undergoing a ghSMART assessment. The following steps can ensure a successful experience:

- *Self-reflection*. Review your career trajectory, focusing on key achievements, challenges, and learning experiences. Be prepared to discuss these in detail, providing specific examples that illustrate your leadership journey.

- *Understand the role requirements:* Familiarize yourself with the expectations and competencies outlined for the position. Reflect on how your experience and skills align with these requirements.

- *Be authentic.* ghSMART values honesty and self-awareness. Openly discussing both successes and lessons learned from mistakes demonstrates maturity and a growth mindset.

By adopting this approach, candidates can present their best selves during the assessment, gaining valuable insights and positioning themselves for leadership success.

Notes

Chapter 2

1. Mark Thompson, "Mark Thompson and Cristiano Amon with the Stanford CEO Summit," Chief Executive Alliance, https://www.chiefexecutivealliance.com/post/cristiano-amon-ceo-qualcomm.
2. Mark Thompson, "The First 100 days," Chief Executive Alliance, https://www.chiefexecutivealliance.com/post/the-first-100-days-with-aicha-evans-hubert-joly-and-carlos-abrams-rivera.

Chapter 3

1. Nancy Colier, "Stop 'Shoulding' Yourself to Death," *Psychology Today*, April 6, 2023, https://www.psychologytoday.com/us/blog/inviting-monkey-tea/201304/stop-shoulding-yourself-death-0.
2. Jim Collins, *Good to Great: Why Some Companies Make the Leap . . . and Others Don't* (New York: HarperBusiness, 2001).
3. Daniel Goleman, Richard E. Boyatzis, and Annie McKee, *Primal Leadership: Unleashing the Power of Emotional Intelligence* (Boston: Harvard Business Review Press, 2013).
4. Robert S. Kaplan and David P. Norton, *Strategy Maps: Converting Intangible Assets into Tangible Outcomes* (Boston: Harvard Business School Press, 2004).
5. Hubert Joly, *Heart of Business: Leadership Principles for the Next Era of Capitalism* (Boston: Harvard Business Review Press, 2021).
6. Ravi Mattu, "Who Would Want to Be a C.E.O.?," *New York Times*, May 14, 2023, https://www.nytimes.com/2023/05/14/business/dealbook/ceo-politics-chatgpt.html.
7. Eric Weiner, *The Geography of Genius: A Search for the World's Most Creative Places from Ancient Athens to Silicon Valley* (New York: Simon & Schuster, 2016).

Chapter 4

1. William Faulkner, *Requiem for a Nun* (New York: Random House, 1951).
2. Spencer Stuart, "Closing the Confidence Gap: Why the Board-CEO Relationship Needs a Reset," April 2025, https://www.spencerstuart.com/research-and-insight/closing-the-confidence-gap-why-the-board-ceo-relationship-needs-a-reset.

3. Julie Daum and Ann Yerger, "2023 S&P 500 New Director and Diversity Snapshot," Harvard Law School Forum on Corporate Governance, August 22, 2023, https://corpgov.law.harvard.edu/2023/08/22/2023-sp-500-new-director-and-diversity-snapshot/; Russell Reynolds, "Global CEO Turnover Index," https://www.russellreynolds.com/en/insights/reports-surveys/global-ceo-turnover-index.

4. Spencer Stuart, "Closing the Confidence Gap."

5. Bill George, "Why Boeing's Problems with the 737 MAX Began More Than 25 Years Ago," HBS Working Knowledge, January 24, 2024, https://hbswk.hbs.edu/item/why-boeings-problems-with-737-max-began-more-than-25-years-ago.

6. The Conference Board, ESGAUGE, Heidrick & Struggles, and Semler Brossy, "CEO Succession Practices in the Russell 3000 and S&P 500: 2024 Edition," The Conference Board, 2024, https://www.conference-board.org/publications/CEO-succession-practices-2024-edition.

7. Rob Maaddi, "Andy Reid Turned a 6-Inch Binder into a Pro Football Hall of Fame Résumé," Associated Press, January 31, 2023, https://apnews.com/article/new-england-patriots-seattle-seahawks-nfl-super-bowl-sports-ce7e0fe97e2bf8490255dc9c36090c06.

8. Elena Lytkina Botelho et al., "What Sets Successful CEOs Apart," *Harvard Business Review*, May–June 2017, https://hbr.org/2017/05/what-sets-successful-ceos-apart.

Chapter 5

1. Blair Epstein, Caitlin Hewes, and Scott Keller, "Capturing the Value of 'One Firm,'" *McKinsey Quarterly*, May 9, 2023, https://www.mckinsey.com/capabilities/strategy-and-corporate-finance/our-insights/capturing-the-value-of-one-firm.

2. Carolyn Dewar, Scott Keller, and Vikram Malhotra, *CEO Excellence: The Six Mindsets That Distinguish the Best Leaders from the Rest* (New York: Scribner, 2022).

3. Kavita Appachu, "Painting the Art of the Possible, with Brad D. Smith," Moves the Needle, September 13, 2022, https://movestheneedle.com/leadership/painting-the-art-of-the-possible-with-brad-d-smith/.

Chapter 6

1. Corporate Finance Institute, "Nomination Committee," 2024.

2. Jeremy Hanson, "CEO and Board Confidence Monitor: Beating the Succession Planning Paradox," Heidrick & Struggles, October 30, 2024, https://www.heidrick.com/en/insights/leadership-succession-planning/ceo-and-board-confidence-monitor_beating-the-succession-planning-paradox.

3. Kevin Wack, "How James Gorman Transformed Morgan Stanley after the Financial Crisis," *American Banker*, October 28, 2024, https://www.americanbanker.com/list/how-james-gorman-transformed-morgan-stanley-after-the-financial-crisis.

4. Hanson, "CEO and Board Confidence Monitor."

5. Nitin Nohria, "Leaders Must React," *Harvard Business Review*, January–February 2024, https://hbr.org/2024/01/leaders-must-react.

6. "Apple's Tim Cook Offered Liver to Dying Boss Steve Jobs," BBC, March 13, 2015, https://www.bbc.com/news/technology-31869113.

7. Lily Mae Lazarus, "Microsoft's Satya Nadella Was Almost Passed Over for CEO. It's a Lesson in Spotting Promising Talent," *Fortune*, March 24, 2025, https://fortune.com/2025/03/24/microsoft-satya-nadella-microsoft-ceo-selection/.

8. Jim Collins and Jerry I. Porras, *Built to Last: Successful Habits of Visionary Companies* (New York: HarperBusiness, 1994).

9. Spencer Herbst, "Ralph Lauren's Short-Lived Outsider CEO," Strategy+Business, February 2, 2017, https://www.strategy-business.com/blog/Ralph-Laurens-Short-Lived-Outsider-CEO.

Chapter 7

1. Bill Alpert, "CEOs Lose Their Jobs in 2024 Activist Campaigns," *Barron's*, October 25, 2024, https://www.barrons.com/articles/ceo-activist-campaigns-c905b2fd.

2. Marshall Goldsmith, *The Earned Life: Lose Regret, Choose Fulfillment* (New York: Currency, 2022).

3. Courtney Vien, "CFO-to-CEO Promotions Are on the Rise," CFO Brew, March 15, 2024, https://www.cfobrew.com/stories/2024/03/15/cfo-to-ceo-promotions-are-on-the-rise.

4. Anjli Raval, "Why More CFOs Are Becoming CEOs," Exec-Appointments.com, May 1, 2024, https://www.exec-appointments.com/article/why-more-cfos-are-becoming-ceos.

5. Douglas Appell, "BlackRock Reports Record AUM of $11.58 Trillion," Pensions & Investments, April 12, 2025, https://www.pionline.com/money-management/blackrock-ceo-larry-fink-reports-record-aum-1158-trillion.

6. PR Newswire, "Elliott Sends Letter and Presentation to the Board Of Southwest Airlines," June 10, 2024, https://www.prnewswire.com/news-releases/elliott-sends-letter-and-presentation-to-the-board-of-southwest-airlines-302168276.html.

7. Bill George and Jay W. Lorsch, "How to Outsmart Activist Investors," *Harvard Business Review*, May 2014, https://hbr.org/2014/05/how-to-outsmart-activist-investors.

Chapter 8

1. Elena Botelho, Shoma Hayden, and BJ Wright, "Beware the Transition from an Iconic CEO," hbr.org, February 1, 2023, https://hbr.org/2023/02/beware-the-transition-from-an-iconic-ceo; Elena Botelho and Shoma Hayden, "When the Heir Apparent Is the Wrong Choice for CEO," ghSMART, July 10, 2019, https://ghsmart.com/insights/when-the-heir-apparent-is-the-wrong-choice-for-ceo/.

2. Ken Favaro, Per-Ola Karlsson, and Gary Neilson, "The $112 Billion CEO Succession Problem," *Forbes*, May 15, 2015, https://www.forbes.com/sites/strategyand/2015/05/12/the-112-billion-ceo-succession-problem/?sh=5f5f2c957688.

3. Quotes are from my meetings with him and his book, Andrew S. Grove, *Only the Paranoid Survive: How to Exploit the Crisis Points That Challenge Every Company and Career* (New York: Currency Doubleday, 2010).

4. Evelyn Orr, Stuart Crandell, and Jane Stevenson, "Unlocking CEO Success," Korn Ferry, March 13, 2024, https://www.kornferry.com/institute/unlocking-ceo-success.

5. Egon Zehnder, "Building the Executive Talent Portfolio: A Strategic Imperative For Energy CEOs," August 2009, https://www.egonzehnder.com/what-we-do/ceo-search/insights/building-the-executive-talent-portfolio-a-strategic-imperative-for-energy-ceos.

6. Christian Jarrett, "How Your Mood Changes Your Personality," BPS, October 25, 2022, https://www.bps.org.uk/research-digest/how-your-mood-changes-your-personality.

7. Raeal Moore, Edgar Sanchez, and Maria Ofelia San Pedro, "Investigating Test Prep Impact on Score Gains Using Quasi-Experimental Propensity Score Matching," working paper 2018-6, ACT, https://www.act.org/content/dam/act/unsecured/documents/R1710-investigating-test-prep-impact-2018-07.pdf.

Chapter 9

1. US Senate Committee on Commerce, Science, and Transportation, "The Courage of Survivors: A Call to Action," July 30, 2019, https://www.moran.senate.gov/public/_cache/files/c/2/c232725e-b717-4ec8-913e-845ffe0837e6/FCC5DFDE2005A2EACF5A9A25FF76D538.2019.07.30-the-courage-of-survivors--a-call-to-action-olympics-investigation-report-final.pdf.

2. Paul A. Argenti et al., "The Secret Behind Successful Corporate Transformations," hbr.org, September 14, 2021, https://hbr.org/2021/09/the-secret-behind-successful-corporate-transformations.

3. David Segal, "An Oasis in a Desert of Customer Service," *New York Times*, June 8, 2013, https://www.nytimes.com/2013/06/09/your-money/at-quicken-loans-a-culture-geared-to-customer-service.html.

4. Rosabeth Moss Kanter, *Confidence: How Winning Streaks and Losing Streaks Begin and End* (New York: Three Rivers Press, 2006).

Conclusion

1. Ruth Umoh, "90 Days, Dozens of Interviews, Billions on the Line: Inside Blackstone's CEO Search Process for Its 250 Companies," *Fortune*, January 28, 2025, https://fortune.com/2025/01/28/blackstone-ceo-search-process-succession-private-equity/.

2. Betsy Rodriguez, "A CHRO's Playbook for CEO Transitions," SHRM Executive Network, April 5, 2024, https://www.shrm.org/executive-network/insights/people-strategy/chro-playbook-ceo-transitions-spring-2024.

3. Rodriguez, "A CHRO's Playbook for CEO Transitions."

4. Anna Penfold and Emma Combe, "Why CHROs Are Playing a More Active Role in CEO Succession," Russell Reynolds Associates, December 13, 2024, https://www.russellreynolds.com/en/insights/articles/why-chros-are-playing-a-more-active-role-in-ceo-succession.

5. Cathy Anterasian and Stephen G. Patscot, "CHRO at the Center: Maximizing the Impact of CEO Succession Planning," Spencer Stuart, August 2023, https://www.spencerstuart.com/research-and-insight/chro-at-the-center-maximizing-the-impact-of-ceo-succession-planning; Penfold and Combe, "Why CHROs Are Playing a More Active Role."

6. Umroh, "90 Days, Dozens of Interviews, Billions on the Line."

7. Umroh, "90 Days, Dozens of Interviews, Billions on the Line."

8. Eton Bridge Partners, "CEO Pathways Report," 2024, https://etonbridgepartners.com/ceo-pathways-2024/.

9. Umroh, "90 Days, Dozens of Interviews, Billions on the Line."

10. Wimbledon press conference transcript, ASAP Sports, July 6, 2018, https://www.asapsports.com/show_interview.php?id=141824.

11. Nasdaq, "2024 Global Governance Pulse," 2024, https://www.nasdaq.com/solutions/governance/resources/global-governance-pulse-report/2024.

12. Nasdaq, "2024 Global Governance Pulse."

13. Joyce Chen, "CEO Tenure Rates: Rising Demands, Falling CEO Tenures," Harvard Law School Forum on Corporate Governance, August 4, 2023, https://corpgov.law.harvard.edu/2023/08/04/ceo-tenure-rates-2/.

14. Nasdaq, "2024 Global Governance Pulse."

15. Rusty O'Kelley and Laura Sanderson, "Global CEO Turnover Index Annual Report," Harvard Law School Forum on Corporate Governance, February 13, 2025, https://corpgov.law.harvard.edu/2025/02/13/the-transformation-of-the-ceo-global-ceo-turnover-index-annual-report/.

16. Srikanth Velamakanni, LinkedIn, https://www.linkedin.com/in/srikanthvelamakanni/, accessed 2023.

17. Hubert Joly, *Heart of Business: Leadership Principles for the Next Era of Capitalism* (Boston: Harvard Business Review Press, 2021).

Index

Abel, Greg, 7, 37, 48
Abrams-Rivera, Carlos, 7, 38–39
Accenture, 143
accountability coaches, 44
accountability to others, 58–60
active listening, 51
activist investors, 113, 123–127
adversity, 195–199
Agrawal, Pranay, 197–198
Alcoa, 176, 189
Altman, Sam, 5
Amazon, 189, 198
American Psychological Association, 211, 213
Amon, Cristiano, 11, 13, 15, 18, 21, 88
Ancestry.com, 114, 131
Ang, Soon, 214
Any Dumb-Ass Can Do It: Learning Moments from an Everyday CEO of a Multi-Billion-Dollar Company (Ridge), 172
Aon, 74
Apple, 35–36, 39, 42, 95, 100
Arch Capital Group, 30
"Are Your 'Shoulds' Really Helping You?" (Colier), 31
Assess International, 143
Assessment.com, 215
assessments
  of CEO readiness, 141–142
  employee engagement surveys, 172–174
  as personal strategy offsite, 144–145
  preparation for, 145–147, 153–156, 187–188
  by recruiting firms, 217–231
  as risk management, 137–141
  types of, 205–215
assessors
  bias in, 151–152
  identifying references, 147–148
  patience with, 149–151
  recruiters versus, 142–143
  as stakeholders, 20
authenticity, 180–181
authority, miscalculating, 26–29

background checks, 207–208
Bain & Company, 173
Ball Corporation, 57
Ballmer, Steve, 101, 140
Banner, Joe, 65
Barclays, 113
Bar-On, Reuven, 210
Barry, Corie, 12, 13, 15, 18, 21, 24, 34
Baxter International Inc., 14, 87
Becoming Coachable (Osman and Lane), 189
Bed Bath & Beyond, 43
behavior, importance of, 17–18, 31–32
Benchmarks 360, 210
Berkshire Hathaway, 7, 36–37, 48
Best Buy, 12, 16, 24, 32, 34, 162, 201
Bezos, Jeff, 189
BFI (Big Five Inventory), 212
bias, in assessors, 151–152
Biles, Simone, 159
Birkman, Roger, 213
Birkman Method, 213
BlackBerry, 43

Index

BlackRock, 122, 131
Blackstone, 185–190
Blake, Frank, 15, 178
blind spots and fears. *See* fears and blind spots
Bloom, Nicholas, 43
Bloomberg, Michael, 6
Bloomberg LP, 6
Blumkin, Rose, 37
BNSF Railway, 36
board of directors
   addressing failures with, 68
   communication of strategy with, 51–53
   credibility with, 58–60
   crossroads mentality of, 60–61, 193–194
   due diligence done by, 47–49
   dynamics of, 56–58
   earning trust of, 47–70
   enterprise risk management (ERM) by, 58
   fears and blind spots, 49–51
   internal versus external candidates, 61–65
   lack of unity, 149
   member histories, 53–54
   preparing pitch for, 65–68
   reasons for rejection by, 68–70
   relationship management, 55–56
   as stakeholder, 19
boomerang CEOs, 5–7
Booz Allen, 60
Botelho, Elena Lytkina, 67
Boyer, Herbert, 40, 42
brand legacy, fear of destroying, 42–43
brand reputation, 174
Branson, Richard, 81, 103, 178
Bratches, Sean, 32
Briggs, Katharine Cook, 211
Buffett, Warren, 7, 36–37, 48, 202
Built to Last (Porras and Collins), 34, 105
buy-side analysts, 122–123

C3.ai, 198
Calico, 42
Caliper Profile, 211

candidates. *See* CEO candidates
capitalization table, 114
career risks, 159–161
Carlson Companies, 32
Case, Greg, 74
case studies, 207
CBS Evening News, 179
CBS News 24/7, 179
celebrity CEOs, fear of failure in following, 34–39
Center for Board Excellence, 49
Center for Creative Leadership (CCL), 210
CEO Academy, 30, 189, 190, 199
CEO candidates
   assessment types, 205–215
   avoiding being overlooked, 101–103
   behavior, importance of, 17–18
   Buffett role models for, 36–37
   career risks, 159–161
   CFO as, 117–118, 188
   elite athlete comparison, 191
   evidence-based versus relationship-based, 103–105
   HR, partnering with, 186–187
   humility of, 11–15
   incumbent CEO relationship, 100–103
   leadership calling of, 193–194
   leadership development by, 90–91
   odds against, 1–9
   personal risks, 181
   preparation for evaluation process, 187–188
   questions for incumbent CEO, 108–110
   questions to ask themselves, 10, 22, 45, 71, 77–78, 92, 112, 136, 157
   recruiting firm assessments, 217–231
   reflection questions, 194–203
   skill development, 14–17
   as stakeholders, 18–19
   as third horse, 152
   transition process, 170–171, 188–190
   unqualified, 5
   See also self
The CEO Life Cycle (Citrin), 144

Index 241

CEO-ready organizations, characteristics of, 65
CEOs
  average tenure of, 192
  challenges for, 97–98
  as chief architects, 164–165, 183
  as chief coaching officers, 171–172
  as chief communication officers, 177–181, 184
  as chief culture curators, 165–166, 184
  as chief customer officers, 162–163, 183
  as chief engagement officers, 16–17, 162, 183
  as chief gratitude officers, 163–164, 183
  as chief transformation officers, 166–177, 184
  as driver of value creation, 188–190
  high-stakes nature of role, 190–191
  public visibility and authenticity, 179–181
  See also incumbent CEO
CEO selection process, risk management in, 137–141
CEO succession planning, 95–96, 192–193
  See also leadership development
CEO.works, 167
CFO
  as CEO candidate, 117–118, 188
  relationship management, 118
challenges for CEOs, 97–98
Chambers, John, 108
change management assessments, 213–214
Change Style Indicator (CSI), 213
Charan, Ram, 33, 127
Charles Schwab Corporation, 13, 37, 160
Chewy, 170
chief architects, CEOs as, 164–165, 183
chief coaching officers, CEOs as, 171–172
chief communication officers, CEOs as, 177–181, 184

chief culture curators, CEOs as, 165–166, 184
chief customer officers, CEOs as, 162–163, 183
chief energizing officers, CEOs as, 16
chief engagement officers, CEOs as, 16–17, 162, 183
chief evidence officers, CEOs as, 17
chief gratitude officers, CEOs as, 163–164, 183
chief human resources officers (CHRO), partnering with, 186–187
chief people officers (CPO), partnering with, 186–187
chief transformation officers, CEOs as, 166–177, 184
Children's National Hospital, 59, 147
Chipotle, 5
Christie's, 125
CHRO (chief human resources officers), partnering with, 186–187
Cisco, 108
Citibank, 123
Citizens Financial Group, 55
Citrin, Jim, 60, 61–62, 68, 144–145
clarion calls, 97–98
Clark, Ed, 26
Clem, Mike, 7, 74–75, 168–170
Clifton, Donald, 214
coaching
  chief coaching officers, CEOs as, 171–172
  importance of, 85–86
  for incumbent CEO, 107, 110–111
  in investor relations, 120
Coca-Cola Company, 119–120
Colgate-Palmolive, 199
Colier, Nancy, 31
collaboration assessments, 214–215
Collins, Jim, 34, 167, 198
communication, CEO role in, 177–181
company ownership types, 127–134
Comparably, 174
competency assessments, 206
competition for CEO, among C-suite peers, 81–84

competitor companies, mystery shopping, 121
Conference Board, 61
Confidence (Kanter), 179
confidence, instilling, 58–60
conflict management assessments, 213–214
Cook, Tim, 35–36, 100
COSO, 58
CPO (chief people officers), partnering with, 186–187
CQ (Cultural Intelligence) Assessment, 214
Creative Artists Agency, 32
credibility with board of directors, 58–60
crossroads mentality of board of directors, 60–61, 193–194
CSI (Change Style Indicator), 213
C-suite peers
 building relationships with, 73–91
 building team of, 87–91
 competition for CEO, 81–84
 disagreement with, 84–86
 earning respect of, 75–81, 82*t*
 as stakeholders, 19
 working relationship with, 67
cultural fit analysis, 205
Cultural Intelligence (CQ) Assessment, 214
culture (of organization)
 chief culture curators, CEOs as, 165–166
 chief engagement officers, CEOs as, 16, 162
 chief transformation officers, CEOs as, 166–177
 earning board trust and, 47
 repairing, 165
 Sweetwater Sound, 168–170
Culture Amp, 173
curiosity, 51
current CEO. *See* incumbent CEO
customers
 chief customer officers, CEOs as, 162–163
 engagement with, 174–177, 178
 evolving needs of, 168–170

 as stakeholders, 20
 stakeholders as, 3–5

Daft, Douglas, 119–120
Daumeyer, Jason, 146
David, George, 190
Dawood, Shahzada, 137–138
DDI (Development Dimensions International), 143
decapitation, 113
Dechra Pharmaceuticals, 199
decision-making ability of owners, 116
decisiveness, 67
Dell, Michael, 5
della Cava, Courtney, 186, 187, 188, 190
Delta, 15
Denhollander, Rachael, 159
Deutsche Bank, 123
Development Dimensions International (DDI), 143
diagnostic tools, 208
Dickerson, John, 179
direct reports, as stakeholders, 20
disagreement with C-suite peers, 84–86
Discover Financial Services, 114
Discovery Learning, Inc., 213
DISC Personality Assessment, 215
Disney. *See* Walt Disney Company
Djokovic, Novak, 191
DocuSign, 174, 200
Donald, Jim, 5
Dorsey, Jack, 5
Dow Jones Industrial Average, 43, 139
Drucker, Peter, 16, 51, 58, 116, 170
due diligence, done by board of directors, 47–49
DuPont, 30, 93

Eastman Kodak, 43
eBay, 139
Edmondson, Amy C., 17
EDS, 139
Egon Zehnder, 141, 143, 208, 217, 218–221

EleVen, 33, 191
Elliott Investment Management, 125
EMC, 139
Emerson, Bill, 170
emotional impact on incumbent CEO, 94–95, 96–98
emotional intelligence, 210
empathy, 79, 81
employees
  engagement surveys, 172–174
  as stakeholders, 20
Engine No. 1, 126
Enneagram, 212–213
eNPS (employee Net Promoter Scores), 173
enterprise risk management (ERM), 58
EQ-i, 210
ESPN, 32
evaluation process, preparation for, 187–188
Evans, Aicha, 189
evidence-based leaders, 103–105
Executive Intelligence (ExI), 225–226
executive team, building, 87–91
  See also C-suite peers
external CEO candidates, advantages and disadvantages, 61–65
external networks, building, 156
ExxonMobil, 126

Facebook, 32
Face the Nation, 179
failures
  addressing with board of directors, 68
  fear in shadow of giants, 34–39
  reactions to, 146–147
Farmer, Kathryn, 36
Fazen, Eric, 102
fears and blind spots, 23–44
  of board of directors, 49–51
  destroying brand legacy, 42–43
  failing in shadow of giants, 34–39
  feeling inadequate, 32–34
  ignoring inner voice, 29–31
  losing noble cause, 40–42
  losing yourself, 39–40
  miscalculating authority, 26–29
  overestimating heir apparent status, 25–26
  reacting to rejection, 31–32
feedback from stakeholders, 20–21
feelers (as leadership type), 104–105
FFM (Five-Factor Model-Based Personality Test), 211–212
Fidelity Investments, 122
FirstMind Behavioral Assessment, 213
Five Dysfunctions of a Team Assessment, 214
Five-Factor Model-Based Personality Test (FFM), 211–212
Five Practices of Exemplary Leadership, 210
Forbes, 137
Ford Motor Company, 191
founders
  fear of failure in following, 34–39
  respect for legacy, 106, 134, 169
  returning, 5–7
Fractal Analytics, 196–198
frameworks for assessments, 209–215
  Egon Zehnder, 218–221
  ghSMART, 229–231
  Korn Ferry, 221–225
  Spencer Stuart, 225–229
Frontier Communications, 174, 200

Gallup, 173
Gallup CliftonStrengths (StrengthsFinder), 214
Gandhi, 193
Gasol, Pau, 193–194
Gates, Bill, 101, 140
Gelsinger, Pat, 139
Genentech, 24–25, 39–42
General Electric, 43
The Geography of Genius: A Search for the World's Most Creative Places from Ancient Athens to Silicon Valley (Weiner), 43
George, Bill, 58, 126
Georgiadis, Margo, 114–115, 131–132, 133–134

ghSMART, 137, 143, 144, 146, 151, 217, 229–231
GLA (Global Leadership Assessment), 210–211
Glassdoor, 174
Glint, 173
Global Governance Pulse survey, 192
Global Leadership Assessment (GLA), 210–211
Goldberg, Lewis, 212
Goldman Sachs, 47, 123
Goldsmith, Marshall, ix–x, 8, 35, 44, 57, 70, 116, 179
Goleman, Daniel, 40
Goodell, Roger, 62
Good to Great (Collins), 34
Google, 114, 198
Google Alphabet, 42
Gorman, James, 96
governance committee, 95–96
gratitude, 163–164, 183
Great Places to Work, 174
Green Bay Packers, 65
Greenberg, Herb, 211
Groupon, 114
Grove, Andy, 139, 140
Guardian, 30
Guardian Life, 30, 93

H&M, 106
Hasker, Steve, 26, 32, 61, 146
Hastings, Reed, 6
Hayes, John, 57
HDS (Hogan Development Survey), 208, 209–210, 219
The Heart of Business: Leadership Principles for the Next Era of Capitalism (Joly), 41
Heidrick & Struggles, 96, 141, 143
heir apparent, overestimating yourself as, 25–26
Hewlett-Packard, 4, 56, 95, 152
Hirshland, Sarah, 15, 159–167, 181, 194, 199, 201–202
Hogan, Robert, 210
Hogan Assessments, 143
Hogan Development Survey (HDS), 208, 209–210, 219

Home Depot, 15, 178
Homestead High School, 100
HR, partnering with, 186–187
humility of CEO candidates, 11–15

Ichazo, Oscar, 212
Iger, Bob, 5, 62, 126
impostor syndrome, 32–34
improving investor relations, 117–121
inadequacy, feelings of, 32–34
incumbent CEO
    candidate relationship with, 100–103
    challenges for, 97–98
    emotional impact on, 94–95, 96–98
    evidence-based versus relationship-based, 103–105
    leadership development by, 93–94
    mentors for, 107, 110–111, 164–165
    questions for, 108–110
    resistance from, 98–99
    respect for legacy, 106, 134, 169
    as stakeholder, 19
    transition process, 93–111
Indeed, 174
independent directors, 95–96
in-depth behavioral interviews, 206–207
Indian Institute of Management Ahmedabad, 197
Individual Style Profile, 226–227
influencers on board of directors, 56–58
Infosys, 197
inner voice, ignoring, 29–31
Institutional Investor, 123
Intel, 43, 139
internal CEO candidates, advantages and disadvantages, 61–65
internal Net Promoter Scores (eNPS), 173
internal references, 155
Intuit, 88
investment timelines, 134–135
"investor days," 118
investor relations, 66, 113–135
    activist investors, 113, 123–127
    blueprint for, 128

buy-side versus sell-side analysts, 122–123
coaching in, 120
improving, 117–121
preparation for speaking, 124
See also owners

Jobs, Steve, 35–36, 39, 42, 100
John, Oliver P., 212
Johnson, Kevin, 5
Joly, Hubert, 12, 16, 21, 32, 34, 41, 162, 163, 201
Jordan, Bob, 125
joy, finding, 201–203
J.P. Morgan Asset Management, 123
judges. *See* stakeholders
Jung, Carl, 211, 215

Kansas City Chiefs, 65
Kanter, Rosabeth Moss, 177
Kaplan, Dan, 187
Kaplan, Robert S., 41
Kelleher, Herb, 178
Kelly, Gail, 88
Kelly, Gary, 125
Kessenich, Eric, 7, 33, 170–171, 174, 175–176, 200
key performance indicators, 51–53
Kilmann, Ralph, 213
Kleinfeld, Klaus, 176, 189–190, 191
Kliatchko, Vlad, 6
Kohler, David, 198
Korn Ferry, 141, 143, 187, 208, 217, 221–225
Kouzes, James, 210
Kraemer, Harry, 14, 87
Kraft Heinz, 7, 38
Krzanich, Brian, 139

Lafley, A.G., 189
Lane, Jacquelyn, 189
Larsson, Stefan, 106
Lattice, 173
Lauren, Ralph, 106
Lawrence, David, 47–49
leadership agility, 14–17

leadership assessment centers, 207
Leadership Assessment Suite, 210
leadership calling of CEO candidates, 193–194
leadership development
  by CEO candidates, 90–91
  in companies, 95–96
  by incumbent CEO, 93–94
The Leadership Pipeline: How to Build the Leadership Powered Company (Charan et al.), 33
Leadership Practices Inventory (LPI), 210
leadership style assessments, 209–211
leadership team, building, 87–91
See also C-suite peers
learning agility, 223
Lencioni, Patrick, 214
Lencioni's Table Group, 214
level 5 leadership, 198
Levinson, Arthur, 24–25, 39–42
LinkedIn, 173
Loeb, Daniel, 125
Lores, Enrique, 4, 56, 152
Lorsch, Jay, 126
Louvet, Patrice, 106
LPI (Leadership Practices Inventory), 210
Lurie, Jeffrey, 65
Lynch, Peter, 120
Lyons, Susanne, 160

MAPP (Motivational Appraisal of Personal Potential), 215
Maroney, McKayla, 159
Marston, William Moulton, 215
Martin, Curtis, 200
Mattel, 114
MBTI (Myers-Briggs Type Indicator), 208, 211
McDonald's, 114
McKinsey & Company, 141, 189
McLaughlin, Mark, 12, 79–80
MDA Leadership, 143
Medtronic, 126
mentors for incumbent CEO, 107, 110–111, 164–165
Mercer, 143, 211

Mercer Leadership Assessment, 211
Merrill Lynch, 123
MeydenVest Partners, 107
Microsoft, 101, 140, 165, 166, 194, 198
Montai Therapeutics, 114
Morgan Stanley, 96
Moskowitz, Howard, 195
Motivational Appraisal of Personal Potential (MAPP), 215
Mulally, Alan, 190–191
Mulligan, Deanna, 29–31, 93–94
Murthy, N. R. Narayana, 197
Myers, Isabel Briggs, 211
Myers-Briggs Type Indicator (MBTI), 208, 211
mystery shopping competitors, 121

Nadella, Satya, 101–102, 140, 165, 166, 194
Naranjo, Claudio, 212
Narasimhan, Laxman, 5
Nasdaq, 49, 53, 192
Nassar, Larry, 159, 161
Nebraska Furniture Mart, 37
Netflix, 6–7
Net Promoter Score (NPS), 173
New York–Presbyterian Hospital, 30
Niccol, Brian, 5
Nielsen, 26, 32
noble cause, fearing loss of, 40–42
Nohria, Nitin, 97
nominating committee, 95–96
Nordengaard, Jesper, 199
normal noise, 97
Norton, David, 41
NPS (Net Promoter Score), 173
Nvidia, 139

Occupational Personality Questionnaire (OPQ), 208, 212
OCEAN, 211, 212
Ogg, Sandy, 167, 168
Old Navy, 106
Olympics (US team), 159–167, 194, 201–202
100Coaches, 189

"The One Number You Need to Grow" (Reichheld), 173
Only the Paranoid Survive (Grove), 139
OpenAI, 5
operating model architecture, 167–168
OPQ (Occupational Personality Questionnaire), 208, 212
organizational culture. *See* culture (of organization)
Osman, Scott, 189
owners
  company types, 127–134
  decision-making ability of, 116
  expectations of, 115–116
  language of, 115–116
  relationship management, 113–135
  as stakeholders, 20
  See also investor relations

Palo Alto Networks, 12, 79
passion (3Ps), 196–197
patience with assessors, 149–151
Patricio, Miguel, 7, 38
Peakon, 173
peers. *See* C-suite peers
Peltz, Nelson, 125–126
PepsiCo, 119, 187
performance (3Ps), 196–197
personality assessments, 211–213
personal risks, 181
personal strategy offsite, assessments as, 144–145
Peters, Greg, 6
Peterson, Christopher, 215
Philadelphia Eagles, 65
Pixar, 100
Plank, Kevin, 5
Porras, Jerry, 34, 105, 195
Porter, Michael, 97
Posner, Barry, 210
preparation
  for assessments, 145–147, 153–156, 187–188
  for evaluation process, 187–188
  for speaking to investors, 145–147

Primal Leadership: Unleashing the Power of Emotional Intelligence (Goleman et al.), 40
private companies nearing IPO, 129–130
private equity-owned companies, 130–132
Procter & Gamble, 106, 126, 189
psychological safety, 17, 50
psychometric testing, 208
public companies, 129
public visibility of CEOs, 179–180
purpose (3Ps), 196–197

Q12, 173
Qualcomm, 11, 12, 79, 88
Qualtrics, 173
quarterly earnings reviews, 119
questions
  for CEO candidates to ask themselves, 10, 22, 45, 71, 77–78, 92, 112, 136, 157
  for incumbent CEO, 108–110
  preparing for board pitch, 66–68
  for reflection, 194–203
Quicken Loans, 170

RadioShack, 43
Raisman, Aly, 159
Ralph Lauren Corporation, 106
RANE Network, 47
recruiters
  assessments by, 217–231
  assessors versus, 142–143
  as stakeholders, 20, 141–145
reference checks, 147–148, 155, 207–208
reflection questions, 194–203
Reichheld, Fred, 173
Reid, Andy, 65–66
rejection (as CEO candidate)
  reacting to, 31–32
  reasons for, 68–70
relationship-based leaders, 103–105
relationship management, 199–201
  with board of directors, 55–56
  with CFO, 118
  with C-suite peers, 73–91
  with customers, 174–177, 178
  with incumbent CEO, 100–103
  with owners, 113–135
repairing organizational culture, 165
resistance from incumbent CEO, 98–99
respect for incumbent's legacy, 106, 134, 169
respect of C-suite peers, earning, 75–81, 82t
RHR International, 143
Ridge, Garry, 171–172, 183
Riley-Brown, Michelle, 59–60, 147
risk management
  for career risks, 159–161
  in CEO selection, 137–141
  for personal risks, 181
Robbins, Chuck, 108
Rock Holdings, 170
role models for CEO candidates, 36–37
Rozanski, Horacio, 60
Ruprecht, William, 125
Russell Investments, 24, 107, 117
Russell Reynolds, 141

S&P 500, 43
Sandberg, Sheryl, 32
Sarandos, Ted, 6
Satmetrix, 173
Schellekens, Ronald, 187
Schmidt, John, 7, 171
Schultz, Howard, 5
Schwab, Charles, 13, 37, 179
Schwab.com, 13, 121
Sears, 43
Seitz, Michelle, 24, 107, 110, 117, 127, 145
selection process, risk management in, 137–141
self
  accountability to others, 44
  fears and blind spots, 23–44
  loss of, 39–40
  as stakeholder, 18–19
  See also CEO candidates

self-awareness, 24–25
Seligman, Martin, 215
sell-side analysts, 122–123
SHL, 212
"shoulds," 29–31
Siemens AG, 176, 189
simulations, 207
Singer, Paul Elliott, 125
siren songs, 98
Situational Judgment Tests (SJTs), 214
16 Personality Factors (16PF), 212, 219
skill development, 14–17
Skillscope, 210
Smart, Geoff, 144, 148, 149, 151–152, 153
SmartAssessment, 229
Smith, Brad, 88
Smith, Orin, 5
sneaky peer syndrome, 83
Society for Human Resource Management, 189
Sotheby's, 125
Southwest Airlines, 125, 178
Spencer Stuart, 50, 60, 141, 143, 144, 208, 217, 225–229
Srivastava, Sanjay, 212
stakeholders, 8
   as customers, 3–5
   descriptions of, 18–20
   earning trust of, 182
   feedback from, 20–21
   recruiters as, 141–145
Stanford University, 100, 105
STAR (Strategic Transition Alignment and Readiness) test, 196
Starbucks, 5
State Street Global Advisors, 123
strategic scope, 14
Strategic Transition Alignment and Readiness (STAR) test, 196
Strategy Maps: Converting Intangible Assets into Tangible Outcomes (Kaplan and Norton), 41
StrengthsFinder (Gallup CliftonStrengths), 214
Success Built to Last: Creating a Life That Matters (Porras and Thompson), 34, 195, 199

succession planning, 95–96, 192–193
   See also leadership development
Surack, Chuck, 7, 169
Swan, Bob, 139
Swanson, Robert, 40
Sweetwater Sound, 7, 74, 168–170

talent acceleration, 15–16
talent capital balance sheet, 168
TD Bank Group, 26
team, building, 87–91
team dynamics assessments, 214–215
Texas Children's Hospital, 59
thinkers (as leadership type), 104–105
third horse, CEO candidates as, 152
Third Point, 125
Thomas, Kenneth, 213
Thomas-Kilmann Conflict Mode Instrument (TKI), 213
Thompson, Bonita, 39, 195
Thompson, Brian, 181
Thomson Reuters, 26, 32, 61, 146
360-degree feedback assessments, 206
TinyPulse, 173
TKI (Thomas-Kilmann Conflict Mode Instrument), 213
transition process
   CEO candidates, 170–171, 188–190
   incumbent CEO, 93–111
transparency, lack of, 51
Treadway Commission, 58
Trian Partners, 125
trust, earning
   from board of directors, 47–70
   from customers, 177, 178
   from stakeholders, 182
truth tellers, 44, 175–177, 191–192
Turner, Mark, 199
Twelve Angry Men (film), 56
Twitter, 5

Umoh, Ruth, 186–187
Under Armour, 5
UnitedHealthcare, 181

United States Olympic & Paralympic Committee (USOPC), 15, 159–167, 194, 201–202
United Technologies Corporation, 190
unity, lack of, 149
unqualified candidates, 5
USA Gymnastics, 161
USCard Services, 114
USOPC (United States Olympic & Paralympic Committee), 15, 159–167, 194, 201–202
U.S. Venture, 7, 33, 170–171, 175, 200

value creation agenda, 167, 188–190
Values in Action (VIA) Survey of Character Strengths, 215
Van Dyne, Linn, 214
Vanguard, 30, 93, 122
Van Saun, Bruce, 55, 57
Velamakanni, Srikanth, 196–198
venture capital-funded companies, 132–134
VIA (Values in Action) Survey of Character Strengths, 215
Virgin, 81, 103, 178
vision memo, 145, 155
VMware, 139
V Starr Interiors, 33, 191

Walt Disney Company, 5, 96, 125–126
WD-40, 171–172, 183
Weiner, Eric, 43
Westpac, 88
Wharton, 189
What Got You Here Won't Get You There (Goldsmith), 70
whisper warnings, 98
"Why Boeing's Problems with the 737 MAX Began More Than 25 Years Ago" (George), 58
Wilderotter, Maggie, 174–175, 200
Williams, Serena, 191
Williams, Venus, 33, 191
Wind, Jerry, 195
WorkBoard, 173
Workday, 173
Working Genius, 214
World Business Forum, 81
World Economic Forum, 34, 35, 137
WSFS Financial, 199

yes folks, 68
YSC Consulting, 143

Zappos, 170
Zoox, 189

About the Authors

Mark Thompson is a globally recognized authority on CEO succession, executive readiness, and high-stakes leadership transitions. He has led more than a hundred board-level engagements to prepare C-suite successors to step confidently into enterprise leadership. He is the founding chairman and CEO of the Chief Executive Alliance and the CEO Leadership Plan Review (LPR). Previously, he served as chief executive of the CEO Academy, a SHRM company, in partnership with Wharton and McKinsey.

Earlier in his career, Thompson reported directly to founder Charles "Chuck" Schwab, serving as executive producer of Schwab.com, the first large-scale digital platform for online investing. Together they introduced the world's first chief customer experience officer role.

Thompson earned a place on the *Forbes* Midas List as a founding board member of Esurance and as chairman of three companies—Rioport, Interwoven, and Integration Associates—ventures acquired by Allstate, Hewlett-Packard, and Silicon Labs. He served as a founding adviser to Richard Branson's Entrepreneurship Centers and Virgin Unite. In 2023 he was inducted into the Thinkers50 Coaching Legends and, in 2022, the Global Gurus Corps d'Elite Lifetime Achievement Award in Coaching among the world's top thought leaders, having already been ranked by Marshall Goldsmith as number one CEO Coach in 2021.

At Stanford University, his alma mater, Thompson cofounded the Realtime Venture Design Lab, a leadership innovation project led by Professor Clifford Nass. As a member of the Stanford Faculty Club, he launched more than a hundred episodes of the *Chief Executive Summit Series* podcast, which formed the backbone of this book and his Strategic

Transition and Readiness (STAR) methodology for executives. His doctoral research at Purdue University builds on that foundation, exploring the leadership skills most critical to C-suite succession.

Thompson is coauthor of *Admired: 21 Ways to Double Your Value*, a *New York Times* bestseller; *Success Built to Last: Creating a Life That Matters*; and *Now . . . Build a Great Business*. He resides in Manhattan and Orlando and is a Golden Visa resident of the United Arab Emirates.

Byron Loflin is a globally recognized leader in corporate governance and boardroom effectiveness. He currently serves as the Global Head of Board Advisory at Nasdaq and is the former CEO of the Center for Board Excellence (CBE), now a part of Nasdaq. With over two decades of experience advising corporate boards, CEOs, and executive teams, Loflin is widely respected for his pragmatic approach to board leadership, integrity, and strategic alignment.

A two-time CEO, Loflin began his career in public service and finance, later channeling his expertise into transforming how boards govern. While engaging in several areas of study at Harvard Business School, he developed the Center for Board Excellence and its unique, scalable questionnaire and evaluation platform. Since founding the Center, he has interviewed well over a thousand CEOs and board members. He continues to pioneer tools and frameworks that elevate board effectiveness, board and peer evaluations, and director development, helping organizations strengthen their oversight and strategic impact.

A frequent speaker and writer on governance effectiveness, innovation, and CEO-board dynamics, Loflin believes effective leadership is rooted in the interplay of confidence and accountability. His leadership philosophy emphasizes transparency, continuous learning, and a commitment to stakeholder stewardship.

Loflin brings his deep experience and measured perspective to his empowerment of current and aspiring CEOs, helping them navigate complex challenges with clarity, integrity, and resilience. His work continues to shape the evolving role of the modern boardroom in a fast-changing world.